A TWO-SPIRIT
JOURNEY

CRITICAL STUDIES IN NATIVE HISTORY
Jarvis Brownlie, Series Editor

A TWO-SPIRIT JOURNEY

THE AUTOBIOGRAPHY OF A LESBIAN OJIBWA-CREE ELDER

MA-NEE CHACABY WITH MARY LOUISA PLUMMER

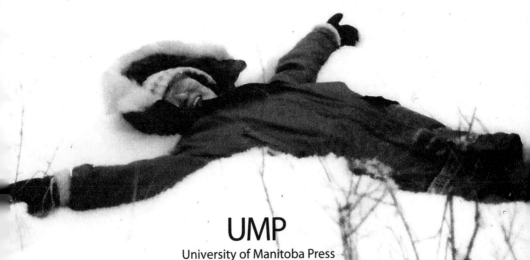

UMP
University of Manitoba Press

A Two-Spirit Journey: The Autobiography of a Lesbian
Ojibwa-Cree Elder
© Ma-Nee Chacaby and Mary Louisa Plummer 2016

26 25 24 23 22   7 8 9 10 11

University of Manitoba Press
Winnipeg, Manitoba, Canada
Treaty 1 Territory
uofmpress.ca

Cataloguing data available from Library and Archives Canada
Critical Studies in Native History, ISSN 1925-5888 ; 18
ISBN 978-0-88755-812-2 (PAPER)
ISBN 978-0-88755-505-3 (PDF)
ISBN 978-0-88755-503-9 (EPUB)
ISBN 978-0-88755-230-4 (BOUND)

Cover and interior design by Jess Koroscil
Cover photo by Ruth Kivilahti, www.ruthlessimages.com

Printed in Canada

The University of Manitoba Press acknowledges the financial support for
its publication program provided by the Government of Canada through
the Canada Book Fund, the Canada Council for the Arts, the Manitoba
Department of Sport, Culture, and Heritage, the Manitoba Arts Council,
and the Manitoba Book Publishing Tax Credit.

Funded by the Government of Canada | Canadä

CONTENTS

ILLUSTRATIONS

A NOTE ON TERMINOLOGY

Ma-Nee Chacaby uses the terms *Anishinaabe* to refer to an Indigenous person and *Anishinaabeg* to refer to all Indigenous Peoples. In the text, Anishinaabe is also used as an adjective ("Indigenous") to describe other nouns, e.g., Anishinaabe medicine, Anishinaabe family, or Anishinaabe history. The Anishinaabe words she uses in this book are Ojibwe. The spellings of Anishinaabe terms were generally standardized with existing dictionaries, except in cases where they did not reflect Ma-Nee's pronunciation or knowledge of them.

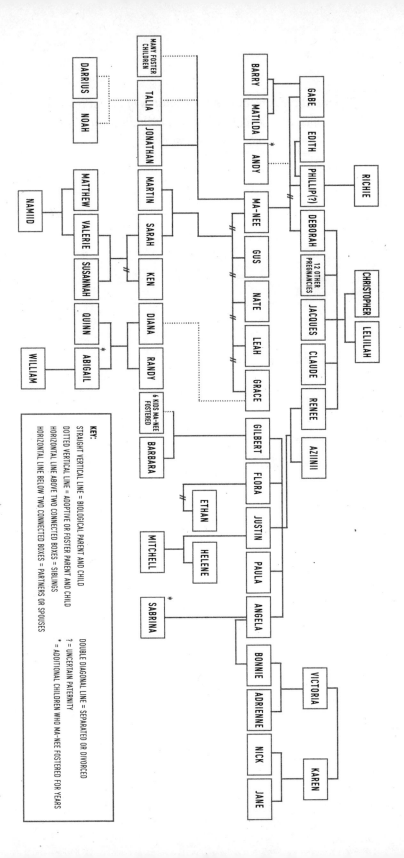

FIGURE 1. PARTIAL FAMILY TREE. THIS DIAGRAM DEPICTS A PORTION OF MA-NEE CHACABY'S FAMILY TREE AS OF DECEMBER 2013. FOR THE SAKE OF SIMPLICITY, ONLY INDIVIDUALS WHO ARE NAMED IN THE BOOK ARE INCLUDED. MANY OTHER BRANCHES IN THE TREE (E.G., SIBLINGS, COUSINS) ARE NOT DEPICTED.

KEY:
STRAIGHT VERTICAL LINE = BIOLOGICAL PARENT AND CHILD
DOTTED VERTICAL LINE = ADOPTIVE OR FOSTER PARENT AND CHILD
HORIZONTAL LINE ABOVE TWO CONNECTED BOXES = SIBLINGS
HORIZONTAL LINE BELOW TWO CONNECTED BOXES = PARTNERS OR SPOUSES

DOUBLE DIAGONAL LINE = SEPARATED OR DIVORCED
? = UNCERTAIN PATERNITY
* = ADDITIONAL CHILDREN WHO MA-NEE FOSTERED FOR YEARS

To protect the privacy and the identities of the individuals mentioned in this book, all names, excluding Ma-Nee's, have been substituted with pseudonyms.

CHAPTER ONE

MY GRANDMOTHER'S AND MY FAMILY'S HISTORY IN MANITOBA AND ONTARIO (1863–1952)

My name is Ma-Nee Chacaby. I am an Ojibwa-Cree elder, and I have both a male and a female spirit inside of me. I have experienced a long, complicated, and sometimes challenging journey over the course of my life. My earliest memories are of gathering kindling, making snowshoes, and hunting and trapping in my isolated Canadian community, where alcoholism was widespread in the 1950s. In 2013, more than half a century later, I performed a healing ceremony and then helped lead the first gay pride parade in my city, Thunder Bay, Ontario. This book describes the extraordinary path that led me to this place.

I will begin with what I have been told about my family history (Figure 1). Almost everything I know about the period before I was born I learned from my *kokum* (grandmother), who raised me. She was a Cree woman named Leliilah. She had a very long life and was the oldest among the elders in my Ojibwa-Cree community. When my grandmother died in 1967, her doctors guessed that she was over 100 years old. They entered her age as 104 on her death certificate, which means she would have been born in 1863. Some of the elders in our community later discussed the events in my grandmother's lifetime, and they agreed that she probably was born in the 1860s.

When I was a child, my *kokum* was well known as a storyteller in our community. Some of the following stories she told to me alone. Many I heard at social events, when other adults and children also gathered around to hear her tales.

MY GRANDMOTHER'S CHILDHOOD

My grandmother came from the prairies of Saskatchewan. She lost her parents when she was a small child, maybe four or five years old. She remembered living with them and other families in teepees on a hill or a cliff that overlooked a sandy, broad river. My *kokum* said her community was in conflict with another Native group in the area. She said the other group did not have enough young people to have babies, so they wanted to kidnap children from her community. Because of that dispute, she and other children had been warned that, if their homes were ever attacked, they must run and hide under a canoe at a certain spot, some distance away.

My *kokum* explained to me that one night her parents woke her in a rush and told her to hide. She and her brother and another child ran to the canoe and crawled under it. They heard yells and screams from their homes, but they stayed quiet for a very long time, until there was silence. Then they waited even longer, as long as they could. They came out from under the canoe in the morning. The air was filled with smoke, and the teepees had been burnt to the ground. Dead bodies lay everywhere. The children were terrified and hid under the canoe again. In the end, they were discovered by travelling Cree families that were canoeing by the area. My grandmother said that those adults buried the dead in a large mound, and then adopted her and the other two children into their own families.

My grandmother's adoptive parents were very good to her. She and her brother were raised in different households within the same extended family. Their new family had also been attacked by another Native group in their original home, so they were migrating across Canada, trying to reach relatives on the coast of James Bay, in northern Ontario. For many years my grandmother travelled with them by foot, horse, or canoe in summer, and dogsled and horse in winter. She said they moved faster on ice and snow, trapping and hunting animals as they travelled. My *kokum*'s strongest memories of those years were of bitterly cold winds that chilled her as she slept in a teepee at night. While they journeyed, she also saw a branch of the Hudson's Bay Company store when she was about ten or eleven years old. The store was on a boat that moved from place to place to sell its wares. In that store, my grandmother saw a mirror for the first time. She also tasted her first orange, which she remembered as being both sweet and sour.

My grandmother and her family must have travelled about 1,500 kilometres as they moved eastward along a northern route that crossed both Manitoba and Ontario. They only created a permanent home when they reached the Attawapiskat River on James Bay (Figure 2) in the early 1880s, when Leliilah was ten or eleven years old.

MY GRANDPARENTS' MARRIAGE

When my grandmother was about fourteen years old, she met my grandfather. His name was Christopher Chacaby. Christopher's father was French,

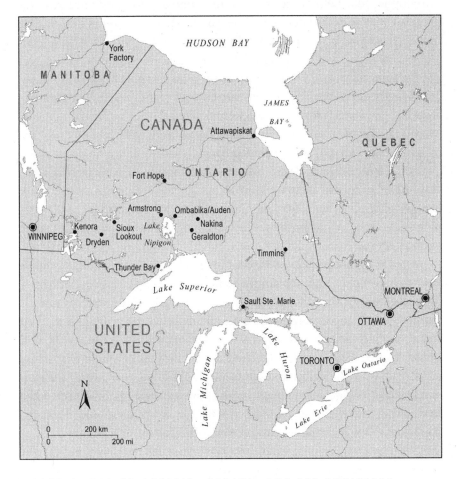

FIGURE 2. MAP OF ONTARIO, CANADA, AND KEY LOCATIONS.

and his mother was Ojibwa. My grandmother explained that Christopher spoke both French and Ojibwe, but he looked like a white man to her. She said he was shorter than her and had pale skin and curly hair. Christopher was about her age, but when she met him he was already working, as was common at the time. He and his father travelled around James Bay trading store-bought goods, like mirrors and blankets, for beaver, fox, muskrat, wolf, marten, lynx, and weasel fur.

Leliilah was shy but quickly drawn to Christopher. She said he was a good talker and very funny. He introduced her and her family to the fiddle, and he played it well for them. Before he left to continue trading, Christopher told Leliilah he would return one day to marry her. And he did return a few years later, when she was about sixteen years old. At that time, Christopher's father asked Leliilah's adoptive family whether Christopher could marry her. Her family said it was for Leliilah to decide, and she chose to marry him. It was normal for a man to give his bride's family gifts as part of the wedding ceremony, but my grandmother said that my grandfather was extraordinarily generous. He gave her family two horses, two moose for meat and *makizin* (moccasins), and some buffalo and deer hides for blankets. His gifts included two rifles, several mirrors, and some Hudson's Bay blankets. Their marriage ceremony followed Ojibwa-Cree customs of wrapping their wrists together in cedar, lighting a sacred fire, and giving each other a feather. Christopher also bought two gold wedding rings from a Hudson's Bay store. Many years later, my grandmother passed hers on to me.

After my grandparents married, they left her community, but Leliilah did not lose touch with her family. Late in her life, when I was a child, I remember her visiting with her brother and adoptive sister. But my grandmother's life changed completely after she married my grandfather. They journeyed together for many years and she helped him in his work as a trader. They travelled with other trading families and a guide who knew the territory. In the summer, each family used a huge *wiigwaasi jiimaan* (birch canoe), which was much larger than the ones people use today. Again, they travelled more quickly in winter, when they used dogsleds. They slept in teepees and conditions were often harsh.

I do not know exactly what routes or schedules my grandparents followed. They may have stopped sometimes for several months, like when my grandmother had her babies, and they may have returned over and over again to areas where they developed good trading relationships. In the course of years, though, they gradually shifted from James Bay, on the northeast border of Ontario, to Lake Nipigon, about 500 kilometres to the southwest (Figure 2). My *kokum* told me she had sixteen pregnancies during that period. Several of her babies were stillborn or died in childbirth. Others died during childhood from diseases, like smallpox, or accidents, like drowning. Only six of my grandmother's children survived into their teen years, including Deborah, my mother, who was Leliilah's youngest child. At home, my grandparents spoke in Cree, Ojibwe, and French, so their children grew up knowing all three languages. Most of my grandparents' surviving children stayed with them into adulthood, except for an older son and daughter who joined a residential school at some point during the family's travels. I don't know whether my grandparents chose for those two children to enroll in school, or it was something that the government forced them to do. I also don't know what happened to that aunt and uncle. My grandparents never saw them again. By the time my *kokum* was raising me in the 1950s, she expressed a lot of sadness about losing contact with them, and she believed they were dead.

My grandmother became blind during her travels with my grandfather. As I understand it, she lost her vision slowly over a period of years, and not as the result of an injury. She later told me that my grandfather wanted to take her to a hospital to have her eyes examined, but she never agreed to it. My grandmother was wary of hospitals, because most of the people she had known who had gone into them had died, and she did not trust white people's medicine. Instead, she and my grandfather adjusted their lives around her blindness and continued on their journey.

Over their years of travel, my grandparents had different ideas about where they would settle in the end. My grandfather wanted to go to Auden, an Ojibwa settlement on the northeastern shore of Lake Nipigon (Figure 2). Auden was quite isolated, but he thought he might get work there, because the Canadian railway was being built and maintained in that area. My grandmother instead had a dream of reaching the northern shore of Lake Superior, some 150 kilometres further south of Auden. She had a vision that she would find a gathering of Native peoples there. They never made it that far, though. While they were still on their way to Auden, my grandfather became seriously ill. He was taken to a hospital where he died. My grandmother ended up settling down near Auden, in Ombabika, with her four remaining adult children, Jacques, Renee, Claude, and—after some time—my mother, Deborah. My grandmother always spoke of my grandfather with a great love and respect. She lived many years after he died, but she never remarried.

While my grandmother lived in Ombabika, she and some other local Native people signed a treaty with Canadian government representatives and became registered as "treaty" or "status" Indians. Ombabika was not part of a reserve when my grandmother lived there. Instead, local treaty Indians became members of the Fort Hope Reserve, which had been formed 150 kilometres north of Ombabika in July of 1905 (Figure 2). In signing the treaty, my grandmother was promised health, education, and social services by the federal government.

MY MOTHER'S EARLY LIFE, AND MY BIRTH AND ADOPTION

I believe my mother, Deborah, was born in 1908, so my grandmother would have been about forty-five years old when she gave birth to her last child. I don't know very much about my mother's childhood, because she never told me about it. What I know I learned from my grandmother and my cousin Flora, who was a young woman when I was a child in Ombabika. I believe my mom spent her childhood travelling with her parents. When my grandfather died, my mother was already a young woman. She continued living with my grandmother, but at some point she had a serious accident. I heard it happened when she climbed a tree and was trying to move from that tree to another one over a river in cold weather, but the trees were icy, and she slipped and fell. Her hips and some other major bones were broken, so she was taken to a hospital in Winnipeg, Manitoba, where she was put in a body cast. My mother had to learn to walk again, and she spent many years recovering from her accident. For a part of that time, she lived with some nurses and they taught her to bake and to speak English.

While staying in Winnipeg, my mother became sick with tuberculosis, so she was transferred to a tuberculosis sanatorium in Thunder Bay, Ontario, where she lived for several years. During her first years at the sanatorium, a woman from Ombabika was staying there as well. She and my mother must not have been sick at that stage, or they left the sanatorium without permission, because the woman later told people in Ombabika that she and my mom sometimes went downtown together to get drunk. At some point during that period, my mother became pregnant with me. I am not certain who my father was, because she did not tell me. A couple of men have been mentioned by others over the years, and one of them seems like he is a strong possibility, but none of them were ever definitely confirmed.

In any case, I was born in the tuberculosis sanatorium on 22 July 1950. My mother was in her early forties, which was unusually late to have a first child. After I was born, my mom gave me up for adoption. I was taken home by a French couple in Thunder Bay. The woman from Ombabika who was staying in the sanatorium mentioned my birth in a letter to someone back home, so my grandmother found out about it afterward. She travelled to Thunder Bay to find me, with the assistance of a young woman named Irene, who spoke English well. Together they went through a long process to find me and get custody of me. I was almost two years old when they finally took me back to Ombabika.

I don't know what name the French family called me during my first two years, but my grandmother always called me "Ma-Nee." She liked that name since it sounded like the name of a French artist who my grandfather admired. Today I believe she must have meant Manet or Monet. More than anything else, though, my grandmother said she named me after a beautiful *miinikaa* (place with many blueberries), because I had been born in the blueberry season.

CHAPTER TWO

FIRST DISCOVERIES, JOYS, AND SORROWS—MY EARLY CHILDHOOD IN OMBABIKA (1952–1958)

From the age of two until I was twenty years old, I lived in the neighbouring settlements of Ombabika and Auden in northwest Ontario. Ombabika lay a couple of kilometres west of Auden. The two communities were separated by both the Ombabika River, which ran north to south at that point, and the national transcontinental railway, which ran east to west. Summit Lake, the source of the Ombabika River, lies about twenty kilometres northeast of Ombabika and Auden. Lake Nipigon, the river's final destination and the largest lake entirely within Ontario's boundaries, lies about twenty-five kilometres to the southwest (Figure 2).

Until I was sixteen years old, I lived in Ombabika, which had an almost entirely Ojibwa and Cree community. Most people spoke Ojibwe, but my family spoke Cree at home as well. The population of Anishinaabeg (Indigenous people; singular Anishinaabe) was spread out across a wide area, with houses as much as one kilometre apart. Like everyone else, my family lived in wooden homes without running water or electricity. Our cabin and nearby shack were built on the shore of Blusky Lake, a large pond that had formed after beavers dammed a stream off the Ombabika River. Blusky Lake may have been a kilometre across at its widest section, so it was not very large, but it was big enough that children were not allowed to cross it on their own.

My family lived several kilometres away from the Auden railroad station. When we visited Auden, we either walked over the railway bridge or paddled our canoes across the Ombabika River. Most of the houses in Auden were fairly close together. Houses around the local branch of the Hudson's Bay store—where most white people lived—were especially dense. The store sold groceries and equipment needed for hunting, fishing, and trapping. Larger Hudson's Bay branches, and hospitals, could be reached in towns further up and down the railway line. Armstrong is about 80 kilometres to the west of Auden as the crow flies, while Sioux Lookout is a further 220 kilometres to the west beyond Armstrong (Figure 2). Nakina lies 90 kilometres east of Auden, and Geraldton and Longlac are 90 to 110 kilometres to the southeast. The cities of Fort William and Port Arthur, which in 1970 combined to become the city of Thunder Bay, lay on the northern shore of Lake Superior, about 250 kilometres to the southwest.

In Ombabika we supported ourselves by fishing, gathering fruits and vegetables, and hunting and trapping animals. Some men also worked for the Canadian government constructing and maintaining the local section of the railway. Others worked for the Abitibi Pulp and Paper Company, which was clear-cutting nearby forests. Depending on where they camped, Abitibi workers loaded logs into the Ombabika River upstream at Summit Lake, Toronto Lake, Goode Lake, or Pigeon Lake. The men then ferried them downstream until they were unloaded in Ombabika or Auden, where they were moved to freight trains or trucks. There was a two-lane gravel road that connected Auden and Ombabika to the main Ontario highways. Cars could not drive on that road when it became covered in snow in winter.

Ombabika also had a Catholic and a Protestant church. The white priest and Protestant minister spoke in English during services and were assisted by Anishinaabe church members who translated their words into Ojibwe for the people gathered there. Those translators may have been the only adult Anishinaabeg who spoke English well. I hardly ever heard other adults speak English in Ombabika, although it is possible some knew it from school, work experience, or living in cities. Some Native people spoke a bit of French, especially if they had French ancestry, like my family.

When I was a child, Ombabika and Auden shared a one-room schoolhouse that had been open for at least twenty years, because some of the adults in their twenties and thirties had attended it as children. The school probably was built and maintained by the Hudson's Bay Company, the Abitibi Pulp and Paper Company, and the Canadian National Railway for their workers' children. The white children whose parents worked for those companies made up only a few of the students, but the schoolteachers were white and spoke only in English.

Many of my childhood experiences in Ombabika were fun and joyful, including days I spent with my grandmother, exploring on my own, or playing with friends. Some parts of my childhood were difficult, though. Alcohol abuse was very common in Ombabika, and I experienced violence in many forms, including beatings and sexual abuse. It is painful to revisit my memories of that time, but I have tried to do so honestly and fully here.

EARLY MEMORIES OF LANGUAGE AND PLAY

Some of my earliest memories from Ombabika are good ones. I was a small child, and I believe I was kept in a *tikinagan* until a fairly late age. A *tikinagan* is a swaddling cradle made out of a flat wooden board, beaded animal skin, and moss on the inside. It usually holds a baby snugly, like a bunting bag, but a similar cradleboard might be used to carry toddlers, leaving their hands free. One of my earliest memories is of being in a *tikinagan* while watching people's heads move up and down as they picked blueberries. I also remember being thrilled when my mother's brother, my uncle Jacques, carried me on his shoulders as I held on to his long, reddish-brown ponytail. Jacques was a musïcian, and I happily danced jigs when he played his fiddle.

During my first years in Ombabika, I didn't speak Ojibwe or Cree. Instead, for a long time, I spoke a language that no one seemed to understand, except for my grandmother. She helped me figure out how to communicate with people using sign language instead. For example, when I wanted water (which I remember calling "wadenama" in my language), she explained I needed to show people what I meant. I realize now that I probably was trying to speak French or English, because the white family that adopted me during my first two years spoke one of those languages to me. I remember my uncle Jacques laughing affectionately at how I talked and moved my hands around when I was trying to express myself. He would say, "That's a little French girl right there!" And my grandmother would chuckle and reply, "Maybe she's following in her grandfather's footsteps." In the end I learned to speak Cree with my grandmother, my uncle Jacques, and my mother. When I was seven years old, my mom married an Ojibwa man, and he began to teach me Ojibwe numbers and other words.

The fact that I couldn't speak Ojibwe or Cree set me apart from other children in my early years. I was different in other ways too. I had a lot of energy, and I had a hard time keeping still. I ran away from situations I didn't like. And I refused to wear skirts like other girls. Instead, I would strip off my skirt and run around just wearing my heavy bloomers, which were held up by a string, a safety pin, or a belt. My bloomers were made of a thick, warm, blue material that puffed out along my thighs, but came together with elastic at my knees. I saw them as pants, not underwear, and they were very comfortable, so I loved wearing them. But no one else wore bloomers the way I did, and some people seemed to see me as strange, stubborn, or dumb. A few called me a "devil's child." Others made it clear to me that I was an unwanted, fatherless child—a bastard. People in Ombabika looked down on children who did not have a father, especially if they were girls.

When I was young, I often played alone. I made up my own games. I loved standing in the middle of a field of tall grasses to listen as they rustled and made music in the wind. I would brush the grasses to my front and sides to hear what different sounds they made. I enjoyed hearing tree leaves rubbing together, wood crackling as it burned, and water dripping or rippling in streams. Underneath a beautiful boulder, I discovered a hidden spot where I could listen to the wind whistling like music. That place gave me joy and comfort for many years. Nobody knew about it, and I felt completely safe when I was in it. From a young age, going outdoors into the fields and woods was a source of comfort and peace when I was sad or afraid. Being in the bush on my own could also be exciting, because I explored the wilderness like a great playground. One of my favourite things to do in winter was to take a toboggan, or anything else I could use as a sled, and go up and down snowy slopes for hours.

I also liked to build things out of wood and other materials I found in the forests. I tried to make nests for birds, carefully crafting little baskets out of sticks and grass, and placing leaves inside of them to make them comfortable. There was a long period, maybe months or years, when I built miniature towns out of mud, sticks, and leaves in the woods. And there were times when I dug deep holes in the ground. I did this once after someone told me that the devil lived in the fires of hell, far underground. I wanted to see what those fires looked like! Another time I dug a massive hole after someone told me China was on the other side of the earth, directly under our feet. Of course, I wanted to see what that looked like too.

I made many discoveries when I was playing outdoors alone. A sad one happened once when I was six or seven years old and hiking by the river. I remember it was a spring day and the sun was shining brightly. Sunlight reflected off the fast-moving water, and the leaves around me gave off a sweet, strong smell. I had a stick in my hand that I had planned to use to fish in the river, but I was nervous about getting too close to the water, which was overflowing the river's banks due to snowmelt. I came across a fallen-down shack with a water-filled barrel inside, so I thought I would try fishing in the barrel instead. I made myself a little fishing pole, using the stick, some string, and a big safety pin that was holding up my pants.

As soon as my stick was in the water, it poked something and I thought, "Oh! I caught a fish, a real fish!" I pulled up a heavy bundle of cloth and placed it on the ground to unwrap it. But the first thing I saw as I opened the soaking bundle was a little human face, so I dropped the cloth and ran right out of the shack. I kept going until I found my grandmother's friend, our widowed neighbour, Renard. I brought him back to the shack with me. Renard murmured, "Ohhhhh...," as he gently loosened the bundle and pulled a baby out of it. He wrapped the baby in something else and took it away, I guess to give it a proper burial. Later that evening, my grandmother told me no one knew whose baby it was or how it had died. She explained the baby's mother probably did not want anyone to know she had had it, so she hid it in the barrel. I was confused and saddened, because I could not understand why someone would do that.

Some of my other discoveries in the woods also shocked me, although most were harmless. Once when I was about the same age, I was jumping from tree to tree when I missed my footing and fell to the ground. I landed near a young couple that I had not noticed earlier. The man was moving on top of the woman in a way that scared me, like he was hurting her. I ran and got Renard again, and I told him something awful was happening. I brought him back to that spot. When he saw the couple, he covered my eyes and pulled me away. As we walked back to my house, he told me that I wasn't supposed to have seen that, because it was something that only happened between grown-up men and women. When I asked him why they were hurting each other, he said they weren't—that in fact they were enjoying themselves. He wouldn't discuss it further. He told me to ask my grandmother if I had any more questions about it.

During my outdoor explorations, I discovered different materials I could use for toys, art, or crafts. When I was about seven or eight years old, for instance, I found clay for the first time. It was at the spot, across Blusky Lake and directly facing our house, where my family buried and stored food in the summer. Right away I saw what fun it was to play with clay, given all the different shapes and forms I could make out of it. After that, I always brought clay home whenever I visited that place. I also had other playthings people had created for me. One of my toys was made out of a large moose bone that had a hole where many small bones were attached to it on a string. The game was to flip each of the small bones into the hole in the big bone. It required a lot of patience and focus, so it kept me busy for a long time.

Around the same age, I discovered I could use charcoal to draw on the inside of birchbark, either by using my fingers or a little stick with a charred tip. Soon I also figured out that I could smash certain berries and mix them with ash to make orange and red paint. I also made paint colours from the rotting, burnt-looking logs that my stepdad used to tan hides. Sometimes I used flattened birchbark for my paintings, and at other times I worked on old, brown wallpaper.

I may have gotten the idea of drawing and painting pictures from comic books. Someone had brought a few comic books to our house when I was little, and I liked to study them and copy their pictures. I also tried to sketch people and things around me. I once spent a long time making a portrait of my grandmother. I had her sit and tell me stories while I sketched her on a large, flattened piece of birchbark. I drew her wrinkled face carefully with ashes from a firepit and a pencil stub. I tried to capture the way she was sitting with a little teapot by her side. When I finished, everybody thought that picture was very good, so they hung it up on a wall. Then one day some white people came to interview my grandmother. A woman from the Department of Indian Affairs admired my painting. She asked my uncle Jacques if she could take it to Ottawa to show to people there, and then bring it back the next time she returned. My uncle and I agreed. That woman did return later, but she never brought back my painting. I tried to ask her about it. When she realized what I was asking, she spoke to me in English, which I did not understand, and hit her head in a dramatic way, as if to say that she had forgotten it.

MY GRANDMOTHER LELIILAH

The best memories from my childhood are those of my grandmother, and our life together. My *kokum* was already very old when I was a child. She probably was in her late eighties when she brought me back from Thunder Bay, and she certainly was one of the oldest people in Ombabika during my childhood. My grandmother did not smoke, drink alcohol, or use other drugs. She tried to take good care of her health, which probably contributed to her long life. One of my strongest memories of my *kokum* is her softness: her beautiful, silky, white hair; what seemed like a thousand fine wrinkles on her face; and the loose folds of her brown skin, which hung gently from her arms and neck. When I was small, I recall once leaning back against my grandmother's knees and wrapping her long hanging breasts around my ears to make her laugh. My grandmother chuckled as she freed herself from me.

Despite her advanced age, my *kokum* still had some of her teeth. I remember this because she used them to bite my fingers playfully. Her eyes were a mix of blue, green, and grey, which may have been caused by her blindness. When she was younger, a priest had given her tiny, round, gold-rimmed glasses. By the time I knew her, the glasses did not help her see, but she put them on when she met white people out of appreciation for the gift the priest had once given her. Despite her blindness, she was very aware of what was happening around her. She knew the small area where we lived extremely well. In fact, she knew the ground better than I did! Often she sensed what was happening even if she couldn't see it. I remember once making faces at her behind her back, until she said, "I know you're making faces at me." And I thought, "Wow, that woman can see everything!"

My grandmother usually wore a long skirt, a blouse, and a sweater or a shawl. I heard that she was a tall woman in her youth, but it is difficult to guess how tall, because by the time I knew her, her back was very hunched over. She told me her back had been injured when she fell through a layer of ice on a lake once, and the ice blocks came back together, pressing against her on both sides. By the time I was fifteen and at my full adult height, five feet and three inches, I was taller than her. She was very fragile and could not walk or even stand easily on her own. She used a walking stick, but still sometimes shook very badly if she tried to stand without support.

There were a number of helpers who assisted my grandmother to get around and do other activities. Through her, they became my helpers too, because they assisted me in ways she could not as I was growing up. My *kokum*'s helpers were adults who took on a variety of tasks, like preparing meals for her, doing needed chores, or fixing her hair nicely. Renard was one of them. He lived in a little hut near our shack with his children. Like a lot of men in Ombabika, Renard wore old, checkered shirts and jeans, and was a bit scruffy looking. He was missing some teeth and always had a hat on his head, so that his hair stuck out a bit underneath, at the back and the sides. I had heard rumors that Renard had not always been kind to his wife, and that he got into trouble when he got drunk, but I never saw anything like that. I only knew him to be gentle and helpful, so I trusted and respected him. He, in turn, admired my grandmother and was devoted to her. He used to tell me that my *kokum* was a wonderful woman, because she chose to look after me even when she was very old.

Another of my grandmother's helpers was Irene, my godmother, who helped my *kokum* find me after I was born in Thunder Bay. When I was little, Irene prepared breakfast for me and my grandmother each morning, and then she did a few other chores before she left. My grandmother called Irene my godmother, because priests had introduced that term in Ombabika to mean a child's guardian if his or her parents died. Before my mother moved to Ombabika, Irene agreed to look after me if my grandmother died. My *kokum* sometimes gave Irene gifts. Once I remember she gave her a beautiful scarf that Irene tied around her long, dark hair right away.

As I grew older, I became one of my grandmother's main helpers. Every day I made her tea, stacked our wood, and got kindling for our stove. I fetched things for her, and guided her wherever she wanted to go. In the summer, I usually took her to the long house, a large building nearby where my aunt Renee's family and several other families lived. Friends and neighbours often gathered there during the day, so my *kokum* enjoyed sitting outside and socializing with people as they came by.

Traditionally, every family had a totem, which is an animal they honoured and identified with. By the time I was growing up in Ombabika, though, most people did not seem to be very concerned about clans. The majority of Ombabika residents were Ojibwe, so they would have been members of clans through their fathers' families, but many people had converted to Christianity, so they did not follow such beliefs and practices anymore. Among children, the topic of a clan usually only came up when someone was being teased, for example, when a boy in the sturgeon clan was told he smelled bad, like a fish.

My grandmother was in the *amik* (beaver) clan. Through her, my mother and I were in the same clan, and this was important to all of us. I do not know if we were members of my grandmother's clan because her particular Cree tradition followed clans through a mother's family, or because we did not have a father's clan to follow. My grandfather had been Métis, so he may not have had a clan, and I do not know who my father was, or what his clan might be. In any case, I have never had any doubt that I am a member of the beaver clan. My grandmother taught me to study beavers, like the hard-working ways they built and maintained their homes, and the smart ways they reused objects. She explained that members of our clan do not kill beavers, and we do not eat them. Most importantly, my grandmother stressed that people should never marry within the same clan, because it would be like sisters marrying brothers.

Most adults I knew in Ombabika were Christian. At times my grandmother also went to services at the Catholic and Protestant churches. She enjoyed the celebrations and socializing that could happen there. My *kokum* said that white people believed their God lived in a house, but she did not believe that. She instead believed that *Gitchi Manitou* (the Great Spirit) lived everywhere. Still, my grandmother told me that we should be respectful whenever we visited church, and that we should listen and always try to find at least one good thing in the minister's sermon to take away to use in our own lives.

My grandmother was a spiritual person. She believed in the sacred powers of *giizhik* (cedar), *wiiskwemushgan* (sweetgrass), *nasemaa* (tobacco), and *mashkodewashk* (sage). She used them to cleanse and bless people when they came to her for spiritual help. She did this by smudging, which means she talked with the Great Spirit while she burned sweetgrass or sage, using her hand or a feather to guide the smoke gently over a person's head and body. I remember her smudging me like that while praying for me to learn to speak Cree and Ojibwe when I was small. From time to time my *kokum* also went into the bush to fast and cleanse herself physically and spiritually in a *madodoigan* (sweat lodge).

In Ombabika, people also sometimes came to my grandmother when they were sick. She prepared herbal medicines for them to drink or rub on their bodies. Because of her blindness, I helped her to find the specific flowers and plants she wanted gathered during the spring, summer, and fall. She also made a *mashkikiiwazh* (medicine bag) for each of our family members to wear, to protect and care for us. These were small, beaded, leather pouches with sacred items permanently sealed in them. They were to be worn around the neck. I recall she once made a medicine bag for my aunt Renee's son, Justin, after his parents complained that he misbehaved. I remember her telling them, "Oh, well, that's just the way he is. You have to accept him." Justin was a few years older than me. He had lived with my grandmother before I came to live with her, and sometimes he still came to stay with us for a few nights. Justin was a bit jealous that I got to live with our *kokum* all of the time. He liked to tell me that he was her first baby.

My grandmother was a storyteller, so at social events people gathered around the open fire to hear what she had to say. One of the main characters in her stories was a traveller named Chacaby, who could transform. Sometimes Chacaby was a man and sometimes Chacaby was a woman, depending on the story. My grandmother also told a legend about a woman who created the first *madayigan* (drum). She explained that, a long time ago, the men in one community had all gone away to war and not returned. When a woman from that same community was walking in a forest one day, she heard a voice that told her to make a song to bring the men back. Soon after, that woman went hunting and killed an elk. After she had prepared the elk's hide, she had a vision of making a large circular shape, like a section of a hollowed-out tree trunk, and stretching the hide tightly over it to make music. And that is how she made the first drum. When she played a song on that drum, it brought many people together, including the men who had travelled far away.

I did not always understand the stories my grandmother told. Sometimes I listened and enjoyed them, and sometimes I found them boring, so

I left. But I remember how adults listened closely to her and often laughed heartily while she told a tale. When I was about seven or eight years old, some white people came to interview my grandmother. I realize now that they wanted to record her stories, but at the time I did not understand what they were doing. My *kokum* was supposed to answer their questions inside of a tent, using an Anishinaabe interpreter. The white men had set up a battery outside the tent, and connected it via wires running underneath the canvas to a machine with big wheels inside. I watched a man set it up and test the equipment by talking into the machine and then playing back his own voice. I understood they wanted to do the same thing with my grandmother's voice, but I feared they might capture her entirely, and keep her inside the machine. So I waited outside the tent until I heard my grandmother say, "*Eya* (Yes)," agreeing to talk. They then played her voice back as a test. As soon as I heard that, I took the little hatchet I carried on my belt, chopped through the wires, and moved away quickly. It took a while for the men to figure out why their machine had stopped working. They said they couldn't repair it there, so they just wrote down my grandmother's responses to their questions instead. Nobody knew who had cut the wires, except for my grandmother, who guessed it was me. She talked to me about it later and tried to reassure me that they would not have hurt her.

My grandmother had a gentle way of teaching me when I had done something I should not have done. When it was something serious, she took me out on Blusky Lake in a canoe to talk to me. On the lake, I could not run away, so I had to listen to her. That worked very well. My grandmother also told me stories to teach me lessons, and sometimes maybe to frighten me away from dangerous activities, like taking off into the snow to go sledding by myself. She probably worried about me being out alone in the bush in winter. One time I remember she told me a story about travellers who stayed overnight in a little dome they built out of snow and branches. While they were there, she said, the people saw someone speed toward them moving incredibly fast. When he arrived at their dome's entrance, they saw he was huge—much bigger than normal people—and he had eyes like blue knives, which they thought might be made of frost. That story frightened me. For a little while, it made me too scared to go far away to toboggan each morning. But soon I got over it, and continued as I had before.

My grandmother was always very loving with me. When other people called me weird or poisonous, she would tell me that I was curious and smart in ways that some people did not understand. She said that in my life I would have a long and difficult *bimose* (walk or journey), and I would have to be courageous, like a warrior. As a small child I did not understand her. I thought she meant that one day I would actually stand up and walk a great distance. She used to touch my hands and tell me, "When you grow up, you're going to be a great teacher of our people. You will help others. You will be a medicine woman."

MY MOTHER DEBORAH

When I was about five or six years old, my mother came to live in Ombabika. Until that time, I had always thought my grandmother was my mother, and I actually called her "*maamaa*" (mother). Then one day she told me a woman would be coming to Ombabika who was her daughter and my real mother. After my mother arrived, I learned to call my grandmother "*kokum*," but I never learned to call my mother "*maamaa*." As a child, I almost always called her Deborah.

The first time I saw my mother, she came into my room as I was lying in my little bed under mosquito netting. She was a tall woman, big-boned, but not fat. She had naturally wavy, black hair, and skin that was paler than mine and my grandmother's. From the start, my mom seemed very unhappy with me. In fact, I think she hated me sometimes. I have never understood why. Maybe my being born made her life worse. Once she told me she wished I had been a boy, because then her life would not have been so difficult. She may have been ashamed that I was a girl who acted like a boy, wearing pants and playing outdoors as a small child, and later working with machinery, and trapping and hunting.

When my mother first came to Ombabika, she lived in a trapper's tent with some other people. They set it up by digging a room about five feet deep into the earth and by reinforcing the dirt walls with wood. They put a white canvas tent on top of it, and used branches, bark, and moss for insulation in the wintertime. I remember my mother was still living in that tent the winter I fell through the ice on the nearby river. She and I had been walking together when it happened. My hood and the back of my coat became soaked as I floated in the freezing water, but I was not very scared. My mom crawled away from me off the ice, maybe because she wasn't strong enough to get me out, or maybe because she was afraid she would fall in too. She got help from people in the nearby tent, so someone else pulled me out.

Most of the time when I was around my mom she didn't talk to me, and usually she just ignored me. Sometimes, though, she became very angry with me. Then she would call me a devil's child and beat me, especially if my grandmother and my stepdad were not around. My mom didn't warn me when she was going to hit me, she would just grab me and start beating me on my back, usually using a homemade wooden broom. There were times when she was more controlled in her abuse, and she seemed to take pleasure in hurting me. Once when I was about seven or eight years old, for instance, I was sleeping at my mother's house because my grandmother was away, and she woke me by pinching my legs, my butt, and my lower back. When I started to cry, she used some kind of flat stick to slap me all over my body. She was drunk as she did this, and she laughed.

My mom was only kind to me once in a while. One time when I was eight or nine years old, again when my grandmother was away, my mother called me into her house. I thought, "Oh no, not again," expecting to be hit. Instead, she made tea for us both and told me stories about her life when she lived in Winnipeg. She described amazing things she had seen in that city, like underground shopping centres and roads built as long bridges, up high in the sky. When she was done talking to me, she asked me if she could brush my hair. Again, I was wary, because I thought that she might beat me with the brush. But actually she just neatened my hair and braided it nicely. Later that day, we were visited by one of my mother's friends and her daughter. So it may be that my mom only was nice to me to make it appear that we got along when her friend visited. But, at the time, it felt like she meant it.

I never saw my mother treat anyone else in the abusive way she often treated me. She got along well with other people, and she was always respectful toward her own mother. My mom was active in the Ombabika community. Sometimes she went from house to house to organize teenagers to do chores for their families, like cutting wood. My mom also attended the Catholic and Protestant churches regularly. Most of her friends went with their children, so she wanted me to attend church with her, too. I did not like to get up so early on Sunday mornings. At first my mom forced me to go, but then my grandmother told her to let me be. My *kokum* said I should be allowed to decide whether I wanted to attend church.

My mom was a fine musician—she played the fiddle and the accordion, and she had a beautiful singing voice. She also was a good cook, and sometimes she hosted big dinners at her house. Her Christmas fish dinners were well known, and everyone agreed she made the best pudding in Ombabika. It was delicious! She prepared her pudding by wrapping it in a flour sack, like a big round sausage. She first boiled it in water on the stove, and then baked it in the oven. My mother also often sewed quilts with other women, and she did beadwork on moccasins and belts on her own. She used a wooden board to brace belts as she beaded them. She even made a small belt for me that I wore for a long time to hold up my bloomers. I don't know if my mother ever earned any money from her sewing, beadwork, or cooking. Every so often she went away for days or weeks. It is possible she earned money by washing clothes or doing other kinds of domestic work at those times, but I don't know for sure.

My mom wore clothes typical of women in Ombabika: homemade dresses that reached her calves; long brown stockings that ran the length of her legs; and long-sleeved sweaters of different colours. Often she also wore a shawl or a kerchief outside, or a white apron while doing housework. She styled her long hair like a lot of other women of her age, wearing it loose, braided down her back, or in a bun held together by bobby pins.

While my mother lived in Ombabika, she still experienced much pain from her earlier accident. One of her legs was shorter than the other, so she limped when she walked. Once in a while her pain became great, and then she used a wheelchair to get around. It was a foldable, wooden chair with a little rubber and metal tire at the bottom of each of its four legs, so it could roll. Sometimes my mom used her wheelchair as a walker, supporting herself as she stood or walked, but if she became very tired she sat down in it. She could wheel herself around fairly well on Ombabika's compacted gravel roads.

A couple of years after my mother moved to Ombabika, she married an Ojibwa man named Gabe. They seemed happy together. I don't remember them ever arguing. They laughed and kissed a lot; they also often got drunk together. Gabe mainly worked as a trapper and a hunter, but at times he was employed by the railroad, or as a fishing and hunting guide for white men who visited the area. Gabe was a dark, rough-skinned man who usually had a light beard or stubble on his face. Like a lot of men in Ombabika, he was missing some teeth. Gabe was shorter than my mom and several years younger than her, but he had two children who were about seven or eight years older than me, Matilda and Barry. Soon after my mom and Gabe got married, they built a cabin and Matilda and Barry came to live with them.

When I was eight years old, my mom told me and other people that she had a baby growing inside of her. Over the following months, I did not pay attention to whether her stomach grew or not. Then one day my mom and stepdad went away for a long time. When they returned, they brought back a baby boy named Andy. From the time Andy was a baby, I was responsible for looking after him a lot of the time, so he always called me "*maamaa*" or "mum." For many years I assumed he was my mom's and stepdad's biological child, which made him my biological half-brother, but when I was in my late thirties my cousin Flora told me that my mom and stepdad had adopted Andy. Flora explained my mom and stepdad did not want it widely known that they were adopting a baby, so they pretended my mom was pregnant before they brought Andy home.

DAILY LIFE

My grandmother and I lived in a little one-room shack made out of wooden boards. It had three windows, two low wooden beds, and a wood stove in the centre. My grandmother's bed was much larger and nicer than mine, but we both had a lot of heavy quilts and blankets, which kept us warm at night. For a number of years I had a dog named Diienge, who stayed outside our shack. She had floppy ears and a large body covered in curly, black-and-white fur. Diienge was my companion and protected me from other dogs when I was out wandering. I was very affectionate with her, hugging her and petting her a lot. She, in turn, comforted me when she sensed I was sad or frightened.

My mother, stepfather, Matilda, Barry, and Andy lived in a large, square log cabin next door to the shack where my grandmother and I lived. There were no homes close to ours, except for the long house, which was some distance away and up a small hill. Inside of the long house, there was a hallway that ran the length of the building, and each room off of the hallway housed an entire family. Most of the families had many children. Grandparents, parents, and children all lived together in one room. My aunt Renee and her husband Aziinii lived in one of those rooms with four of their children: Paula, Angela, Justin, and Flora. They also had some older children who had already left home to attend a residential school or start their own families.

My mom's and stepdad's cabin was very comfortable and had a lot of space, unlike the single rooms where families lived in the long house, or the shack where my grandmother and I lived. The cabin had a main room with an open kitchen and living area. My mother and stepdad had a bedroom of their own. Barry and Matilda had beds which were separated from the main room, and each other, by blanket dividers. Later, when I was about twelve years old and my grandmother was becoming more frail, we also moved into the cabin and slept on beds in the main room. During the first years, the cabin only had one central wood stove for heating, but in later years my mother had a cooking stove installed as well. We all used candles, bear grease lamps, and kerosene lamps.

My stepbrother Barry was a kind, soft-spoken, and gentle person. He was a smooth-skinned boy with a long, black ponytail. Barry always treated me with respect, listening to me and never yelling at me. He was affectionate and sometimes hugged me or held me to comfort me. I remember him offering to help me with chores when I had too many to do, and telling me stories under the stars at night. I could not see stars well, but I enjoyed lying beside him and listening to tales he wove about the bear star, the dog star, the moose star, and others. Sometimes I fell asleep listening to his stories.

Barry tried to protect me from Matilda, who was very mean to me. Matilda enjoyed playing tricks on me, like sometimes she messed up my bed after I had made it in the morning, and then told my mom I had not done it. Another time, when I was older, she asked to cut my long hair for a dime. I knew that would be enough *zhooniyaa* (money) to buy ten hard candies, so I agreed, not understanding how much my grandmother and others valued my long hair, which had never been cut. Of course, Matilda did a terrible job, leaving me with a crude bowl cut, and my mom and stepdad were not pleased. Still, Matilda and my mother usually got along very well. They both liked to sew with the other girls and women at the long house. My mom and Matilda often made fun of me together, and sometimes Matilda watched and laughed when my mom hit me.

Within our shared household, all of the people who were big enough were responsible for carrying water from Blusky Lake to the cabin. Water was carried in buckets on the ends of a long wooden bar that rested on a person's shoulders. Inside the cabin, we used water for cooking, bathing, and washing clothes in a large bucket. We heated water on the stove to fill the big bucket for baths, and then we all shared the same bath water. Whoever lined up first got the first bath. I almost always was first, because I didn't like to clean myself in dirty water! In warm weather, Barry and Matilda sometimes bathed in Blusky Lake instead, but I didn't because I didn't know how to swim. We cleaned our teeth using a mixture of boiled water and minty herbs that my grandmother prepared. My mom was very concerned about cleanliness and kept an eye on us to make sure we rinsed and gargled with that solution once a day. We all shared an outhouse, which was not much different from outhouses today. It was a moveable shack, so once a hole was filled up, we'd put sawdust on top of it, dig a new hole further away, and move the whole structure there. My mom talked a lot about the importance of keeping our outhouse clean. She did that chore herself to make sure it was done right. At night, we all used a small bucket inside our homes as a toilet, so we did not have to go outside after dark.

During the summer, my family stored food in a cool spot near a stream on the other side of Blusky Lake, where my stepdad had dug a pit in the clay. We kept a large food supply there, including fresh and dried meat, and other dried goods like fish, blueberries, raspberries, rosehips, and willow sticks, which we used to make string. Our stockpile was covered in clay, so it stayed cool and preserved, and my stepdad put a big woodpile on top of it to prevent bears and other animals from unearthing it. Year-round we ate dumplings made out of flour and lard, as well as fish, berries, and, now and then, fresh, smoked, or dried meat. I tasted jam for the first time after my mother married my stepdad. He used to mix jam with milk and bread, squishing them all together in a bowl, and I found it wonderfully sweet. Later, there were times when my mom bought macaroni, oats, and butter at the Hudson's Bay store, so we began to eat those at home too. When we ran out, I didn't miss the macaroni and the oats, but I missed the butter!

In addition to caring for my grandmother, I had a number of chores to do each day. Starting when I was about six years old until my teens, I was responsible for cleaning fish with my friend Pascal, who was a cousin by marriage. That was not a popular chore—other kids got to do easier tasks, like sewing or washing dishes. The fish were gathered in nets and dumped into a big bathtub at the lakeshore each morning. Then Pascal and I would skin each fish, cut it open, remove its bones and guts, and fillet it. Before we started, an adult combed bear grease into our hair and spread it over our skin to repel bugs. That worked pretty well to protect us from mosquitoes and horseflies, but it was still a smelly job. Pascal and I always tried to finish before the heat of the day. After we were done with our chore, we sometimes played together. We liked to pretend to go hunting, or we would explore plants and bugs. At times, Pascal helped me build tiny mud-and-branch homes for the miniature village I had created in the woods.

LEARNING TRADITIONAL SKILLS

During the few times when my mother was kind to me, she taught me useful skills. She knew I didn't like sewing quilts, but once she called me to her and asked if I would like to make my own clothing, and I was eager to do it. She taught me how to make moccasins, shirts, and bonnets. Our indoor moccasins were small and made of thin leather, while those for outdoors were made of thick leather that could be wrapped around the lower leg, to prevent snow getting inside our pants. We used deer sinew to sew moccasins because of its strength, but it took a long time to turn sinew into thread, requiring hours of pulling and cutting large pieces into very thin strips, so we used store-bought thread for other sewing jobs. I wore a bonnet in summer to protect myself from insects and the sun. I used cardboard to make the wide brim to shade my eyes in the front, and it was long in the back to protect my neck from mosquitoes. My mom was surprisingly patient when she taught me the detailed tasks involved, like how to cut the leather or cloth, or how to stitch beadwork. Both of us were pleased by what I made with her.

My stepdad taught me many other skills when I was a child, skills which normally were only taught to boys. When I was eight years old, he made me a pair of snowshoes. While he was working on them, he allowed me to use the material and pattern to make a smaller model pair at the same time. First, we carefully bent pieces of cedar wood over steam. Once we had the right shape, we tied the wood in place until it held that shape on its own. Then we put those pieces of wood together to build a frame. My snowshoe frames were flat at the back but came to long, upturned points in the front. That style was best at preventing our feet from sinking into snow. Inside of the frames, we made strong nets from fishing line and we sewed thick leather on to the centre, where my moccasins were attached with straps. Finally, we decorated them with a set of red-and-white pompoms. My stepsister Matilda came upon me and my stepdad while we were working on those snowshoes. She was very jealous. Matilda hardly ever went outside in winter, so she did not really need a pair for herself. To make her feel better, my stepdad created an additional set in a quick, circular style, but Matilda remained angry. Later, she took the model pair I had made and broke them on purpose.

My stepfather also let me help him when he worked on machinery, like his boat's motor. When I was about seven years old, he brought home a radio for the first time, and I was fascinated by it. He turned it on, and when I heard people talking and playing the fiddle, I wanted to see where they were inside of that radio. So one day, when everyone else was busy, I took the radio apart. But I couldn't find any people inside of it, not a single soul! When my stepdad found me with the radio in pieces around me, he exclaimed, "What have you done?!" Then he told me to take it all to the kitchen table and put it back together again. And I did. It took me quite a while, but I got it back in working order. The whole time I was worried that my mom was going to punish me when she got home, but luckily my stepdad was there and explained to her that it was not a problem, because I was fixing it.

I learned skills from other people in the community as well. When I was eight or nine years old, Renard made a bow and arrow for me and showed me how to use them. I watched him make the bow out of cedar and a kind of elastic twine. The arrow was cedar whittled to a fine point at the end, but Renard also showed me how to hammer a piece of a metal to make an even stronger and sharper arrow tip. I didn't use my bow and arrow for hunting. Instead, we lined up old cans for target practice.

From the start, I was pretty good when I used my left arm, but over time I became a decent shot with my right arm too. Later I made another cedar bow and arrow set just like the one Renard had made for me.

Sometimes my grandmother arranged for me to learn special tasks from other adults. Once she sent me to help a family tan a moose hide over a period of several weeks. I was their gofer, doing chores and fetching anything they needed as they worked. But I learned how they treated the moose hide until it became tough leather, and how they dyed it in the process. In Ombabika, people tanned different kinds of hides at different times of year, depending on what they wanted to make and what plants they needed for it. For instance, if we wanted to tan hides to make moccasins, we did it in springtime, because that was when we could find the rotting, burnt-looking logs we needed. Bears loved that kind of decaying wood for the insects that lived inside of it, and we used it for the beautiful red and brown tanning colours it produced. We placed a bucket full of the rotting wood on to a fire and hung the hide above it, so over time the smoke would tan the hide. We used animal hides for many purposes. A deer hide, for example, could become clothing, a blanket, a door covering, or strips used to tie things.

ALCOHOL ABUSE

My grandmother told me that, when she was travelling with her husband and children in the early 1900s, they did not see very much drunkenness. She said my grandfather sometimes drank a glass of wine in the evening, like his French father, but he never drank a lot at once. She herself had only tried wine one time. She thought it tasted awful, so she never drank it again.

Ombabika was different, though. It was a large settlement on a railway line. By the time we lived there, beer and wine were delivered often and in large quantities from the nearby towns of Armstrong and Nakina. Many people bought alcohol with the cash they earned from fishing, hunting, trapping, and paying jobs. Some made their own homemade brews. My mother and my aunt Renee were skilled at making blueberry wine.

During my childhood, my *kokum* was the only adult I knew who did not drink alcohol, and most of the adults I knew drank heavily. In my earliest memories of people drinking, I did not understand exactly what was happening. It just seemed like everything was normal, and then suddenly the adults would start acting in strange and sometimes frightening ways. As I got older I started to understand more. Usually, my mother, my stepdad, and their friends had gatherings on the weekends, when everyone brought cases of bottled alcohol and drank together until they passed out. By the end of a party, the adults lay unconscious all over the floor. They looked like dead bodies to me, and they stank. Many times my grandmother tried to convince my mom and stepdad not to get drunk. Normally they respected her wishes, but they ignored her when it came to parties. Once in a while my mother also got drunk with just a couple of her girlfriends.

My stepbrother Barry also drank alcohol, but he was not a heavy drinker. Barry was worried about my grandmother's and my safety during drinking parties. He and I agreed that, when the adults began to drink, we would try to settle my grandmother somewhere safe in the woods, where no one could accidentally fall on her or hurt her in some other way. It was not easy to wait outside in winter, though, so my grandmother and I ended up sitting through some parties, silent witnesses to everything happening all around us. I saw a lot of drunken accidents and violence during my years in Ombabika. Once, when I must have been about four or five years old, I saw two men attacking a woman. They ripped her clothes off while she screamed and cried. I ran away from them and found Renard, but he didn't understand what I was trying to tell him. He kept saying, "No, no, no," when I tried to pull him back to that place. Finally he came with me. When we got there, the men had left and the woman was lying on the ground, naked and bloody. Renard picked up her clothes to cover her. He told me to go stay with some other adults, and I don't know what happened after that.

Then when I was about six years old, my uncle Jacques died in a drunken accident. It happened not long after my mother came to Ombabika. That night, at a party in the long house, I saw a woman mixing liquids from different bottles on the floor. Then she gave the drink she made to four men on the couch, including my uncle. They continued drinking like that for some time. After a while the men on the couch passed out, like all of the adults. The next morning I woke up to people wailing. My uncle and the other three men had died in the night. They had drunk alcohol mixed with antifreeze, and it killed them.

A joint memorial service was held for the four men at a church. I remember looking out the church window as their coffins arrived, one after the other, each one drawn by a workhorse struggling to pull a cart up a slope. My mother and grandmother were sobbing. My *kokum* asked me to hold her, and I did. At that point, I don't think I understood that my uncle was gone forever. Mostly, I just wanted to comfort the upset adults. My uncle Jacques had been like a father to me for as long as I could remember. I didn't really believe I would never see him again. Sometime later, my grandmother suggested that I should take my uncle's fiddle and try to play it like he did. I tried, but I did not like the noise I made, so I stopped. It did not sound anything like the music my uncle Jacques had created.

A few times men bothered me at drinking parties. Once a couple of men were acting strangely, swaying and singing and slobbering. Then suddenly they tried to grab me and touch me. They were so drunk, though, that I was able to run away from them. After Andy was born, I had to look out for him at parties as well. I remember one party that took place in an unfamiliar house when I was about nine years old, and Andy was about one. He was small enough that he was still wrapped in a bunting bag. Our mother and the other adults all became drunk and left the house for some reason, so Andy and I were left alone. After a while we fell asleep. I woke up in the middle of the night, when the house was freezing cold. I tried to make a fire in the stove to warm us, in the same way we did at home. I guess I built a fire, but it must have gotten out of control because suddenly the house was in flames. When I smelled the smoke and saw the fire, I grabbed some heavy object and threw it at the nearest window. The glass broke, and then I lifted up Andy in his bunting bag and threw him outside. I climbed out after him, cutting myself on the jagged glass as I did. I still have the scar from that glass on my left hand. A woman passing by took us to her sister's house, where we were given a bed for the night. I don't know what happened after that.

PHYSICAL AND SEXUAL ABUSE

My mom had a lot of anger toward me, and sometimes she was very violent. I tried to avoid her as much as possible. After she came to Ombabika, I kept living with my grandmother, but most mornings I would jump out of bed, do my chores quickly, and try to get out of sight, so my mother wouldn't see me and hit me. But it was impossible to completely avoid her. Once, for example, my mom wanted me to join her and the group of women who sewed quilts at the long house together. She told me to sit down with all of them at the big, round table to sew. I was very restless, and I had a hard time keeping still. When I tried to sneak away, my mom grabbed me and smacked me. My grandmother was there that time and said, "Let her go, that's enough." My mother gave me a dirty look and let me go. She did not stop so quickly at other times, when my grandmother or others weren't there.

There were times when I rebelled against my mother's abuse. One day when I was about eight or nine years old, after she badly beat me with a broom that morning, I pretended to take revenge against her. First, I went to her room and took some loose hair off of her pillow, as well as some cloth, a button, and a safety pin from her dress. I brought those things outside to the miniature town I had made out of mud and sticks in the woods. After I got there, I crafted a little doll out of leaves and the things I had taken from my mother's room. Then I hit the doll on the head, pinched its body, and wrapped it in birchbark to bury it in the graveyard I had made for the miniature town. While I was doing that, Renard came up to me, saying, "*Aniinah!*" meaning, "What are you doing?!" He must have been watching me for some time, because he knew exactly what I was doing.

Renard took the doll to my grandmother and told her what he had seen. Then she took me out on the lake in the canoe to talk to me. She said, "Why are you taking what I teach you about medicine and using it like that? That is not how I want you to use the medicines I give you. I don't want you to hurt anybody. You must forgive, love, and respect your mother. No matter what she does to you, turn away. Don't let it get to you. Leave it alone, and things will get better for you down the road." Afterward, she took my medicine pouch away from me. I promised her I would not do it again, and I didn't. Still, it was a long time before my grandmother gave me back my medicine bag.

My mother was only one of many people who abused me when I was a child in Ombabika. Once, when I was seven or eight years old, my grandmother and mother were travelling, so I stayed with Gilbert, one of my aunt Renee's adult sons, and his family. Gilbert always had a miserable, unhappy expression on his face. He was an angry person, and he seemed to hate me. While I was staying with him, he said that our grandmother was wasting her life raising me. He called me a stupid devil's child. One time he got so mad that he picked me up and threw me right across the room. And he did not want to feed me. When he, his wife, and children ate a meal together at the table, I was told to sit nearby and watch. One time his wife got up from the table and brought me a bowl of food, but Gilbert said I did not deserve it. He stood up and took the bowl away from me. His wife asked him not to be like that, but he did not give me back the food.

I also experienced sexual abuse when I was left in some of my relatives' care. When I was about five years old, I had to stay with my aunt Renee and her family for some nights. I slept near a stairway in the long house. On one of those nights my aunt's husband, Aziinii, came and sat on my bed in candlelight. He was a stocky man, with a smooth, hairless face and shoulder-length hair. He started touching me. His hands felt coarse, like he did not cut his fingernails. He grabbed my hand and made me touch something slimy and squishy on his body. It felt awful. I wanted to scream, but he covered my mouth. He kept saying, "Shhhh! Shhhh!" with a lot of force. I did not understand what he wanted, but I knew it felt terrible. I felt like I was going to throw up. He came back during other nights and molested me again. Sometimes he was very rough.

My uncle Aziinii was the first of several men and teenage boys who sexually assaulted me during my years in Ombabika. Some of those men told me that what they were doing was okay, that it was normal, and that I should enjoy it. From an early age, though, even when I did not fully understand what they were doing and I didn't have the words to describe it, I still knew it was wrong. But I also felt confused. I felt ashamed, like somehow what was happening was my fault. Those men and others made it very clear to me that I should not talk about such things, because if I did, the men would be sent away and their families would suffer.

I once tried to tell Renard that I had been molested, and he replied, "Well, I don't really know what to say. You shouldn't be telling me this, you should be telling your grandmother." And I did try to tell my grandmother, but when I went to her, I found I couldn't say it out loud. My mother was often with my *kokum*, and I didn't feel comfortable talking about it in front of her. I tried to ask my grandmother about it indirectly, like it was a question about someone else. She said that when that kind of a thing happens, the adult knows what he or she is doing, not the child, so the child is not responsible for it. But I was still afraid to tell her. I feared I would hurt a lot of people.

Many other girls in Ombabika learned to keep heavy secrets like this. Three times I came upon a girl being raped, or right after she had been raped, and each time it was kept secret afterward. When I was about nine years old, I was out hiking and listening to musical sounds around me when I heard someone crying and sniffing quietly. I followed the sound and found a naked girl who was tied to a tree. I had seen her before, but I didn't know her name. She had already freed one of her feet, and I quickly untied her other leg and both wrists. Then she grabbed me and shook me, saying, "Don't ever say anything to anybody about this! If you do, we'll both be in trouble!" She made me feel like I had done something wrong.

Then, when I was ten or eleven years old and I was on my way to a friend's house one morning, I heard someone screaming in the woods. I didn't know why the person was screaming, but it scared me, so I ran the rest of the way to my friend's house. She wasn't home, so I waited for her to return. When she got there, she was naked and crying, and I realized with horror that she had been the one who was screaming. Her mom shoved me into a corner and grabbed a blanket to cover her daughter. She washed her and put her to bed. My friend continued crying the whole time. She never saw that I was there. Afterward her mother told me, "You can't ever tell anybody what you just saw. Never tell anyone!" Then she told me to leave. Later, there were times when I tried to talk to my friend about what had happened to her, to let her know that things like that had happened to me too. But she never wanted to talk about it. She was angry when I brought it up and told me that nothing had happened. She said I was just looking for trouble.

Then a third time, when I was about the same age, I was again walking in the woods when I heard men yelling, "Yeah!", so I went to see what was happening. I found them in a clearing, gang raping a teenage girl I knew. She also had been tied to a tree by her arms and legs. I was terrified. I think I must have gone into shock. I ran to look for someone to help, but when I found my godmother, Irene, I wasn't able to speak. I stuttered as I tried to tell her what was happening. She made fun of me, saying, "What, is somebody bugging you again?" When I finally got my breath back, I didn't tell her what I had seen.

CHAPTER THREE

SEASONAL ACTIVITIES, FIRST FRIENDSHIPS, AND THE BEGINNING OF ADDICTION (1958–1960)

After my mother and stepfather got married, from the period when I was about eight to fourteen years old, my whole family went on long canoe trips during the summer to fish and pick berries to stock up for the winter. My mother, stepfather, Barry, Matilda, and Andy travelled in one large, metal motorboat. My grandmother and I followed them in our smaller birch canoe, which was tied to their boat by a short rope. I sat in the front of our canoe to paddle when needed, and my grandmother sat at the back. Some years we travelled with other families, whose canoes were tied behind ours. From time to time, we also met and visited with other travelling groups at campgrounds along the way.

When my family left Ombabika on those journeys, we travelled up-stream close to the shoreline. Over weeks and months we passed through a network of lakes and rivers. We sometimes portaged, which means we carried our canoes and supplies over land between bodies of water. When we saw geese start to fly south in late summer, we turned and headed back to Ombabika. By then, our boat and canoe were packed full of fish and berries. The rivers and lakes at that time often were filled with long, floating logs, which were pulled downstream by tugboats from the Abitibi Pulp and Paper Company. We always passed the tugboats because we were faster in our motorboat and canoe.

During summer trips, we fished with nets like we did at home, and picked blueberries, raspberries, and any other berries that could be gathered nearby. We washed our clothes by hitting and rubbing them against stones in streams and lakes. Then we wrung them out and hung them to dry on lines strung between trees. In the evening people met at the central campfire to talk, make music, and dance. My grandmother told stories, my mother sang and played the fiddle or accordion, and I danced on a board that I used as a kind of a platform. People gathered around to clap to the music and watch me dance. Now and then someone joined me when I jigged, but usually I was the only one who danced. It gave me a lot of joy. People did not bring much alcohol on those trips, because space was limited in the canoes. So there was not much drinking or drunkenness at the evening parties.

At the Summit Lake campground there was a huge teepee that many families could share. Whoever stayed in it helped to maintain it, patching up holes with birchbark, cedar, and leaves. I enjoyed staying in that teepee, because we could tell stories and dance even when it rained. People had built small teepees nearby for tasks we did not want to do in the big one, like gutting fish or cooking. The teepee frames were made of willow trunks placed together to form a cone, with the logs all meeting and then going in different directions at the top. The frames were covered in layers of birchbark, moss, and animal hide. During our first summer trips, most families stayed in small teepees at other campsites, although there were a few families from southern Ontario who preferred dome-like *wiigiwaam*. In practice, the two structures often blurred, and it was not unusual for people to build a lodge that had the characteristics of both.

In later years, many families started using store-bought tents made of metal poles and heavy canvas. I remember being at a campsite the first time my family and others tried to put together such a tent. We could not read the instructions, so it took us a long time to figure out how to do it. There was a lot of laughter at the failed attempts. I closely studied the drawings in the instructions, and in the end I helped my stepdad to put up the tent.

Usually our summer journeys were pleasant, but once in a while we encountered dangerous, difficult situations. Once when we were camped in a cedar grove during a storm, a lightning bolt struck one family's tent. Suddenly people began screaming and running. When I came out of our tent, I saw a naked woman shivering on the ground, so I put a blanket over her. Two people were killed by that lightning strike, and some others were injured.

Another summer, we were returning to Ombabika in a large group of several families. We had reached a point in the river where the rapids were too rough, so most of us had gotten out of the water to portage the canoes, supplies, and goods to where the water was calmer downstream. My stepdad was the only one from our family who stayed in the river. He succeeded in getting his boat and all of our gear through the cascades. The tragedy occurred afterward, when we were all getting back into our boats and canoes. I am not sure exactly how it happened. I think my stepdad's boat turned over first, and then my grandmother's and my canoe did as well. Suddenly she and I were underwater. I was very frightened, because neither of us knew how to swim. Someone hauled me out of the water by my neck and shoulders. Someone else pulled out my grandmother. We lost everything that had been in the boats—our packsacks, gear, and all the food we had gathered for the winter. In the confusion, other boats had turned over as well and suffered worse outcomes. One adult and one child drowned that day.

When we gathered on the shore again, we were dripping wet. People yelled and cried. An Abitibi Pulp and Paper Company camp lay on the other side of the river, so the adults in our group built a big fire and made smoke signals to get the attention of the camp's staff. My stepdad also got a white cloth and waved it back and forth like a flag. After a while some white men came across the river in a huge boat and brought us back to their place. They gave us blankets and hot food and drink as we recovered.

I experienced other frightening events during the summers when I was picking berries or filleting fish close to Ombabika, but they did not end as badly. One summer day when I was picking raspberries with my stepsister Matilda, I must have upset a beehive, because a swarm of bees attacked me. I tried to run away from them, and Matilda ran in the other direction. They stung me all over my body, even inside my mouth. I did not know it until then, but I am extremely allergic to bee stings. My body began to swell up everywhere, and I passed out. Someone carried me to a train gas car, which is a kind of wagon that railway foremen drive up and down the train tracks on their own. They took me to see a doctor in Armstrong. By the time I reached him, my neck was so swollen that he had to make a cut in it to put a tube down my throat so I could breathe. The doctor was a black man, the first person of African heritage I had ever seen. I didn't think he was real when I recovered consciousness in the hospital. His skin was a rich, dark colour, and beautifully smooth. He was very gentle and patient with me. He carefully explained how I needed to avoid bees in the future because of my allergy.

The other incident happened during the summer when I was eight or nine years old. My cousin Pascal and I were filleting fish early in the morning by the lakeshore, as usual. My stepdad had been out hunting since very early that day. He returned in his canoe, and left it and his shotgun by the waterside. My mother was yelling at me about something. She was mad at me, I can't remember why. I also became angry. She turned her back, and on the spur of the moment I picked up my stepdad's gun and pointed it in her direction. I could not actually see her very clearly, but it didn't matter, because I was only pretending to shoot her. Until then, my stepdad had always been careful to remove the bullets from his gun when he wasn't using it. So I had handled his gun and even pulled its trigger many times before, without ever firing a shot. That time, though, my stepfather hadn't removed the bullets. The gun went off, and I was thrown backward by the force of it.

As it turned out, my mother had bent down just at the moment when I shot the gun. The bullet only grazed her shirt and skin, leaving her with a ripped blouse and a surface wound. But I did not know that at the time. I was shocked and horrified that I might have killed her. My instinct was to run, so I ran and ran and ran, right into the woods and onward for what might have been hours. I only stopped in the evening, when the night was falling. Then I hid myself under an old, bent over, dead tree, and I cried for a long time. I felt sad, guilty, and fearful that I might have killed my mother. I worried about what my grandmother was feeling. I was scared of what would happen to me if they found me, and of the animal noises I heard around me. Mosquitoes swarmed and sucked my blood. In the end, I must have cried myself to sleep.

Later, people in Ombabika said that I spent a week in the woods on my own. I remember it as being eight nights, because I counted the nights on my hands and I had two fingers left when they found me. The days are a blur in my memory. At first I spent a lot of time running and hiding. I was completely lost. I ate leaves and juicy mosses. I sucked water and dew off of plants, until I found a stream where I could drink. I was extremely hungry—my stomach growled so loudly, it seemed like it was talking to me. After a few days, I saw a rabbit. I chased it for a long time before giving up on catching it. I also watched chipmunks, trying to figure out how I could catch them. Once, when I had climbed a tree, a doe and a fawn came into the clearing below me. I climbed back down to see them better, and the mother let me play with the fawn for a little while. I must have been all skin and bones by that point, so I guess I did not seem very threatening to her.

During the days and nights I spent in the bush, I was most scared when I came face to face with a *makwa* (bear). I had never seen one before, and I wasn't sure what it was. It just seemed like a huge, furry beast to me. The bear saw me and growled, and then stood on its hind legs. I was frozen with fear. After a while, it got back on all fours and walked away. But before it disappeared, the bear turned around to growl at me one last time. I was so frightened by meeting the bear that I climbed a nearby tree and did not come down again for the rest of my time in the woods. I slept in that tree for a couple more nights. I continued to cry a lot. When I woke up on the final morning, my eyes were so swollen that I could barely see the sunrise. And then I heard people calling me: "Ma-Nee! Ma-Nee!" I still thought about running and hiding. I didn't want to face the possibility that I had killed my mother, or that, if I hadn't, she would beat me for almost killing her. But my dog Diienge found me, followed by some other dogs. And then Renard appeared. He talked me down from the tree by assuring me that my mom was not badly injured and that she wouldn't hurt me either. And it was true. When I returned home, my grandmother checked me all over with her hands, to make sure I wasn't seriously hurt. And my mother didn't hit me. They all must have been so amazed to see me alive, to know that I had survived that long on my own in the bush, that no one wanted to punish me.

TRAPPING AND HUNTING IN WINTER

Starting when I was about eight years old, and continuing until I was about twelve, my stepfather took me with him when he set traps and snares to catch animals for their fur and meat. Each autumn we left Ombabika after the heavy rains ended, when the snow began to fall. We travelled up north by dogsled, sometimes just the two of us, and sometimes with other adult men. We slept overnight in a canvas tent or in trapping huts. These huts had been built at isolated spots in the wilderness and were shared by whoever needed them. Some of them were teepees, and others were small log cabins or shacks made out of wooden planks and boards. If we were caught in a storm, we would build an emergency snow shelter by making a small structure out of branches and sticks that we covered in snow. My stepdad also taught me how to make other types of snow houses. I learned a lot from him about how to survive in the wilderness. I enjoyed being out in the bush, and not having to go to school, but I didn't like killing animals. There were days when I cried after I did it. Still, I learned to do it over time, first by watching my stepdad, and then by following his step-by-step instructions.

My stepdad had a large sled that was pulled by five or six dogs. On very long trips, he took seven or eight dogs. I had a little sled that was pulled by my own dog, Diienge, who was as big as a sheepdog and worked just as hard. The dogs wore harnesses that my stepdad made during the summer, when he shaped a leather collar to each dog's head, and connected them all together with hooks and thick canvas-like cloth. He always picked females to be his lead dogs, because he said they understood him better than male dogs did. The dogs ran in a single line, with the main lead dog in the front and the second lead dog at the very back, ready to take over in case anything happened to the first one. My stepdad showed me how to feed Diienge in the bush by cooking a meal of dried meat for myself first, and then one for her.

On our winter trapping trips, I was responsible for catching rabbits, weasels, and muskrats. We usually made a *nagwaniian* (snare) out of a round, gold-coloured wire attached to a stick, but if we were out of wire, we used deer sinew instead. My stepdad only bought gold-coloured wire, because he believed the silver-coloured type was more visible against the snow or ground. To catch a weasel or a muskrat, we set up a snare in the water with two sticks on either side. Then we put mud over the trap to camouflage it, as well as mosses and branches which those animals like to eat. Depending on which animal we wanted to catch, we rubbed smelly oils from its glands on the snare to attract one of its kind. We set muskrat snares deeper in the water, and weasel snares near the surface. That usually worked very well. Sometimes we trapped a muskrat, and then a weasel would come to check out what had happened and would get trapped in the water above it. My stepdad also snared geese. When we saw them in a swamp, he crawled on his belly right through the muck to lay snares for them. But his biggest task on those trips was to set a large *onaagan* (trap) for beavers. He did not let me watch him do this, because I am a member of the beaver clan.

After we had set our snares and traps, my stepfather and I would move on. We returned later to collect any animals that had been caught, resetting the traps and snares at the same time. When it was cold and we were far from home, we cleaned the animals in trapping huts. My stepdad removed the guts and other parts that we couldn't use, and left those pieces nearby, for birds and other creatures to eat. While he was cleaning a beaver, my stepfather always told me not to come near him. He also did not keep beaver meat or pelts at our home in Ombabika. If he needed to cook beaver, he used a shed about a kilometre away from our house, because he did not want my grandmother or the rest of us in the beaver clan to see or smell dead beaver.

In addition to his trapping skills, my stepfather was widely known as a very good hunter. People used to say, "If Gabe goes hunting, we'll eat well before Christmas." He mainly hunted moose using a rifle. Once in a while he shot geese, if he wasn't able to snare them first. Sometimes he hunted deer, wolf, or bear, but I never joined him for that. When he hunted bear, he travelled far out into the bush to find truly wild bears. There were other bears that lived close to Ombabika, but they ate from our trash piles, and my stepdad did not want us to eat their meat.

I went moose hunting with my stepdad a few times. I already felt troubled about trapping animals, and it was even more disturbing for me to hunt them. More than once I scared a moose on purpose, before my stepdad could shoot it. But my stepfather wanted to teach me that hunting was not a bad thing, and that it was an important part of our survival. When we went hunting, we would leave Ombabika early in the morning searching for moose tracks. He explained which tracks were two or three days old, and which ones were fresh and worth following. One day when I was about twelve years old, we came upon a moose and my stepdad suddenly gave me the rifle. He checked the way the wind was blowing, and told me he was going to circle around the moose and chase it toward me. And he did just that. I clearly remember that huge moose rushing toward me, with my stepdad running right behind it. It looked like a giant was charging at me! I pulled the trigger and flew backward, because, as usual, the force of the gunshot lifted me right off the ground. The moose fell, and was dead. My stepdad ran up to me and exclaimed, "Oh good, good, good. I knew you would be a good hunter!"

Then my stepdad paused to express his respect and gratitude to the moose and to the Great Spirit, by leaving a small offering of tobacco, as is our custom. Afterward he started cleaning the moose right there, on the spot. He opened her abdomen and felt around inside of her. He told me he wanted to remove the heart, but he couldn't reach it, because there was something blocking the way. He asked me to crawl inside and pull out whatever it was. I did and pulled out a baby moose. I hadn't known the moose was pregnant. My stepdad might not have known that either. He told me to put the baby moose in my backpack to bring to my grandmother. I think he wanted my grandmother to see that I had become a capable hunter. Also, he wanted to honor her with the baby moose, because it was the choicest meat from our hunt. Then he cut up the rest of the moose. When he got to the heart, he told me to eat a small bite of it and lift the rest toward the sky in all four directions. He explained that this was something a young hunter did after killing his or her first large animal, to show pride and to honour the animal and the Great Spirit. To carry the meat back to Ombabika, he used the moose's hide as a kind of extra dogsled. My stepdad told me, "When we get home, we're going to celebrate!" And in fact, there was a big feast after we returned. But my hand and shoulder hurt for days after I shot that moose, and I did not touch a gun again for a long time.

At first, when my stepfather took me away on trapping or hunting trips, I was grateful to him. I thought he just wanted to teach me and to protect me from my mother. But at some point during our years of trapping together, he molested me. I can't remember exactly when it started or how often it happened, but I believe it happened more than once. I have a clear memory of one incident. We had been caught in a snowstorm far from a trapping hut, so we built an emergency snow shelter. It only had enough space for our bodies, so we were lying down, packed close together. He was behind me. Then he suddenly grabbed my body, and started groaning and making strange noises. I felt something hard on my back. At first I thought he was sick, and then I realized what that stiff thing against my body was. After that experience, I was afraid of my stepdad. When we returned to

Ombabika, he kept telling me not to say anything about what had happened. I avoided him. I think we went trapping again together, but I had nightmares and I screamed when he touched me. In the end he told me, "You're going through a rough time right now, and I am part of it, so I won't bring you trapping with me anymore."

I stopped going trapping with my stepfather, but I did not stop it completely. I knew the grounds around Ombabika well enough that in the fall and winter I still caught weasels, rabbit, mink, and otter. One time I took Renard with me to check my traps, but otherwise I went alone. I sold the furs to the Hudson's Bay store, which kept an account in my name. It was unusual for a young teenager to have an account at the store, especially a girl. I believe my stepdad and Mr. Jones, the store manager, set one up to recognize the work I was doing, and to teach me how to save. I hardly ever withdrew money from my account. Maybe once a month I bought myself a Coca Cola, hard candy, or crayons. Sometimes I shared those things with my friends, but mostly I forgot about that money until I was older.

By my teen years, I was sad to see many changes in my familiar trapping grounds and in the bush surrounding them. The Abitibi Pulp and Paper Company continued to set up new camps in the area, and at each one they clear-cut the nearby forest. So sometimes, when I went trapping, I found that familiar stretches of woods had entirely disappeared. It was devastating. Beautiful, sacred forests that I had grown up with had been destroyed. The land looked naked and scarred, as if it had been raped and left to die.

MY BIOLOGICAL FATHER

In my early childhood, my grandmother was the only parent I knew. When my mother moved to Ombabika, I got used to her and, soon afterward, to my stepdad being my parents as well. Other people still called me a bastard sometimes, but I did not wonder who my biological father might be, and I was not interested in meeting him. Over the years, some Ombabika residents told me that a man named Phillip was my father. At that time, Phillip lived 150 kilometres north of Ombabika in Fort Hope with his wife Edith and their five children, who were all about my age or younger.

I have a few memories of meeting some of Phillip's family when they passed through Ombabika, during the period when I was probably eight to eleven years old. I met Richie—Phillip's father, and possibly my grandfather—several times. People told me that he was my grandfather, but I did not really believe or understand what they meant, because he was a stranger to me. One time when he saw me, he gave me a little money and bought me my first bottle of Coca Cola. As we sat together, I noticed that he had very thick eyebrows, so I asked him if he had to comb them. He told me he didn't, but that I should expect to get thick eyebrows when I got older, so I might need to comb my own one day. Another time when I met him, he was wearing a heavy, dark navy jacket with gold buttons. He had on a sailor's cap that covered most of his shoulder-length white hair. I admired his hat, so he bought me one too. I liked it a lot, and wore it often.

I also remember Phillip's sister visiting Ombabika. She wore a dark green trench coat, and she picked me up and swung me around and around in the air. One night, after she had been drinking with my mother and others, she wandered on to the railroad tracks, where she was hit and killed by a train. Richie came to Ombabika the next day, upset and in mourning for his daughter. At some point, he tried to talk to me and to hug me, but I stayed away from him. By that age I had been molested by different men, so I avoided unfamiliar ones.

The only time I met Phillip, the man who may have been my father, I was nine or ten years old. I remember him as a very large man, like a giant to me. Again, I was wary and avoided him, so we hardly spoke. Many years later, Phillip tried to contact me when he was on his deathbed. One of his adult sons came to tell me that Phillip claimed me as his child. I was in the hospital myself at that time, so I was unable to go see him. Later still, I received a copy of my birth certificate and saw that Phillip was recorded as my father on it. Over the years, though, some members of Phillip's family and other people who knew my mother around the time when she became pregnant told me that they did not believe he was my father. One woman mentioned that my mom had a different, long-term partner while she was in the sanatorium. She believed that Phillip only claimed to be my father out of kindness toward me and my mother. To this day I do not know whether he truly was my biological father.

FRIENDSHIPS BEFORE STARTING SCHOOL

One of my earliest memories of playing with another child is of being in a canoe with a girl named Adrienne, who was about my own age. She was on one end of the canoe and I was on the other. We dragged our socks through the water to see if we could get fish to bite them, until Adrienne lost one of hers. She left Ombabika soon after. In my child's point of view, she disappeared suddenly. Later, I learned that the authorities had taken Adrienne and her brother away from their mother, Victoria, and that they were adopted by a French Canadian family.

As a young child, I mainly knew my aunt Renee's kids—Paula, Justin, Angela, and Flora—who lived in the long house nearby. I liked my cousin Paula a lot. She was one or two years older than me. Sometimes I imagined that she and I would live together when we grew up. I also got along pretty well with Justin and Angela. Angela was a year younger than me. Flora, who was a young woman at that time, babysat me when I was little. She always treated me well. Flora wore her hair in a simple bun, but she liked to style my hair with ribbons. She didn't seem to mind that I pulled them out the first chance I got. My aunt Renee had several other teenage and adult sons, and some of them were pretty mean and aggressive. When I was little, her adult son Gilbert was the cousin who beat me severely, and her husband Aziinii was the uncle who sexually molested me. So although I liked Angela, Paula, Justin, and Flora, I learned to avoid their household when I had a choice.

One of my first friends outside of my family was a white boy named Max, who I met when I was around nine years old. He was about the same age as me. My stepdad had been working as a fishing guide for Max's dad, and one day he brought Max and his father home. My stepfather told me to take Max and go play down by the river. Max was the first person I met who had hair the colour of sunshine and naturally blue eyes. The only comparison I had was my grandmother's blind eyes, which had some blue in them. So I guessed Max was blind and gave him a little stick to use to guide himself. Then I took his other hand in mine, and I walked him carefully down to the river. Once we were there, I prepared a long stick for him to use as a fishing rod, and I put it in his hands so he could fish with me. He smiled at me the whole time, but it wasn't until I put my hands in front of his eyes, crinkled up my nose, and made funny faces at him, that he finally burst out laughing. At that moment I realized he could see. He grabbed my hand and put his fishing rod in it, the way I had done with him. Next he found a smooth round rock and gave it to me as a gift.

Max and I became friends. He would bring books, which we looked at together, and paper that we used for drawing. He tried to teach me the ABCs. He drew each letter and said it out loud, and I repeated it back. Then I taught him sounds that I made up. I tried to understand what he was teaching me, but I didn't really grasp it until I started school later and learned more about reading and writing.

Max wore suspenders and strong, brown farmer's pants with many pockets. Before he and his dad left Ombabika the first time, my stepdad asked whether they could bring me a similar set of pants and suspenders the next time they visited. They agreed, and brought me a set when they returned the next year. That was when I finally stopped wearing bloomers. The pants they brought were too long for me, so I had to roll them up, but I grew into them over time. Max and his dad came back to visit us every year for several years, and they always brought me pants. Then one year Max's dad came alone. He said that Max had become ill with leukemia, and died. I think Max once tried to tell me he was sick, but I had not understood him. His death came as a very sad shock to me.

Around the same time I got to know Max, I met a local boy named Shiigohbii, who also became a good friend of mine. We first came across each other at an abandoned, rusted-out truck. It stood halfway between our two houses, which were about a kilometre apart. That truck had been one of my hideouts for a long time. I had made myself a little nest out of rags and blankets inside of it. As it turned out, the truck also had been a private hangout for Shiigohbii, because when we first met each other there we both claimed it as our own. After a while we learned to share it. Shiigohbii was about my age, or maybe one or two years older. He always seemed older to me, because he knew about a lot of things that were new to me.

I was with Shiigohbii the first time I saw a train. Of course, I had seen the train tracks before, but adults always told me to stay away from them. They explained that a dangerous black beast lived on the tracks. They called it a *windigo odaabaan*—a beastly or monstrous vehicle. For a time that discouraged me from going near the tracks, but in the end I wanted to see the beast for myself. So Shiigohbii and I went to a place everyone called the "rock cut," where railway workers had blasted a path in a hillside. Perched high on the rock cut, we had a clear view of the tracks below. When the train finally appeared, it barrelled toward us roaring, "Choooooo! Choo,

choo!" It was a terrible, frightening sight! It came at us like a monster, arms pumping and smoke pouring from its stack. At first I feared it would hit us, but it just stayed on the tracks and quickly disappeared out of sight.

At that time, the railway still used black steam engines fuelled with coal. Not long after, those trains were replaced by round-faced diesel engines in yellow and green colours. In later years, I went to the railway station if I heard that famous people were scheduled to stop briefly in Auden, when their trains passed through. I remember a large crowd once gathered to see Queen Elizabeth, who waved from her decorated train. Other times singers and their bands got off a train to perform a few songs for us on the station platform, and then they moved on.

Before I went to school, Shiigohbii and I sometimes hung out with two boys named Edmond and Hank. Edmond was only a bit bigger than us, but Hank was much taller and chunkier. He would probably be considered overweight today. Fishing was one of the activities we all did together. I made my rods out of wooden sticks, string, and hooks of different sizes that my stepdad gave me. I created bobbers out of bright baby bird feathers, because they floated on the water surface and attracted fish. We mostly caught pan fish, like Yellow Perch. I enjoyed fishing, but I did not enjoy cleaning fish. Usually I brought my catch home and then left again quickly, so someone else had to do it.

Shiigohbii, Edmond, Hank, and I also got into mischief together. Once, for example, when I was still about nine years old, my grandmother was away and all of our parents had been on a drinking and eating binge, so there was nothing left for us to eat. We were very hungry, so we started searching for food around Ombabika. We looked inside the window of a house owned by a white man named Fritz, and we discovered that he had a lot of food. Edmond or Shiigohbii decided to break the window, and then Shiigohbii and I crawled in, because we were small enough to fit through the hole. We threw a few things up to Hank and Edmond. Then I picked up a big blue bottle of honey with a picture of a hive on it. We had never eaten honey, so we squeezed it out to see what it was, and of course we loved it. We ate some right there. Suddenly, though, Hank and Edmond called our names and told us that Fritz was coming back. I pushed Shiigohbii up and through the window, and he tried to pull me up after him, but he dropped me. I fell right into a bucket of flour.

While I was getting my bearings, a large white man entered the house and exclaimed something like, "Who the hell are you?" He picked me up in his big hands and looked me straight in the eye, with our faces very close together. I remember he had a smooth face and blue-green eyes, like lake water. After that he turned me around and made me look at myself in the mirror. White flour and honey covered my head and my long black hair. He wiped my face a little so he could see me better, and then he said something in English like, "Oh, you're one of the Chacabys."

Fritz shook his finger at me to scold me for stealing, so I thought I was in trouble and I would be beaten when I got home. But he must have understood that I was hungry and felt sorry for me, because all he did was give me something to eat. I think he might have made me a peanut butter sandwich; I remember it tasted strange but nice. Next he opened a can of something and heated it, probably some kind of stew. He fed that to me, and was it ever good! I wolfed it down. Finally, he filled my pockets with oranges, and I took off. Shiigohbii, Edmond, and Hank met me outside and quizzed me about what Fritz had said and done. They were surprised that I didn't get into trouble, and they were disappointed that they didn't get to share in my feast. I saw Fritz again many years later. Once he recognized me, he laughed and teased me about the day he caught me stealing from him.

BECOMING AN ALCOHOLIC

I first drank alcohol at one of my parents' parties when I was about ten years old. Some of the adults had passed out, and others were getting into arguments, so I hid under a bed. While I was down there, I noticed a brown beer bottle that had been forgotten on the floor next to the bed. I decided to drink some of the liquid inside of it. I don't remember how many sips I took before I passed out. When I woke up the next day, adults were still unconscious all over the floor. I got up too fast when I came out from under the bed, and I became very, very sick. It was horrible!

But then I did it again. I don't know why, given how ill I'd been after the first time. I drank at another party, and then at another, and I began to feel good when I drank. I tried drinking from bigger, rounder bottles as well, which I later understood held wine instead of beer. I thought alcohol tasted bad, but I drank it anyway. After that I started to steal it during parties when all of the adults were drunk, because they didn't know the difference. I poured alcohol from their bottles into my own empty bottles, put their bottles back where I found them, and stored mine outside in the bush to drink later. Shiigohbii also stole alcohol at parties, and we started to drink secretly together.

Then when I was about eleven years old, Shiigohbii and I began to sniff car exhaust and gasoline fumes to get high. We were introduced to sniffing exhaust by a boy about my age named Ivan. Sometimes Ivan put a paper bag around the exhaust pipe of a car to capture as many fumes as possible before breathing them in. Once in a while, when a driver was drunk and did not notice, Ivan rode a car's bumper for as far as he could, breathing in fumes directly from the exhaust pipe. There were even times when Ivan held on to a car and breathed in the exhaust as it dragged him behind it. Afterward, he laid on the ground and told us how good he felt. So we tried it too.

Shiigohbii and I learned to breathe gasoline and diesel fumes from Hank. We got the gasoline out of automobiles and the diesel out of railway gas cars. Once we had the fuel, we soaked a rag in it and placed the rag in a paper bag, which we opened to inhale fumes. Hank, Shiigohbii, and I also tried to get high with any pills we could find. They probably were just headache pills. We tried squishing them into wet rags to inhale their fumes, crushing and rolling them up with tobacco as cigarettes to smoke, and swallowing their powder mixed with Coca Cola.

At first my grandmother didn't realize that I had started drinking alcohol, or sniffing exhaust and gasoline fumes. But then she started to comment about how I smelled of gasoline. I made excuses, saying I spilled gas on my clothes by accident. When I had been drinking, she told me I smelled of alcohol, and I lied again, claiming I had picked up the odour when cleaning up after the adults' parties. Soon she knew I was lying. She asked me, "Are you doing what all of the others are doing, drinking and getting high?" And I replied, "Yes, I am, because I feel better when I do that." She told me to stop, of course, but she couldn't make me stop. I was angry, and I was tired of being afraid. When I was high or drunk I felt brave, strong, and fearless, at least for a short time. When I drank with my friends, we relaxed and laughed together, and I felt like I belonged somewhere.

I only stopped sniffing car exhaust and fuel when Hank died doing it. He and I had gone to Ombabika River one day. We were fishing under the railway bridge while sniffing fumes from gas-soaked rags. After a while he told me, "I'm going to set down my bag and fishing pole. If I fall asleep, don't wake me." And then he slept. Some other kids arrived and we left him alone. When it was time to go home, I tried to wake him, but he wouldn't get up. At first I just thought he was in a deep sleep. Then one of the others noticed that he was not breathing, so we ran to get adults. But Hank had already died. The adults smelled gasoline on him, so they realized he must have been sniffing it. Of course, they talked to all of us about it afterward, and told us that we would die too if we kept doing it. Losing Hank scared me enough that I did stop for a long time.

Still, I kept drinking alcohol. I drank the most during the school vacations, a bit less when I was attending school, and not at all when I travelled with my family on fishing or trapping trips. I mostly drank with other kids, although, when I did, I often spent a good part of my time worried that someone would steal my alcohol. I knew some people who became violent when they got drunk, and others who took wild risks, but usually I was a pretty boring and mild-mannered drunk.

CHAPTER FOUR

SCHOOL, TEENAGE FRIENDSHIPS, AND HAVING TWO SPIRITS (1960–1965)

I registered to go to the local school in the fall of 1959, but I travelled up north for the winter trapping season soon afterward, so I did not actually start school until the spring of 1960. Auden and Ombabika had a small, one-room schoolhouse that stood just off the railway line, about a two-kilometre walk from my house. Students arrived there in the early morning and stayed until afternoon, when they returned home to do chores. Children of all ages from a wide area attended school, and there were many of us crammed into the room, maybe a few dozen. We each had our own chair. The students were mostly Native, but there were a couple of white kids whose fathers worked for the Abitibi Pulp and Paper Company. At any given time, two white teachers taught at the school, either two men, or a man and a woman. They tried to teach reading, writing, and arithmetic in English. I didn't understand very much of what they said.

I got my first pair of store-bought shoes when I started school. They were black-and-white Oxfords which I found very uncomfortable compared to my flexible and light-weight moccasins. When I wore my Oxfords, it felt like my toes were being squeezed into a rock-hard box. At first I took these shoes off as soon as I left school, and many times I forgot them somewhere on my way home, so I had to return to find them again later. In the end, though, I got used to them and did not mind them too much.

I also got my first pair of eyeglasses not long after I started school. From the start, I had difficulty seeing what teachers wrote on the blackboard. At some point they realized that I could not see what they were writing unless I sat at the front of the class, so they moved me and informed my parents. When I first started wearing glasses, I was surprised by the detail I suddenly saw around me. I had not known how poor my eyesight was, and being able to see better gave me a new sense of freedom. Before then, people often called me clumsy when I bumped into things. They told me to watch where I was going, without realizing that I already was trying to do that, but I couldn't see well.

Despite the positive role that teachers played in me getting my first pair of glasses, most of them were mean to me. They did not hit all of the kids, but they hit me a lot. The main reason was because I was left-handed, and they wanted me to use my right hand to write. Each time they caught me using my left hand, they took me to the front of the classroom, unfolded my hands, and strapped them with a wide belt or a fire hose. Sometimes they lashed my hands until they were numb, swollen, and bloody. Once in a while they hit me for other reasons. One morning, for instance, some children taught me to say a few bad English words, which I did not understand. When I said the words out loud in class, the teacher punished me, because he thought I knew what I was saying. Another time some kids took my long hair, which reached all the way down my back, and tied it to my chair. I cried out, "Don't! Don't!" The teacher thought I was causing a problem, so again he strapped me.

One morning when the teacher had already lashed my hands, he called my cousin Pascal's older brother, Joshua, to the front of the classroom to be beaten for something else. Joshua was one of the oldest kids in our class. Like some other teenage boys in Ombabika at the time, he dressed in black pants, a black shirt, and a black leather jacket, with his hair slicked back. Because he was older than most of the students, he looked out for us. That day, Joshua rebelled against the teacher when the teacher went to strap him. Joshua grabbed the belt from the teacher's hand and swung it around and around, in the air, before tossing it out the window. Then he took hold of the teacher and lifted him like he was going to throw him through the window too, but he didn't. I think he realized what he was doing and stopped himself. Instead, he dropped the teacher and walked out the door. My hands were painfully swollen and I was angry too, so I ran after him. We walked to the rock cut and sat there for a while together. Joshua warned me not to fight back against the teacher like he had done, because I would get an even worse punishment than him. He told me that school was not meant for us, but that we needed to pretend that we were listening and understanding the teachers, nod in response to them, and try to behave to get by. Joshua never went back to school after that day.

During all my time at school, there was only one teacher who was always kind to me and never hit me. Her name was Mrs. Jones. She was the wife of the Hudson's Bay store manager. Mrs. Jones knew I liked to draw, so she gave me extra pieces of paper in class. She also stepped in and stopped the male teacher when he wanted to strap me. Once when I was nine or ten years old, I was very dirty for some reason, so she took me to her house to have a bath. That was where I saw a white porcelain tub for the first time. It had clawed feet, and stood by itself in the bathroom. It looked big enough to swim in! Mrs. Jones filled the tub with water and bubble bath. I was eager to play with the bubbles, so I got right in with my clothes still on. Mrs. Jones laughed and laughed. Then she helped me get my clothes off to wash myself.

When Mrs. Jones was gently soaping my back, she made a sound of surprise and then said a lot of English words. I didn't understand most of what she said, but I could tell she was upset. I thought I must look terribly ugly to her. I wanted to see what she saw on my back, so I got out of the tub and stood in front of her mirror, twisting around to see it. I realized she had been looking at the scars left by my mom's beatings. After I finished cleaning and dressing myself, Mrs. Jones hugged me and spoke to me for a long time. Again, I did not understand much of what she said, but she had very kind eyes, so I trusted her. Then she gave me food that I had never eaten before, an apple and a box of Lucky Elephant Pink Popcorn from the store, which I gobbled up. Later, she went to talk to my mother and stepfather about the marks on my back, but they were just mad at me for going to her house and having a bath. They told me never to do it again.

My social world grew in other ways through school. I met many more children than I had known before. I became friends with two cousins, Jane and Bonnie, who were both a couple of years older than me. Jane's mother, Karen, and Bonnie's mother, Victoria, were sisters and my mom's best friends. Sometimes our three moms got drunk together at my mother's house. Victoria's younger daughter by another man, Adrienne, was the girl who had been my first playmate and was taken away from her mother and given up for adoption. I had seen Jane once or twice, when her dad came to pick up her mom when she was drunk. But Jane and Bonnie lived a couple of kilometres away from our house, so I did not really get to know them until I started school.

Jane became my best girlfriend. From the start, I liked her a lot. She was protective of me, and sometimes helped me when bullies bothered me. She introduced me to many new things. She taught me how to ride a bike, and she gave me her old clothes. That was very helpful, because I did not have much clothing, and what I did have was usually worn out. In my eyes, Jane and Bonnie were rich. I liked visiting Jane's house, because they ate butter with yummy foods that I had never tasted before, like blueberry jam on toast, or baloney on bannock, or mashed potatoes. Jane's dad adored her and treated her kindly, and I was fascinated by that.

Getting to know new children at school was not always a positive experience, because I also met kids who bullied and even assaulted me. Between the abusive teachers and the violent bullies, I often felt afraid to go to school. I had to work hard to overcome my fear. My worst experiences of bullying happened when certain boys caught me on the way to, or from, school. One time when I was about eleven years old, for example, some fourteen- to sixteen-year-old boys grabbed me when I was alone and tied up my hands and legs. It was Jane's half-brother, Nick, and his friends. First they threw snakes on my body, some dead and some alive. I was terribly frightened. I couldn't open my mouth and call for help, because I was scared that a snake would enter it. Then they untied me, picked me up, and threw me into a swamp, which was very hard to get out of. To this day, I am really afraid of snakes. I just can't see myself ever becoming friends with snakes.

Another time, when I was about the same age, some older boys caught me alone when I was on my way home from school in wintertime. One of the boys was white, and the rest were Anishinaabeg. They gagged my mouth, tied my long hair to a tree, and stripped me naked. They put snow all over my chest and back. Laughing the whole time, they slapped my butt and played with different parts of my body. I peed all over myself. Finally, they hung me from a tree upside down and left me. They said they would come back with my clothing later. I was freezing cold by the time a woman passed by and found me. She was one of Jane's relatives. I remember she cried as she got me down from the tree. Then she went to get her boyfriend, a white man, to help carry me home. Afterward, my mother was angry and beat me for being outside naked.

I attended school off and on for about three years when I wasn't trapping or hunting with my stepdad. During those years, the teachers had me skip one grade. By the time I was twelve years old and in grade four, I only went to school once in a while. Most of my friends had dropped out, or had been taken to residential schools, or had graduated and gone on to attend high school in cities. Jane and Bonnie, for instance, went to the high school in Thunder Bay, where they lived in dormitories during the school year and only returned to Ombabika for the summer holidays. Without my friends, I did not feel strong or brave enough to face the bullies at school, unless I got drunk first. One morning, I drank an entire small bottle of whiskey that I had stolen from my parents when they were drunk. Only then did I feel courageous enough go to school. That day, some kids picked on me in the classroom, but I didn't think anything could hurt me and I told them to fuck off. Someone told the teacher, and he made me go home.

Later, the teacher told my parents I had been drunk in school. That may have been the first time my mother and stepfather realized that I drank alcohol. They asked me how long I had been drinking, and I said I couldn't remember. They told me to stop, and warned me that if I ever went to school drunk again, my mom would give me a beating. In fact, I was caught drunk in class a few more times, and those times my mother did hit me as she had promised. Before long, I dropped out of school completely.

WHEN OTHER CHILDREN WERE TAKEN TO RESIDENTIAL SCHOOLS

When I was about twelve years old, some white men came to Ombabika and took away most of the children to residential schools, including my brother Andy, my cousins Angela and Justin, and my stepsister Matilda. Parents did not understand why their children were being taken from them, but they were unable to stop it. Only a small number of school-age children were left behind. They did not catch us because we were not in Ombabika the day they rounded up all of the other kids. I had been at the trapping grounds with my stepdad. When we returned later, Ombabika was strangely quiet. I remember waving to some people as I walked by their house, but they just looked angry, and then they shut their windows. After we got home, my mother started screaming and crying. She told my stepdad that white men wearing trench coats and strange hats had arrived at the railway station, given her and other parents a piece of paper, and taken all of the children away on a train.

In the following months and years, some parents left Ombabika to try to find their children and bring them back. In the end, a few were success-ful. Some children ran away from residential schools and made their way back to Ombabika on their own. Others only returned after many years, when they were already young adults. But a number of those who were taken away that day never returned. There were parents who never saw their children again.

For a long time after the children were taken away, life in Ombabika seemed out of balance. There were many adults and many babies, but very few kids in between. Those of us of school age had to do even more chores than before. We only got help when teenagers who had gone away to high school, like Jane and Bonnie, returned during their vacations. Not many students remained in the local school, and most of them were white. My stepbrother Barry had not been taken away, because he was old enough that he already worked for a logging company.

Andy and Angela were taken to the McIntosh Indian Residential School in Kenora, about 500 kilometres west of Ombabika (Figure 2). Justin and Matilda, on the other hand, were taken to schools 500 kilome-tres to the southeast, in Sault Ste. Marie. Andy was one of the youngest children to be taken away, and Matilda was one of the oldest. At that time, Andy was too young for school but he was big for his age, so the white men who took him may not have realized how young he was. I think Andy was gone for months, but I don't remember exactly how long. He was one of the first children to return to Ombabika. One day my stepdad received a letter saying that Andy was very ill, so he was being sent back home. When Andy arrived, he was not the same child that my mom and I had raised until then. He was very skinny and sad. The McIntosh School was Roman Catholic and was taught by nuns and priests. Andy said they did not hit him, but they cut off his long hair, which traumatized him. In Ombabika at that time, many young boys wore their hair in a neat, long braid and never cut it. By their teen years a lot of them cut their hair short or wore it only to their shoulders, especially if they had been told to do so in school. Andy said he had missed our mother so much when he was away that he did not want to live anymore, so he had stopped eating. After that, he got sick, and they decided to send him back. My grandmother carefully nursed him back to health, and over time he grew his hair long again.

My cousin Angela stayed at the McIntosh School for a year. She was allowed to return to Ombabika the following summer for the school break, and she never went back. Like many other residential school students, Angela had left Ombabika with long hair and returned with a rough, short cut, like a bowl had been placed on her head and her hair had been trimmed around it. Angela told me that the McIntosh students had to pray for long periods many times each day. She said the priests did not treat her badly, but the nuns sometimes were mean and favoured certain kids over others. Angela tried very hard to use English and to obey all of the rules, so she would not be punished. Still, the nuns sometimes punished her along with all of the rest of the kids when a few of them did not follow the rules. At those times, none of the children were given their meals, and Angela said the kids got very hungry and fought among themselves, blaming each other. She told me she did not like the school much, but she did appreciate that she had her own bed there, and she did not have to deal with people getting drunk, like in Ombabika.

Angela's brother, Justin, returned to Ombabika sometime after Angela. He told us he never went hungry at his school, because most of the kids there did not want to eat the food they were served, so he ate what the others left behind. Justin seemed to have learned and changed a lot during his time away. When he came back, he spoke a completely different language, which I now realize must have been English. Not long after he returned to Ombabika, I saw him stab a guy when they were drunk and fighting at a party. The other young man was pretty badly injured, so he was taken to a hospital. Justin was arrested and sent to a juvenile detention centre or prison. He returned to Ombabika some years later, after he was released.

My stepsister Matilda was away for the longest time. We didn't see her again for years. In the end, she ran away from her residential school with a group of other kids. They walked the 500 kilometres back to Ombabika. It took them many months, and at least one child died along the way. They were not able to bury him, because it was almost winter and the ground was already frozen. They covered his body in branches and leaves, and left him there in the woods. By the time Matilda returned, she was already a young woman. She did not talk about the school much. She said the children hadn't been given enough food, so they were often hungry. She explained that, when she and the other kids waited in line for a meal, they tried to stand tall and be still, polite, and well behaved, because they didn't want to risk not being fed. If they acted out, they were beaten or taken away from the school, and nobody knew where they were taken. Matilda stayed in Ombabika for a few years after that. Then she got married and moved to live with her husband in Aroland, about sixty-five kilometres east of Ombabika.

Many times people have told me that I was lucky that I was not forced to go to residential schools like my brother, cousins, and stepsister, because I didn't experience the kind of suffering that they and other children knew in those institutions. I know that it was wrong for the children to be taken away from their parents. I also understand that some of them experienced horrible abuse and neglect in residential schools. But it is hard for me to feel lucky. I experienced molestation and beatings in Ombabika, both before and after the other kids were taken away. So it is difficult for me to know whether it was better to stay, or to have been taken away.

PRE-TEEN AND TEENAGE FRIENDSHIPS

After I started going to school, I developed more friendships that involved larger groups of kids. During the period when I was about ten to twelve years old, for example, I sometimes tagged along with my stepbrother Barry and his teenage friends when they were having fun. The first time I joined them I had followed Barry out onto the lake when it was frozen over and the boys were playing hockey. When Barry saw me following him, he stopped to wet my moccasins. Once they had frozen, I could slide in them easily. Later, he got a small, box-shaped toboggan and towed me in that while the hockey game was on. After it was over, the teenagers built a bonfire in a tub, which they dragged around the lake. It amazed me to see that giant flame sliding around on the lake surface, and I was excited and happy that Barry pulled me on my toboggan behind it. I continued to join Barry and his friends when they played hockey on other days. I became their mascot or gofer, because I ran and fetched anything they told me to get. Sometimes they even let me take part in the game and chase the puck around with my little stick. There usually was a lot of drinking around their hockey games. I already drank secretly, but I had not yet started drinking openly in groups like that.

When I was twelve and thirteen years old (Figure 3), I also played with a bunch of boys and girls, my age or older, in an ongoing game of "Cowboys and Anishinaabeg." Almost all of us were at least partly Ojibwa or Cree, so the "Cowboy" and "Anishinaabe" categories weren't divided along actual racial lines. Jane's brother Nick and his friends were on the Anishinaabe side, and I usually was Anishinaabe too, although sometimes I played on the cowboy side. We were fairly serious about that game, and had a lot of fun with it. We "shot" people with slingshots and pine cones, and not just each other, but also adults. Once I hit Renard on the head and then tried to hide, but he caught me. Another time I was hanging on a beam in the railway station when I saw someone enter who I thought was a cowboy, so I jumped down onto him. In fact, it was an old fellow who worked in the building. One of the other kids dropped down from the ceiling after me, to help me explain and apologize to him. The man just kicked us out of the station.

Once in a while, I still played with my cousins Angela and Paula at the long house, if their father and older brothers were not around. We were playing hide and seek there the day their mom died. I was about twelve years old, so Angela must have been eleven and Paula thirteen. It all happened very quickly. My aunt Renee had not been drinking, but suddenly she became upset and panicked. She started acting strangely. First she put some of her clothing in the wood stove fire, and then she told us to put our socks in there too. She asked me to help her take off her socks to add them to the flames. None of us understood what she was doing. Then my aunt fell on a bed, holding her chest. She stared at the ceiling and foam came out of her mouth. Angela and Paula started screaming and crying. I didn't know what to do, so I just held her and turned her head to the side. I cleaned her mouth and tried to hear her heartbeat. Some adults ran into the room, but there was nothing they could do, because she was already dead. People later said that she had had a heart attack. My uncle Aziinii was still alive, but after my aunt died, Paula and Angela were taken in by two women in the community, Edna and Rose. Those women often took care of orphaned and abandoned children in our area. A few months later, my cousins moved out of that household and in with some of their dad's relatives in another part of Ombabika.

FIGURE 3. IN OMBABIKA (THIRTEEN YEARS OLD, 1963). THIS PHOTOGRAPH OF ME WAS PROBABLY TAKEN BY SHIIGOHBII.

When I was about twelve years old, I started spending a lot of time with Jane and her cousin Bonnie while they were at home on vacation from high school in Thunder Bay. I joined them and some other older girls to form a baseball team that we called the Ombabika Hounds. Jane had red-and-black sweaters made for us in Thunder Bay, which had an impression of an Indian head and the words "Ombabika Hounds" on them. They were very nicely made, and we were happy to wear them. We played baseball against other groups of kids in Ombabika, including some of the white kids who lived in Auden. We used regular, store-bought bats, balls, and gloves. Playing baseball was rough, though. I remember getting the wind knocked out of me when I got hit in the chest once, and another time I was knocked unconscious when I was hit in the head.

Jane and Bonnie began to dress differently once they went to high school. When they returned to Ombabika, they copied the styles teenage girls wore in the city, and the pictures they saw in teen magazines. Both of them wore modern dresses and skirts, and styled their straight black hair in beehive fashions. They often wore makeup, and at one point Bonnie dyed her black hair brown. For a long time I did not understand how her hair had changed colour, but finally someone explained it to me. Both of them sometimes curled their hair too, but I knew how they did that, because I had seen my mother curl my stepsister Matilda's hair at home. My mom combed Matilda's wet hair into sections and rolled each one up around a slip of paper that she tied into place. Matilda then slept with her hair like that, and when she took the paper slips out in the morning, her hair was curly.

Some teenage boys in Ombabika also imitated styles they saw in the city or in magazine photographs of James Dean, Elvis, or other famous men. Jane's older brother Nick, for example, went through a period when he only dressed in black and combed his hair back with bear grease, to make himself look like Johnny Cash. Secretly, I wanted to imitate those men's hairstyles myself. Jane had seen Elvis dance on television and showed me how he moved, and I wanted to look and dance like him. I did not do that, though. Instead, I continued wearing clothes similar to most teenage boys and men in Ombabika: a checkered, lumberjack shirt, jeans, black rubber boots, and some kind of a hat. I liked to have a hat on at all times, either a knitted toque in winter or a baseball cap in summer. Also, like some of the older, traditional women, I did not wear a bra, because I found bras very uncomfortable.

Jane and Bonnie wanted me to dress more like them, and I wanted to please them, so sometimes I wore the clothes they gave me and let them style my hair into a beehive (Figure 4). Once, when I was about thirteen years old, Jane arranged for the two of us to go on a double date with two white boys. She instructed me to wear a skirt, which I did, but I also wore my rubber boots as usual. Jane became annoyed with me, because she thought my boots did not go well with the skirt. During the date, Jane and I and the two boys all got into a car together, with Jane in the front seat with one of the boys, and me in the back with the other one. I didn't know what was expected of me, and I couldn't talk easily with him because I didn't speak much English. I was bored, so I started rolling cigarettes. Jane thought I wasn't taking the date seriously, so she got angry at me. I got kind of mad too, so I left.

I started smoking when I was thirteen or fourteen years old. For several years, smoking made me gag and feel nauseous, but I kept trying to do it because all of the kids I knew smoked and I wanted to fit in. Mainly I pretended to smoke by puffing on a cigarette without actually inhaling. Sometimes other kids made fun of me for that. Most of them probably were addicted to cigarettes by then, because they could not go to sleep at night without having a final smoke. I liked to roll cigarettes and I became very good at it. I took rolling paper and tobacco from my parents when they were drunk, or other kids gave them to me when they wanted me to make cigarettes for them.

When I was in my early teens, Jane, Bonnie, and I got matching leather jackets with fancy buttons. I didn't have any money, so Jane bought mine for me. She also gave me a nice pair of hand-me-down pants to go with the jacket. We dressed up like that to go for strolls on the train tracks together. We thought we were so cool! Once in a while we stole alcohol at the railway station, after crates had been unloaded from trains and stacked on the platform. One of our strategies was to roll a case under the train to the other side, where we could hide it in the woods. That was foolish and dangerous, because the trains could have started at any time when we were under them. People usually didn't notice right away when alcohol disappeared like that. Once they realized it, they couldn't figure out who had

FIGURE 4. IN OMBABIKA, ON A DAY WHEN JANE STYLED MY HAIR (FOURTEEN YEARS OLD, 1964). THIS PHOTOGRAPH WAS PROBABLY TAKEN BY SHIIGOHBII.

taken it. When we got into mischief together, Jane participated but also somehow held herself apart. She never drank as much as Bonnie and I did. Jane had a good relationship with her father, so she carefully hid activities that might make him unhappy.

By the time I was fourteen or fifteen years old, Bonnie, Jane, and I often went to dances and parties, like those that were held at a local store, where the owner had a small hall with a jukebox in the back. Many teenagers hung out there. One day the owner told us he was planning to rent out the hall and sell the jukebox, because he needed the cash. We organized a twenty-four-hour dance-a-thon to raise enough money to keep the jukebox and hall open to us for another year. Adults sponsored us, with the agreement that half of the winnings would go to the store owner, and half to whoever was still dancing at the twenty-four-hour mark. My cousin Pascal and I took part in the dance-a-thon together. At that age, he was about my height, had a fair bit of acne on his face, and cut his hair to look like one of the Beatles, because he loved their music. Pascal and I danced every style of dance we knew during the dance-a-thon: jigs, the twist, waltzes, square dancing, and free dancing. Sometimes we slowed down to eat and drink, but we didn't stop. People began to drop out, some by choice, and a few by fainting. Pascal finally fell down and said he couldn't continue. But I kept going! I was the only one left dancing when they stopped the music at the twenty-four-hour mark, so I won. Of course, when my mom found out that I had made all of the dance-a-thon money, she asked me for it, and I gave it to her.

At one of the jukebox hall gatherings, Bonnie and Jane encouraged me to dance with a certain boy. He and I kissed afterward, outside of the store. He was the first person I ever kissed. It wasn't awful, but it wasn't exciting either. In summertime, we also went to parties that were held at Frank Lake. Those gatherings started at about 6:00 p.m., when the sun was still shining. We would build a big bonfire and almost everybody got drunk. I remember having a lot of fun at those parties. One time, though, we were riding in a truck when it rolled over. Bonnie's arm was broken, so she wore a sling for a long time after that.

There were several times during those years when I was sexually as-saulted at a drinking party. Once, when I was eleven or twelve years old, some older boys and girls did sexual things to me when I was drinking with them. I don't remember much of what happened, except feeling sick to my stomach when the guys touched me. Another time, four boys gagged my mouth, and took off my pants. One of them held my arms and two held my legs, while the fourth guy tried to rape me. When he did that, I remember feeling like I left my body. It was as if I was standing behind and above them. I watched what they were doing without feeling it. I don't think that guy succeeded in raping me, because when they stopped they didn't seem satisfied. They said that it wasn't working.

Two of my closest friends, Jane and Bonnie, knew about some of the difficulties in my life, and I knew about some painful things that had happened to them. But we did not discuss them. One of our ways of coping was to laugh things off—to pretend frightening experiences hadn't occurred, or to joke about them—as if we did not take them seriously. I wanted to say more. I wanted to talk honestly about how I had been hurt. But I got a strong message from them that we did not talk about unpleasant things. I admired both Bonnie and Jane, and I envied them having loving parents and studying in high school. I wanted to be like them, and I wanted them to like me and accept me. So I quietly studied them, followed their example, and tried to do anything they encouraged me to do.

HAVING TWO SPIRITS

Starting when I was a young child, probably when I was four or five years old, my grandmother told me that I had two spirits. She would gently poke me in the chest and say, "Little girl, you have *niizhin ojijaak* (two spirits) living inside of you." Over the years she explained this to me by saying that some people were special and had both a male and a female spirit inside of them. She said that two-spirit girls often were drawn to activities that boys usually did, like me when I explored the bush and went fishing and trapping.

As I got older, my *kokum* told me more about people who had two spirits. She said that when they grew up, some married a person of the opposite sex and had babies, but others never married, or chose to live with someone of the same sex as a couple. My grandmother had been very happily married to my grandfather. She believed that, one day, I also would have a powerful, deep connection with someone like that. She told me I would feel great love and trust for that person, and that person would feel the same for me. She said that I would experience pleasure with my partner, and sensations so wonderful that I would feel like I had died and gone to heaven. For many years I did not understand what her words meant.

My grandmother told me that two-spirit, same-sex couples used to play an important role in Anishinaabe communities, because they adopted children who had lost their parents. Sometimes, she said, individuals with two spirits had other special duties, like keeping fire, healing people, or leading ceremonies. My *kokum* explained that two-spirit people were once loved and respected within our communities, but times had changed and they were no longer understood or valued in the same way. When I got older, she said, I would have to figure out how to live with two spirits as an adult. She warned me I probably would experience many hard times along the way. I remember her rubbing my head and shoulders, saying, "I feel for you. You're not going to have an easy life when you get older." She tried to teach me how to cope with difficult problems by thinking about different ways to solve them. For example, she asked me what I would do if I was on a journey and found boulders blocking my path. Every time I had an answer to how I would get around or over the boulders, she listened to what I had to say. Then, even if she approved of my strategy, she asked me to go away and think about it more, and only return when I had come up with another answer.

My grandmother usually talked about two-spiritedness in private with me, but she also mentioned two-spirit people in a few of the stories she told at campfire gatherings. One story was about a young man whose partner had died, so he went on a great journey to find another. After a while he came to a settlement where he met a healer, and those two men made a life working and raising children together. I also remember a story my grandmother told about a woman with two spirits. She was responsible for painting marks on stones along well-travelled paths. My grandmother said that those signs were how the woman's family communicated with other families travelling through the same area.

In Ombabika, I only remember a few other people who might have had two spirits, including Edna and Rose, the two women who took in Paula and Angela after my aunt Renee died. Edna and Rose were Christian women and very active in their church. They lived together and took care of children who had lost their parents or who were abandoned. One of the women—I cannot remember which one—had only one arm, so she always pinned her empty sleeve to her blouse. Once when I was seven or eight years old, I went to Rose's and Edna's house to play with one of their kids. Their cabin had one big bed for the two of them, with a divider between it and the several children's beds on the floor. My playmate referred to both of the women as his mother, so later I asked my *kokum* how he could have two mothers. She explained that those women had a special job as caregivers, because they raised kids whose biological parents had gone away or died.

Two-spiritedness can take different forms. Ethan, the husband of my older cousin, Flora, may have had two spirits. He sometimes dressed up in women's clothing at parties. I don't know if he did that to make people laugh, because he enjoyed it, or both. I do remember, though, that after he had dressed up a few times on his own, other people started to dress him up when he was drunk and passed out. More than once, people took off his clothes and put women's clothing and makeup on him, to make fun of him. They also played other pranks on him, like shaving off all of his hair, or tying him to a chair when he was drunk. I never understood why some people treated him so badly. I was curious about Ethan, not because he dressed in women's clothes once in a while, but because he had a raven companion. The raven knew a lot of Ojibwe and English words that Ethan had taught it, and it came whenever he called it. Looking back now, I realize that Ethan may have had some African blood, because he had quite dark skin and tight, curly black hair. His father looked like other Anishinaabe men, so Ethan might have gotten his looks from his mother, but I never met her, so I am not sure.

My earliest memories of attraction to other girls are from when I was about ten years old. Around that age, I started to feel strangely excited, nervous, and shy around certain girls. The first time I remember it happened was when I met a girl named Claudia, who came with her grandmother to visit my grandmother. Claudia was older but not much taller than me. She had a sweet, shy smile, and her long, black hair shone. When she looked at me, I felt like my stomach was full of butterflies. I sensed that she liked me too, but, like me, she did not know how to express herself well. I tried speaking to her, but I stuttered, saying something like, "You wanna, you wanna, you wanna go play?" Finally, I grabbed her hand and pulled her outside. We played with my moose-bone toy, and then I showed her how to use my bow and arrow. I saw Claudia around Ombabika a few times after that, and each time I experienced those same sensations of excitement and uncertainty.

The other girl I had a crush on in Ombabika was my friend, Bonnie. She was a warm, likeable person. I remember watching Bonnie one day when she was combing her hair in the mirror, before she put makeup on to go out. Her hair and skin looked soft and smooth, and I was struck by her beauty. She smiled at me, and I felt those butterflies in my stomach again. Bonnie was always very affectionate with me. When we hung out together in a large group, she often held my hand or put her arm around my shoulder, and I liked that a lot.

Looking back, there were three other kids in Ombabika who I now think might have been gay, lesbian, or bisexual. Bonnie and my cousin Angela were two of them. I don't know how they felt when they were growing up in Ombabika, but years later, when we were all living in Thunder Bay in our twenties, the two of them were lovers. While I was still in Ombabika, my friend Shiigohbii also told me he was attracted to other boys. He and I discussed those feelings one day when I was ten or eleven years old and we were sitting on top of the rock cut, watching teenagers go by. I saw Claudia in the distance and my stomach began to flip-flop. I told Shiigohbii how I felt when I saw her, and he explained that he felt the same way when he saw our friend Edmond. Shiigohbii said his parents had told him it was wrong for a boy to like a boy, or a girl to like a girl, in such a way. His parents had strong Christian beliefs and they said that people like that went to hell. Shiigohbii pointed out a man and a woman who were walking together, and he said, "That's what grownups are like. That's what they're going to make us do when we get older. You're going to have to marry me or another man, and I'm going to have to marry you or another woman, and we'll have to make babies." I asked him if he wanted to do that, and he said no, because we didn't like each other that way. Shiigohbii suggested that we should marry each other when we got older, but only pretend to be married. He said that he would invite Edmond over to visit him, and I could invite Claudia or another girlfriend over to visit me. We agreed on that plan, but we never followed through on it. Shiigohbii and I stayed close for a few more years, but then he left Ombabika when he was a teenager.

I did not act on my attractions to girls while I was in Ombabika. I would not have known how to do so. At that stage I couldn't even imagine kissing a girl. I didn't understand my own feelings, and I assumed that I was the only girl in the world who felt the way I did. It was many years before I made the connection between those feelings and what my grandmother told me about people who have two spirits inside of them.

CHAPTER FIVE

LOSING MY GRANDMOTHER AND MOTHER, BECOMING A PARENT, AND SURVIVING AN ABUSIVE MARRIAGE IN AUDEN (1965–1970)

During my early teens, several of my close family members became seriously ill or died in accidents. My stepbrother Barry was killed while he was working as a logger. A bulldozer backed up and accidentally ran over him. Barry was dearly loved by many people, and we were all heartbroken by his sudden death. My mother also became extremely ill when I was fourteen or fifteen years old. She had cancer, and she needed to have surgery to remove one of her breasts. She also had a serious condition that led doctors to operate on her head, but I don't know why. The wounds on her chest and head were terrible. I was the main person to nurse her after her surgeries, cleaning her and changing her bandages as she healed. She was not well for a long time, and she never fully recovered.

AN ARRANGED MARRIAGE

When I was fifteen years old, my mom sat me down and told me that she had arranged for me to get married. She explained that she was very ill, and my grandmother was very old, and this was the only way she could be sure I would be taken care of after they both died. My mother said that, as soon as I turned sixteen, I would marry a man named Gus. Gus was an Ojibwa man about twenty years older than me. He had never been married and he lived with his mother. My mom said that she and Gus's mom had already come to an agreement about the marriage. My *kokum* disagreed with this plan. She told my mother that I should wait and marry someone who I knew and liked, but my mom ignored her.

I was confused about what was happening. I was frightened and saddened about the possibility of losing my grandmother, and even my mother, despite the abusive way she often treated me. I believed my mom when she said she wanted me to get married for my own good. But I did not know Gus, and I did not want to marry anyone. Still, I met with Gus and his mother as my mom instructed. I didn't learn much about Gus during that visit. He was a big man, about six feet tall, and neither skinny nor fat. He had short, straight black hair and a smooth face. I later found out he was deaf in one ear, so people needed to speak loudly for him to hear them. My only other memories from that first visit are that he wore an all-green outfit, and that he shook my grandmother's hand.

Afterward, I decided to run away from Ombabika rather than marry Gus. I tried to do that twice, but both times I did not succeed. The first time, I just got on a train when it stopped to pick up passengers. I tried to pay the conductor with the one-dollar bill I had. He said that I was too young and that I did not have enough money, so I had to get off the train. The second time, I tried to walk eastward along the railway line, hoping to reach a big town or a city on foot. That was in October 1965, just before the winter snow began falling. I only had a jacket and a spare shirt and scarf with me. I walked all day. Someone had seen me leaving Ombabika, though, and told my family. By evening my cousin Justin and my cousin Flora's husband, Ethan, had caught up to me in a railroad gas car and brought me back.

When I returned to Ombabika, my mother sat me down again, and again she insisted that marrying Gus was for my own good. She said it was important that I started acting like I liked Gus and was eager to marry him. She told me to tell people that I was in love with him. My stepdad also talked to me privately and said similar things. He explained that my mom was dying and did not have long to live. He told me my mother had arranged the marriage to make sure I didn't struggle on my own after she and my grandmother died.

So I did what they asked. I told Jane, Bonnie, and my other girlfriends that I really liked Gus, that I even loved him. They did not know the whole story—that my mother had arranged the marriage because she was dying, that I had tried to run away, and that I didn't really know Gus at all. Bonnie and Jane came from homes where their moms and dads loved them, where they were safe and cared for, and where they made their own choices. They did not know enough about my life to know that I was lying. So they may have believed me when I said I was in love with Gus. They planned a big party for me the night before the wedding.

Gus and I got married in the summer of 1966, just after I turned sixteen. I don't recall much about the wedding or the celebrations around it. I do remember that Gus asked me to have sex with him during the party on the night before the wedding. He wanted to have sex at least once before we got married. I agreed. We went to an outhouse and I stood there while he did what he did. It was very painful for me, and I started to bleed heavily. At first, I thought I had gotten my period. I knew what that was like, because I had started menstruating a few months earlier. I didn't understand that a girl or a woman may bleed during first sexual intercourse. I went home to clean myself up. When I came back to the party, I heard Gus bragging that he had just taken my cherry. It upset me to hear him speak like that. I must have drunk a lot of alcohol afterward, because I don't remember much more from that night.

The next day, for the wedding, Jane and my other girlfriends dressed me in a lime green jacket that I thought looked ugly, and even kind of slimy. They also put makeup on my face. When I saw myself in the mirror, I thought I looked strangely old. But I didn't tell them. I never complained, because I was trying to go along with what everyone expected of me. Gus and I said the words the minister told us to say at the ceremony. Then another big drinking party was held at Gus's mother's house. The party was actually spread out between her house and the house next door, with people going back and forth between the two. When I went into the other house at one point, I found Gus there having sex with someone else. Gus apologized, but I was upset and disgusted. It took me several months to forgive him.

FIRST YEARS OF MARRIAGE

My first years with Gus were not terrible. I bought our first house with the money I had saved in my Hudson's Bay store account from my trapping work. Before we got married, the store manager told me that some white people were moving away from Auden, and I had enough money in my account—eleven dollars—to buy their house from them. I agreed to buy it. The house was close to Gus's mother's house. It was cold and much larger than anything I had ever known. During the winter I always stayed near the pot-bellied wood stove to keep warm. We also had a gas stove for cooking. We mostly used kerosene and gas lamps. Like many buildings in that area, our house was on the electric grid that was connected to the railway station, so I had electric lighting for the first time. I wasn't comfortable with it, though, so I didn't use it.

Soon after Gus and I were married, he started claiming some of my most prized possessions as his own, like my gun and my grandmother's canoe. He did not share his valued belongings with me, though. For example, he had a snowmobile that I knew how to maintain and drive, but he did not let me use it. So if he was at home during winter, he might haul wood to our house in his snowmobile, but if he wasn't, I had to carry the wood myself, wearing snowshoes. Gus and I went hunting together during our first years of marriage, and that was when we bonded the most. We hunted moose, duck, and geese together. He was surprised and impressed that I was a good hunter and could survive on my own in the bush.

Gus appreciated that I had such skills, unlike most women in Auden and Ombabika, but he still wanted me to dress and act more like those women. At that time, I wore jeans and a lumberjack shirt every day, without a bra. I usually also wore some kind of hat—a baseball cap, a straw hat, a cowboy hat, or a knitted toque. Gus especially disliked me wearing men's hats and going without a bra. I tried wearing a bra for a while, but I found it very uncomfortable, like the life was being squeezed out of me. I also tried to replace my hats with kerchiefs. Many women in Auden wore kerchiefs over their hair. They usually tied theirs under their chins, but I tied mine at the back of my neck, like a bandana. Once in a while I still wore one of my favourite hats, though. There were times when Gus tried to hide my hats, but I always found them sooner or later.

Despite the time that Gus and I spent together, we did not talk a lot. I never learned much about his life before he met me. He told me that he grew up with several older brothers who spoiled him. I asked if anyone had ever beaten him as a child, and he said no, that both his mother and his stepfather had treated him well. He had gone to school in Auden and seemed to speak English pretty well, although he had never gone away to residential school. I got the feeling that Gus had not wanted to marry me, but, like me, he agreed to do it because his mother told him to. Sexually, I never felt any pleasure with Gus. After our first painful experience, I did not really feel anything at all during sex with him. It was like I left my body and could watch what was happening from a distance.

In Auden, just like in Ombabika, many people drank large amounts of alcohol on a regular basis, but Gus was unusual because he never drank. He also did not like me to drink, so while we were married I reduced my drinking a lot. Gus worked for the railway, fixing and maintaining the train tracks, and sometimes that required him to be away for several days in a row. When that happened, I bought a lot of alcohol and had a drinking binge alone in the house. While Gus was in Auden, I secretly drank small amounts of alcohol, or breathed in some of the fumes from his snowmobile tank, but I did not get drunk or high. Quickly sniffing fuel relaxed me and, unlike with alcohol, Gus did not notice the effect it had on me.

At one point during our first year together, Gus needed to work in a very isolated spot about twenty kilometres from Auden for several months. Another Anishinaabe man who was working there had brought his wife with him, and Gus wanted me to move there to set up house for him too. I became friends with the other woman who was living there. She played guitar, and we spent much of our time together doing chores, singing songs, and baking lemon, blueberry, and raisin pies.

During my first years of marriage I had a few other memorable experiences. When I was sixteen years old, I delivered the baby of a woman named Helene, who was my cousin Justin's girlfriend. I had never seen childbirth before, and I had not expected to be involved in that one, so I wasn't prepared. Helene went into labour when all of the midwives were drunk. I was sober, so her mom grabbed me and asked me to help her deliver the baby. When I entered the room, I remember there was a foul smell in the air, not like the smell of blood and other birth fluids, but like someone had not bathed for a long time. I thought I was just there to fetch and clean things for Helene's mom, but when the baby started to come out feet-first, Helene's mother fainted. Even though I was frightened, I stayed calm and focused. I felt like somebody else entered my body and moved my hands around, doing all of the work for me. The baby was stuck. The umbilical cord was wrapped around its head and neck, which were inside

Helene's body. Helene cried and screamed in pain, but she was aware enough to give me some instructions. I squeezed my hand inside of her to reach the umbilical cord. Then I pulled it away from the baby's head and helped the baby out when Helene pushed down.

When the baby came out, he was bluish. He didn't breathe at first. I turned him upside down and patted him a bit, and then I put my mouth on his mouth to try to give him air, like Helene instructed. Finally, he started to cry. Helene told me to cut the cord. Her mother woke up about then, right as the placenta was coming out. I was frightened when I saw the placenta, because I thought she was having another baby. It looked like a very strange baby! But Helene's mother told me it was the sack that had held the baby inside of Helene. Helene and Justin named their boy Mitchell. He was a healthy, good-sized baby, with a lot of hair. He grew very fast.

MY GRANDMOTHER'S DEATH

When I was sixteen and seventeen years old, I spent a lot of time nursing and taking care of my mother and my grandmother. My mom had been ill for longer than my *kokum*, but my *kokum* died first. She had become very weak and frail. When she first became ill, my family took her to the hospital in Sioux Lookout. The doctors there said my grandmother was healthy and did not have any diseases, but she was dying because she was very old. They thought she was over 100 years old.

We returned to Ombabika and I helped to take care of my grandmother in my mother's cabin. I washed her and tried to convince her to eat and drink. I smudged her with cedar and prayed for her, as she had once done for me. My *kokum* told me that she was tired and she did not want to live any more. She was upset by the drunken and disturbing behaviour that had become normal in our community. She described it as a bad air that was destroying our people, and she didn't want to witness it any longer.

My grandmother knew who I was until the end. When I was in my fourth or fifth month of pregnancy, she was the first person to tell me that I was pregnant, correctly guessing that I would have a baby girl. She reminded me that I had two spirits inside of me and that I would have a difficult life, so I would have to work very hard to take care of myself.

My *kokum* passed away in September 1967. I was not with her when she was pronounced dead. I got there about ten minutes later, and I broke down crying. I held her hand, wishing that I had been able to say good-bye to her in her final moments. All of a sudden, she lifted her head up, squeezed my hand, and told me that everything was going to be alright. She said, "*Giizaagiyin*"—I love you. Then she laid her head back down and she was gone. I'll never forget how she came back and comforted me like that, even in her final moments. My grandmother's death was one of the greatest losses in my life.

MY DAUGHTER SARAH'S BIRTH

In December 1967, three months after my grandmother died, my daughter Sarah was born. My pregnancy had been difficult. I often felt nauseous, so I had not been able to keep down much food or drink. That probably was for the best, because it meant that I hardly drank alcohol when I was pregnant, even when I had the opportunity. I gained very little weight, so I was skinny up until my ninth month, except for my big belly. No one ever talked to me about what to expect during childbirth, but I had already delivered Helene's baby, so I had a basic understanding of what was involved. Still, I ended up having a very long and painful labour. I was in labour for four days in Auden before they took me to a hospital. My mother was the main person helping me during that time, although she was ill and weak herself. Local midwives sometimes assisted her.

I really suffered when my labour did not progress as it should have. I didn't understand what was happening. The people helping me feared they would lose me or the baby, but they waited a long time to take me to a hospital because it was winter and conditions were very bad. Snow had blocked the roads out of Auden, so we could not travel by car. The freight train had derailed near Armstrong, so they weren't able to transport me by railroad. Instead, we blazed a trail in a caravan of snowmobiles until we reached Abitibi Pulp and Paper Company Camp 40, where I could be picked up by an ambulance. Before we left Auden, members of my family and my neighbours made a bed for me out of two lightweight cedar sleds, which they had tied together. They put planks across the sleds and covered me in blankets. Given that my mom was ill, they made a similar bed for her on two sleds, although she was sitting more upright. Once we left, it took a full day to get to the logging camp. I was in terrible pain. I have several memories of that journey: the snowmobile blowing exhaust in my face; the snowfall soaking my blankets; and how I felt like I was dying when they stopped midway to warm up and have tea. My mother tried to comfort me, telling me that I had my *kokum*'s strength and that I would get through it. Finally, we reached the logging camp and the ambulance took me to Geraldton Hospital. Once there, doctors performed a Cesarean section on me and gave me a blood transfusion, because I had lost a lot of blood.

At nine pounds and three ounces (4.2 kilograms), Sarah was a very large baby when she was born. I called her "Sarah" because that was the name my friend Jane had asked me to give her, and we had agreed to name each other's first child. I produced a lot of milk, and Sarah never had difficulty nursing. When she was born, she was very fair and mostly bald, but she had a small amount of reddish-brown hair. Later her skin became darker and her hair became browner. Gus was shocked, though, by Sarah's colouring at birth. He became convinced that I had cheated on him, and that Sarah was not his daughter. The night I brought Sarah home from the hospital, he hit me for the first time. He paced back and forth angrily, saying, "That's not my baby. That's not my baby at all. That's someone else's baby, someone who you were with while I was working." I tried to reassure him that was not true. I reminded him that, even though he and I had darker skin and hair than Sarah, my mother's grandfather was French, and I didn't even know for sure what my father's family looked like. I told him that Sarah's hair reminded me of my uncle Jacques, who passed away before Gus had a chance to meet him. But Gus didn't believe it. He rejected Sarah, and said ugly things about us both.

During Sarah's first months, I spent most of my time with my mother. My mom was ill and needed help around the clock. Fortunately, she got a lot of joy from holding Sarah. Unlike Gus, my mother adored Sarah. I didn't understand why she loved my baby so much when she had not loved me in the same way. But I appreciated that she had such positive feelings for Sarah, especially because Gus didn't. I started leaving Sarah with my mom even when I returned to my house. I squeezed breast milk into jars that my stepdad used to prepare baby bottles, which my mother then gave to Sarah.

MY MOTHER'S DEATH

My mother passed away in April 1968, when Sarah was four months old. I took care of her until her end, cleaning and bandaging her wounds, bathing her, and changing her clothing and bedding. When she was on her deathbed, she asked me to take care of my little brother Andy after she died. She wanted me to finish raising him. I agreed that I would. She never thanked me for caring for her, or for him. She never told me she loved me. I admit I was hoping she would say it before she died, but she didn't.

Andy immediately came home to live with me and Gus. The night after my mom was buried, my stepdad came to see me. He told me to take care of Andy as my mother had instructed, and I promised him I would. And then he left. I assumed he had gone to his cabin, but the next day I was told he had left Ombabika completely. I only saw my stepdad again a few years later, when he came to see Andy at my house. At that time he asked whether his daughter, my stepsister Matilda, could start looking after Andy. I refused, because I had raised Andy since he was little, and I already was like a mom to him.

SURVIVING IN AN ABUSIVE RELATIONSHIP

After Sarah was born, Gus became more and more violent. At first he pushed and shoved me, but then he began beating me on a regular basis. I was only five feet and three inches tall, with fine bones and a slim frame, and he was much taller and larger than me, so there was not much I could do to defend myself physically. At that point, we had traded our house for a smaller one that was next door to Gus's mother's house, and Gus spent a lot of time there. Gus's mom had developed a strong dislike for me. Often, she was very mean to me. I think her hatred fuelled his anger toward me too. Most days Gus came home from work, went straight to his mother's house, and then came home and beat me. I could tell if I was going to be hit by the way he walked as he came toward our house. Andy sometimes saw Gus abusing me. He cried and begged Gus to stop, but Gus just threw him out of the room and locked the door. I still didn't drink alcohol, but as Gus's abuse increased, I started sniffing gas more. I did it about once a week. It numbed my pain and helped me forget my worries, at least for a little while.

Soon after Sarah was born, there was an opening for a local post-mistress position. I applied for it and was accepted. The postmaster from Geraldton brought a contract for me to sign. In our neighbourhood, I had become friends with a bright teenage girl who helped me read and sign the contract. I had already begun thinking about how I might get away from

Gus, so I asked the postmaster to keep all of the money I earned at the post office in Geraldton. He agreed. I knew that Gus would get my income if it was sent to Auden in the usual way. My new job was to drop off and pick up mail bags at the train station twice a day, and to sort and distribute the mail from my house. During the summer I pulled the mail bags on a little red wagon, and in the winter I pulled them on a toboggan. When Sarah was still a baby, I carried her in a *tikinagan* or a sling made out of a blanket. I couldn't read some of the names that were written on envelopes, but people could read their own names when they came to my house to pick up mail. Luckily, the teenage neighbour continued to visit me often, and she helped me read and sort the mail.

FIGURE 5. DURING MY SECOND PREGNANCY IN AUDEN (NINETEEN YEARS OLD, 1969). THIS PHOTOGRAPH WAS TAKEN BY MY COUSIN FLORA.

MY SON MARTIN'S BIRTH

When Sarah was about eight months old, I became pregnant again. I was very nauseous throughout my second pregnancy, as I had been during my first one. Again I hardly drank alcohol and I stopped sniffing gas. Gus continued to be angry and sometimes violent as my pregnancy grew. There wasn't a day that went by when he didn't insult me, and often he shoved and hit me. I was deeply unhappy, but I felt trapped. That can probably be seen in a photograph my cousin Flora took of me during that time, when she came upon me while I was hauling water (Figure 5).

One day when I was almost seven months pregnant, Gus grabbed me and pushed me, knocking over a bottle in the process. He told me to clean up the broken glass. As I knelt to do so, he started kicking my butt. Andy was in the room and tried to stop him. Gus told him to leave, and then he started dragging me across the floor. Suddenly, I started bleeding and having contractions. I went into labour. My labour continued for another two days before neighbours transported me to Geraldton Hospital by freight train.

My son Martin was born at that hospital six or seven months into my pregnancy, in February 1969. I did not need to have a Cesarean section. He was only four pounds and ten ounces (2.1 kilograms), half the size that his sister had been when she was born. His lungs were not fully developed, so he was put in an oxygen tank. Martin stayed in the hospital for another two months, until he reached the date when he would have been born, if he had been a full-term baby. I returned to Auden during that time, but I came back to the hospital once a week to see him and to deliver breast milk for the hospital staff to feed him. On one of those trips, while Martin was asleep in my arms, I watched a television for the first time. Late one night when the program ended, a newscaster came on the screen to sign off the air. I was shocked when that stranger spoke to me directly, saying "Good night." I waved to him and politely replied, "Good night." Only later did someone explain to me that people on television could not see or hear me, even when they seemed to be talking to me personally.

Martin was dark-skinned and bald when he was born. When his hair grew in, it was black and slightly wavy. Gus believed Martin was his own son, and didn't reject him like he rejected Sarah. Martin was a colicky baby, and very needy. In his first year, I almost always carried him in a sling on the front of my body, to comfort and soothe him. From the start, he developed more slowly than Sarah had. In fact, all of his life Martin has experienced developmental delays that probably resulted from his premature birth.

EVER INCREASING VIOLENCE

I lived with Gus's abuse until Martin was almost two years old and Sarah was three. During that period, I almost never drank alcohol or sniffed fuel, but I became a heavy smoker. I learned to inhale deeply, and I no longer felt like throwing up when I smoked. I began smoking many cigarettes a day.

Throughout those years, Gus continued to hit me, but he also began to torture me sexually and in other ways. Once he beat me so badly that I could hardly move. Then he grabbed me by the hair and shoved my face into a lit candle until the candle burned out on my hair and skin. I smelled my skin, eyelashes, and eyebrows as they burned. The next day I had blisters all over my face. It was too much to ignore, so my neighbours asked me what had happened. As usual, I said I had had an accident, and as usual, they didn't ask me any more questions. That time, though, my sores became infected, so I had to go to the hospital in Geraldton to get help. I was treated there by a white man with greying hair named Dr. Lambert. He was worried that the burns might affect my eyesight, and explained that my eyebrows and eyelashes might never grow back. Dr. Lambert told me he had never seen injuries like mine from an accident. He said that if someone was hurting me at home, he would help me to get away from him. He spoke to me in a respectful, calm tone, trying to convince me to leave Gus. But I didn't believe he could really help me. I thought, "How the hell is he going to help me in Geraldton when I'm in Auden? I'm the one who has to live with Gus."

I went to see Dr. Lambert one other time, again after Gus had tortured me so much that I was very injured and infected. That time, Gus had twisted clothes hanger wires around my breasts until I was in great pain. Afterward, one of my breasts became swollen and infected. Gus also had put out lit cigars and cigarettes on my thighs and calves. On one of my legs, I developed infections that were so bad that I could hardly walk. When Dr. Lambert saw my legs, he was shocked. He exclaimed, "Oh my God, these are cigar burns! Who would do such a thing?!" Again, he gently talked to me and strongly encouraged me to leave Gus, and again I denied that Gus had done it. I said I had just fallen down and burnt myself accidentally. Dr. Lambert treated my infected wounds and they healed, but they left behind many small, circular scars that I still have today.

During those years, no one else tried to help when Gus abused me. I was isolated and I had very little social support. I was living in a part of Auden where I did not know people well, except for my husband and his mother, who both hated me. My grandmother, my mother, and my stepfather were all gone. My closest friends from Ombabika had died, gone away to high school, or found jobs in Geraldton, Nakina, Armstrong, Longlac, or Thunder Bay. I still had some family in Ombabika, like my cousin Paula, but they lived pretty far away and never visited me. Maybe they didn't come to see me because they didn't like Gus, I don't know. Some of my neighbours in Auden must have heard Gus beat me and also seen my injuries afterward. Maybe they were too scared to try to stop him. Or maybe they thought it was not their business, or that it was my fault. I, in turn, was too ashamed to ask them for help. Gus told me that I deserved to be beaten, and on some level, I believed him.

LEAVING AUDEN

For all of the times that Gus hit me, I never hit him back. In fact, I had never hit anyone, ever. But there came a day in late 1970 when I reached my breaking point, and I fought back. That day, before Gus came home from work, Gus's nephew and his wife visited me. The three of us were drinking tea together when Gus came inside and demanded that I also get him tea. I put a kettle on the stove. While I was waiting for the water to boil, Gus came up behind me and lit a cigarette lighter under my butt until he burned my pants. When I realized what he was doing, I yelled, "Stop it!" As I put out the fire, Gus told his nephew, "This is how you treat a woman who doesn't listen." Something in me snapped. I picked up the kettle of boiling water and threw it right at Gus. The kettle hit him squarely on the forehead. He put his hands to his head and bent over. I quickly grabbed a piece of wood—a two-by-four—and I hit him so hard that he fell to the ground. Then I straddled his chest and held that two-by-four across his neck, using all of my strength to press it as hard as I could. I was so enraged that Gus's nephew could not pull me away, so he ran outside to get more men. Together they dragged me off of Gus.

When I realized what I had done, I ran. I was afraid Gus would kill me. I fled into the forest and hid myself. Later, I came out long enough to borrow a change of clothing, a tarp, and a blanket. Then I went back into hiding in the bush. I camped there for a couple of weeks. I remember often being cold and wet during that time. I later learned that, while I was away, some neighbours finally spoke to Gus about his abuse. Gus's mother's boy-friend was one of them. He was a shy man who didn't like to get involved in other people's problems, but the situation had become so terrible that he talked to Gus. I heard he told Gus that there is only so much a woman can take, and if you beat her every day, sooner or later she will fight back. He convinced Gus to let me go. Gus wrote me a letter saying that he didn't want me anymore, but he wanted me to come take the kids. Someone found me where I was camping and gave me that letter.

My final weeks in Auden are kind of a blur to me. I am not sure of the exact order of events. I may have blocked some of it out because it was so traumatic. I know that at one point I went to see Jane's brother, Nick, to ask him for help. He gave me a small tape recorder and told me to turn it on and wear it secretly, inside my shirt, the next time I saw Gus. The plan was to record Gus giving me permission to take the kids, so he could not chal-lenge me legally later. Also, if Gus beat me up, I would have a recording as evidence, if I went to court against him.

I arranged to pick up my kids at the house and take them straight to the train station to leave Auden. Someone gave me money to buy the train tickets. I went to Gus's house with Nick, Gus's mother's boyfriend, and another man. Gus met them at the door and told them that he would not hurt me. He asked them to wait some distance away, which they did. I had the tape recorder on under my shirt. At first Gus talked to me and tried to make me feel guilty for leaving. Then he agreed that I could go, and said that I could take the kids. But before I left, he grabbed me by the throat and said I had not seen the last of him. Then he punched me in the face, over and over again.

When I got out of the house, I took Andy, Sarah, and Martin straight to the train station, where we boarded a freight train. I left almost everything of value behind—my beloved dog, my canoe, my gun, and a beautifully carved dresser and mirror that my grandmother had left me. The four of us got off the train in Longlac, and from there we walked the thirty-five kilometres to Geraldton. A teacher from Ombabika was walking the same route and helped me carry my bags. Martin was almost two years old, but he did not yet walk, so I carried him in a sling across my chest. Andy held Sarah by the hand as they walked beside us. Along the way it started to rain, so we got off the road for a break, and I made tea. I remember the teacher was surprised that I could make a fire in the rain. The children were hungry, but all I had to give them was tea with sugar.

When we finally arrived in Geraldton, I went straight to the post office. The people there were very kind. They fed the children and made me lie down to rest. They also brought me all of my paycheques and cashed them for me, leaving me with more than $1,000. The Geraldton post office was right next to the Greyhound bus station, so the children and I were able to get right on a bus to Thunder Bay. Once we arrived there, I made my way to my friend Jane's house to drop off the kids. Then I went straight to the emergency room at McKellar Hospital. My face was very swollen on one side, so I couldn't open one eye. My nose and my jaw were broken in different places. I had lost several teeth, and my mouth was badly infected. The doctors at the hospital put me into surgery right away and began the long process of repairing my injuries.

CHAPTER SIX

LIVING AND PARENTING IN THUNDER BAY AND SAULT STE. MARIE BEFORE SOBRIETY (1970–1975)

In December 1970, when I was twenty years old, I began living in Thunder Bay with my twelve-year-old brother, my three-year-old daughter, and my two-year-old son. At that time, my friend Jane was twenty-two years old and worked day and night shifts as a nurse in the tuberculosis sanatorium. She lived in a basement apartment with her daughter and her mother Karen. Not long after I arrived, Jane's brother Nick also moved into the apartment with his daughter. Nick's and Jane's children were one or two years younger than mine. Jane gave me and my kids one bedroom to share. She also helped me obtain medical and legal services. I started receiving social assistance, so I was able to contribute to the household financially.

Over my first year in Thunder Bay, I had a series of surgeries to fix my broken bones. My female surgeon explained that some of the breaks in my nose and jaw were old ones, which had healed in place, but others were new and had resulted from Gus's most recent beating. My health care providers also arranged for me to replace the teeth I had lost. Twenty years later, when I began to have problems with my nasal passages, doctors x-rayed my face and were surprised to see how many times my nose and jaw had been broken, and how well they had been repaired. They said I was very lucky that the original surgeons had done such a good job.

Not long after I arrived in Thunder Bay, I went to court to get a divorce from Gus. The judge told me, though, that my marriage had never been legal, since it was arranged for me when I was only sixteen years old. Instead of granting me a divorce, he annulled the marriage. The judge also reviewed my medical files from Geraldton and Thunder Bay. Based on those documents, the court issued a restraining order forbidding Gus to come within fifty yards of me. Gus was also forbidden to see Sarah or Martin until they reached the age of sixteen, at which time they could choose whether they wanted to meet him. So in the end I never needed to use the tape recording of Gus beating me to get a divorce or legal protection from him. I kept that recording for many years as a kind of insurance. I never told Jane or my other friends about it. Once in a while I listened to it when I was alone, but finally I threw it out, because hearing it just made me want to get drunk.

I settled into life in Jane's household in Thunder Bay, sometimes babysitting her son and niece when I was taking care of my own children, and at other times leaving my kids with Jane, her mother, or Andy when I went out to explore the area on foot. In the early 1970s, Thunder Bay had a population of about 100,000 people, so it was far larger than Ombabika and Auden. I found life in the city strange and surprisingly easy, because I had so few chores to do. There was no wood to chop or water to haul, tasks which I had done every day since childhood. We only had to turn on a lamp, a faucet, and the gas stove to have light, water, and a cooking fire. I knew those services somehow had to be paid for with money, but I did not yet understand how. At first I enjoyed not having to work as much as I was used to, but over time I started to feel bored. I missed the household chores, trapping, and hunting I had known all of my life. I felt lonely too, although I spent a lot of time with the children, and also with Jane, Nick, and their mother when they were home. I liked walking the streets and seeing new places and different kinds of people, but I did not enjoy the fast pace of city life. People always seemed to be pushing past each other in a rush while they hurried somewhere else.

RAISING MY KIDS

When we arrived in Thunder Bay, my brother Andy had long, wavy hair that he wore in a ponytail, because he had not cut it since he returned from residential school seven or eight years earlier. Once we were in the city, he cut his hair in order to attend the local school. At that point, Jane, Bonnie, and most of my other friends had gone to residential schools or the high school in Thunder Bay, so they often spoke English together. Jane's mother and I did not understand them when they did, but we had fun when we talked to each other. For one hour each day, Karen and I watched *Sesame Street* with the four small children, because it helped us to learn English and the alphabet too. Jane's brother, Nick, also helped to teach me the alphabet. I bought some hard-backed journals to practise writing A to Z, and Nick checked that I got all of the letters in the right order. After I had learned that well, I practised writing full English words and sentences.

Often I took the four little kids to parks, where we played hide-and-seek, or cowboys and Anishinaabeg. The Anishinaabeg always won. If the park had a little patch of woods, I explained to the children how the trees in the city were similar or different from the bush where I grew up. I told them that wild forests were not planted by humans, and they were not as neat and tidy. The kids and I climbed trees, slid down slides, and swung on swings. Martin liked to play with cars in sandboxes, so I built sand mountains with him for the cars to drive up and down. The other mothers at the parks usually sat on benches watching their kids play, but it never made sense to me to just sit and watch them. My children loved it when I played with them, and I enjoyed it too. When I got down on the ground with them, they told me things that they didn't tell me at other times, so I also got to know what they were thinking about.

From an early age, it was clear to me that Martin developed more slowly than other children. When he was two, he still behaved like an infant. He did not crawl or walk. By the time he was three, he started to move around, but he didn't seem to understand what we said to him, whether we spoke to him in Ojibwe, Cree, or English. When Martin was four, he still did not understand me well, but he had become strong and mobile. He was very good at moving large appliances, opening doors, and getting over fences, so I had to keep tabs on him at all times. I made a little vest and a leash for him that I tied to my wrist or pants when I took him to the store. When he, Sarah, and the other kids were playing in the front yard on their own, I attached the leash to the clothesline, so he could run back and forth without leaving the yard.

One day, while Martin and Sarah were playing in the yard, Sarah ran inside and said, "Daddy is outside!" I rushed out of the house and found Gus talking to Martin. I told Gus that it was against the law for him to come within fifty yards of us. Gus said he just wanted to talk. Jane was home at the time, so I asked her what she thought I should do. She said to let him come into the house, so I did. As he came in the house, Gus handed Sarah a twenty-dollar bill and pushed her away, saying, "Get out of here. You're not my kid." Then he told me he wanted to give Martin to one of his sisters, Stacey, for adoption. Stacey lived about 200 kilometres northeast of Thunder Bay, in a town called Jellicoe, not far from Geraldton. I had met her and Gus's other sisters only once, at our wedding. Stacey had never had children of her own. Gus only wanted to take Martin, because he still believed that Sarah was not his daughter. I refused to let him take our son, and he left.

The next day, Martin had been playing outside on his own when he went missing. We didn't realize what had happened at first. We looked all over for him. Then my landlady told me she had seen a man take a child from the yard. Gus must have unhooked Martin's vest from the clothesline and taken him away in a car. We called the Thunder Bay police and explained the situation. They contacted the police in Jellicoe, so the Jellicoe police went to Stacey's house, where they found Martin. I took a Greyhound bus to go pick him up. When I arrived, Stacey told me she had already paid Gus to let her adopt Martin. She showed me the adoption papers that Gus had signed, releasing his parental rights. I refused to co-sign them, but Stacey wouldn't let me take Martin. I had to go to the police station, and some officers came back to Stacey's house with me to make sure she let Martin leave. Gus was charged with abducting a child. Stacey wasn't charged. Gus went to court, but he didn't go to jail. I don't know what punishment he received, if any.

Back in Thunder Bay, Martin continued to have developmental difficulties and also began to have some behavioural problems. Sometimes he got up during the night and went to the kitchen, where he ate a lot of food. He wasn't eating due to hunger, because he always had full meals during the day. He also was not careful about what he ate—he just ate as much as he could of whatever he found. Jane and I were worried that one night he would eat something poisonous. We put locks on the refrigerator, the cupboards, and the door. I also pushed the washing machine in front of our bedroom door to block it at night, but Martin seemed to have an almost magical ability to get past any barriers we created. I started keeping him in a large crib at night, tying one of his arms to the side so he could not get out. I also took him to a pediatrician to ask for advice. The pediatrician suggested that we admit Martin to McKellar Hospital for observation for a while, and I agreed. At that time, Martin was only four years old, but they ended up keeping him at the hospital for an entire month. He slept in a tall, smooth, steel hospital crib, but somehow he still managed to climb out of it and find food in the hospital refrigerators. The hospital staff did not understand his behaviour or know how to stop it.

Martin's doctor then told me he wanted to transfer Martin to Lakehead Psychiatric Hospital. He asked me to come to his office to sign some papers allowing this. I asked Jane to explain to me what a psychiatric hospital was. She said it was where doctors put people who they thought were crazy, although she did not believe that everyone who went there was truly crazy. Still, she said, once someone entered the psychiatric hospital, they almost always stayed there long-term. I knew Martin was developing slowly, but I did not think that he was mentally ill. He was my son and I wanted to raise him. I did not want him to grow up in an institution. I also did not trust that his doctor would give him back to me at that point.

I made a plan to get Martin back. I went to the doctor's office as agreed, taking Sarah with me. She was five years old at the time. The doctor wanted to meet her, to make sure that she did not have the same condition as Martin. Once he had spoken with her, he let her wait outside. I took Sarah to the hospital entrance and instructed her to stand near the taxi phone, keeping her foot in the exit door so it couldn't be locked shut. I told her to act like she was just playing, but to make sure she kept the door open the whole time. She understood. I returned to the doctor's office. He let me sit with Martin on my lap while he left to get his paperwork. As soon as he was gone, I picked up Martin, ran to the taxi phone, called a taxi, and then waited outside with both of the children. The taxi came very quickly. As we got into it, I heard the hospital alarms go off, but we were already on the road by then. I took the children to a friend's house, and we stayed there for several days. Later, my landlord said that a social worker had come by my apartment and left a letter for me, but police had not visited as I had feared. I moved back to my apartment and continued to care for Martin patiently, as I had before. By the time he was six or seven years old, he stopped his strange eating habits. In terms of his behaviour, he continued to develop a few years behind other kids, but otherwise he was a gentle and contented boy.

DRINKING WITH BONNIE AND ANGELA

I still had a strong desire for alcohol after I moved to Thunder Bay. Whenever I could, I drank to chase away bad memories and to feel good for a little while. Sometimes I drank secretly at home with Jane's mom, Karen, who years earlier had been one of my own mother's favourite drinking partners. Like me, Karen continued drinking after she got to Thunder Bay, although she hid it from Jane and Nick because they disapproved. When I was out exploring the city on my own, I also discovered bars. At first, bars seemed like happy, comfortable places where I could go to lift my spirits when I was sad or lonely. I did not have much money to spend on alcohol, so I didn't drink a lot. But soon I began going to bars with my cousin, Angela, and Jane's cousin, Bonnie. Both of them were heavy drinkers, and they often bought me drinks.

Like Jane, Bonnie had finished high school and worked in a local hospital, but she only had a part-time job. Angela had never gone to high school, and she was living from day to day on social assistance. When we lived in Ombabika, Angela wore dresses and skirts like the other girls, but by the time we met again in Thunder Bay, she wore jeans, T-shirts, and button-down shirts like me. She no longer put on makeup or styled her hair in fancy ways. Instead, she left her straight black hair shoulder-length. Angela was an inch shorter than me, while Bonnie—like Jane—was a bit taller. Bonnie and Jane looked even taller when they wore heels and beehive hairstyles.

After Bonnie, Angela, and I had been hanging out together for a while, Angela told me there was another way that she sometimes earned money. She said she'd show me if I was interested. That sounded good to me, because I would have been glad to have extra cash. I assumed she was talking about some kind of a cleaning job. Instead, she took me to a street corner one day and said, "This is how it works. A guy will come by in a vehicle. When he stops, you have to say, 'How much?' He'll offer you twenty to forty dollars. Make sure you get the money before you get in the car. Then you get in and do whatever he wants you to do." She told me about different possible sexual acts. The idea of doing those things sickened me. I thanked her for trying to help me, but told her that I didn't want to earn money that way.

By the time I was twenty-two years old (Figure 6), Bonnie, Angela, and I regularly visited different run-down hotels—the Adinak, the West Hotel, the

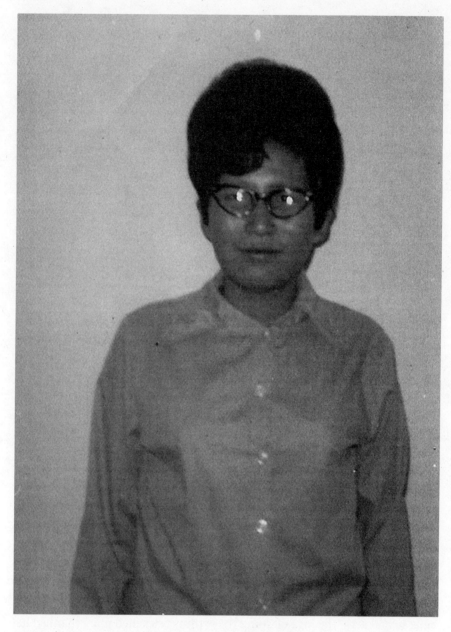

FIGURE 6. AFTER I HAD COMPLETED MY SURGERIES AND MY INJURIES HAD HEALED (TWENTY-TWO YEARS OLD, 1972). JANE WANTED TO CELEBRATE BY STYLING MY HAIR, DRESSING ME IN ONE OF HER BLOUSES, AND TAKING A PHOTOGRAPH.

St. Louis, and the Empire—where people played shuffleboard and darts in the bar as they drank. Usually, once I arrived at a bar, I had one or two beers and became relaxed and comfortable talking to other people. I was quite good at playing shuffleboard, and people bought me more alcohol when I won. After a couple of more drinks, though, I became drunk and no longer played well, so I lost. Still, the next time I returned to that bar, the regulars would buy me a beer or two to get me to join their shuffleboard teams, and the whole process repeated itself. Regular drinkers at the hotel bars often rented rooms upstairs, so many of us drifted back and forth between the hotel rooms and the bar as we drank together. Before long, I was drinking frequently and heavily. I started to sneak away from home, leaving my kids with Jane's family when I shouldn't have. There were times when I was gone for days.

When I was out with Angela and Bonnie, I realized pretty quickly that they had become lovers, although I did not understand it fully. One day when I was having a beer with Bonnie at the Empire Hotel bar, she said, "Do you know about me and Angela? She likes me a lot. Oh, it's more than liking. I know you don't like me like that, because I've tried to give you a hint and you've ignored it." I replied, "What do you mean? I do anything you ask me to do. I run all kinds of errands for you. I'm like your best friend!" The conversation stopped there, because my cousin Angela arrived and wanted to take Bonnie to a hotel room alone. Bonnie insisted that I join them, so I tagged along. We all went upstairs and had another beer. Soon they started touching and kissing each other, but I didn't really know what to make of it. Bonnie went to the washroom and that's when Angela told me to take off, because she wanted to be with Bonnie privately. I didn't want to go yet, so I just stayed where I was. When Bonnie returned, they started making out intensely. I finally understood why they wanted me to leave, so I did. In that moment, I was not struck by the fact that two women were being sexual together, but rather that they were two people who needed privacy. I went back to the bar and drank some more beer. A little while later they came downstairs, happy and talking. Bonnie came over to me and wanted to kiss me on the lips, but I said, "Oh no, no thank you. I don't want anybody to kiss me."

Bonnie continued to flirt with me every once in a while, saying things like, "I still haven't got you yet. One of these days I'll get you, and we're going to have it!" I remember answering her with a joke, saying, "Have what, pork chops?" She laughed and replied, "No, much better than pork chops. You'll be so happy!" Sometimes she tried to kiss me on the lips again, but I turned away. I had had a crush on Bonnie since Ombabika, and I wasn't trying to be virtuous, I just didn't want to get beaten up by Angela or one of Bonnie's other admirers. Bonnie was a beautiful, affectionate girl, and she liked to flirt with both men and women, so a lot of people wanted to be with her. But I know she had a special relationship with Angela. Bonnie told me that she loved the way she felt when she was with Angela. She said men didn't satisfy her in the same way. Bonnie and Angela were casual and open with me about their relationship, but they warned me to not tell anyone else about it, especially their mothers, Jane, or Nick. I kept their secret.

One day, Bonnie, Angela, and I were in a hotel room on Mark Street, drinking with a guy from up north. He and Bonnie began flirting with each other. I felt uncomfortable, because Angela was right there. I decided to go down to the bar to play shuffleboard. Angela followed me downstairs and asked me to go outside to talk. She told me she was in love with Bonnie, and that Bonnie loved her back. Angela felt very jealous when she saw Bonnie talking with that man. She said she was torn up about whether she should leave Bonnie, or stay and fight for her. I said I didn't know either. Then Angela took off. I thought about the conversation after she left, and it really hit me emotionally. I had never heard her talk about how much she loved Bonnie before. I had seen her flirt with other women, putting her arm around them and teasing them by saying that they were her girlfriends and she was their boyfriend. But she clearly loved Bonnie. I felt lonely and jealous, because I also had liked Bonnie for a long time. I felt like I had missed my opportunity to be with her when I turned her down, those times when she tried to kiss me. I fantasized about kissing her, and felt those familiar butterflies in my stomach again. I asked myself: "How did they know? How did they end up together? I feel the way they feel, so why am I alone?" That night, I got very drunk.

The next day, I woke up to Jane banging on my bedroom door. There had been a fire in the hotel on Mark Street. Someone had left a lit cigarette on a mattress, and Bonnie had been badly burned. She died soon afterward. Jane had to go to the morgue to identify her body.

After Bonnie died, my cousin Angela drank more than ever before. She went on a massive drinking binge. At one point, she tried to commit suicide by drinking a bottle of chlorine, but she survived. I don't know if she ever really recovered from losing Bonnie.

MY SON JONATHAN'S BIRTH

Bonnie's death was one of many traumas I experienced during my early years in Thunder Bay. While I was still drinking, I was beaten and abused more times than I can remember. One of the most violent assaults happened in May 1973, when I was on my way to a bar. I was walking by the river near Cumberland Street. I had not yet started drinking that day, so I was sober. On the path I ran into two brothers I knew from Ombabika. In Thunder Bay, the three of us sometimes drank together within a larger group at hotel bars, so I considered them to be friends. The brothers were short men, about my height, with shoulder-length hair. That day I remember that one of them was wearing suspenders and a bolo tie, and the other one wore a button-down shirt with snaps instead of buttons. Both of them smelled like they already had been drinking for some time and needed a bath.

I stopped and chatted with the brothers in Ojibwe. We talked about maybe going to find some beer together. Then suddenly the conversation turned. They started laughing and asked me if I wanted to have sex with them. I immediately refused, saying no, that I definitely did not want to have sex with them. They attacked me, taking me by surprise and overpowering me. They raped me there on the rocks by the river, one after the other. When I finally got away from them, I went straight home. My clothes were ripped, and I had cuts and bruises on my arms, legs, and hips. As I came through the door, my brother Andy saw the state I was in and brought me a towel. I took a long hot bath to clean myself. I told my brother never to tell anybody what he had seen. For many years I did not tell anyone else that I had been raped that day.

A few weeks later, I missed my period. Not much longer after that I met a man named Frank, and we quickly became involved. Frank was a nice and funny man, and I liked spending time with him. He was Anishinaabe, but he only spoke English. He had very dark skin and short, straight, black hair that he combed back with some kind of hair oil. When my pregnancy began to show, Frank believed it was his. He was pleased and proud because none of his other girlfriends had ever become pregnant before. It is possible that the baby was his, and I didn't deny it. I felt ashamed and guilty that I didn't know for sure. Given the timing, though, I guessed that one of the two rapists had made me pregnant.

Frank wanted to leave Thunder Bay, because he had heard he could make good money working in construction near Sault Ste. Marie, 425 kilometres southeast across Lake Superior (Figure 2). After having been raped, I was ready to leave Thunder Bay too. I packed up my kids and my brother and left with Frank. First we all lived in a small run-down apartment in Sault Ste. Marie, and Frank and I got jobs outside of the city. I cleaned houses, while he worked in road construction. I became friends with a woman from the Longlac area. My brother Andy, who was fifteen or sixteen at the time, became close to her teenage daughter.

My son Jonathan was born in Sault Ste. Marie in February 1974. He was a bald, healthy, good-sized baby. I had complications during labour, so he was delivered by Cesarean section. I also had difficulty producing milk. Jonathan never latched on to my breast, so I was not able to nurse him. I remember feeling that this was somehow my fault, that Jonathan must not like me and that he was rejecting me, because he had been conceived during a rape. I loved him, and I felt like I had failed him. I fed Jonathan with bottles of cow's milk instead, and he grew well.

After Jonathan was born, Frank and I moved fifty kilometres north of Sault Ste. Marie to Batchawana Bay, to be closer to his construction site and a hotel where I could work cleaning cabins. My friend from Longlac invited Andy to stay in Sault Ste. Marie with her family. Andy wanted to do that, so he did not move with us.

WORKING IN BATCHAWANA BAY

In Batchawana Bay, I took Jonathan to work with me when I cleaned cabins, and I left Sarah and Martin with another maid who was off duty. Frank and I were earning well in our jobs, so we sometimes took the three kids out for fancy dinners. We also drank heavily. Frank and his co-workers always had a lot of beer and wine around. After a long day of construction, people came to our place to drink and to do other drugs. I did not know all of the different substances people were using—some were smoked, some heated in a spoon, some snorted, and some injected. I mostly drank alcohol, but I tried a few of the other drugs. I never tried injecting anything, because needles frightened me.

A couple of times when I was in a bar near Sault Ste. Marie, people approached me about quitting alcohol and other drugs. They would drink soda and encourage me to go to Alcoholics Anonymous (AA) meetings to get sober. They didn't explain, though, how AA meetings or the broader program worked. There were days when I thought I could handle my alcohol use, so if I wanted, I could stop on my own. And then there were days when I thought it was impossible to quit, so when people told me there were ways to stop drinking, I thought they didn't understand me or my situation.

Once in a while I visited Frank at his work site, where he drove a bulldozer. One day, a worker there came up to me and said, "Hey, you're young and I bet you run fast. I'll pay you a lot of money if you take this bag, run up that hill, cross over those rapids, and leave the bag right there. Then run back as fast as you can." I agreed, so he lit the string hanging out of the bag, and I did just as he instructed. Of course, he had me setting off dynamite, but I didn't really understand how explosives worked at the time. I thought the dynamite was like a big matchstick. I continued doing that job for a few weeks. Sometimes the workers lit the bag before giving it to me, and at other times I lit it once I got to the drop site. In the end, though, I realized they were using me to do a very dangerous task. I worried that, if I died, there would be no one left to raise my children, so I stopped.

I didn't feel content in my new life in Batchawana Bay. It seemed like all I did was clean rooms and drink alcohol with Frank after work. A woman at the restaurant told me that the Greyhound bus stopped at Pancake Bay, further up the highway. I told Frank I wanted to leave, but he had a well-paying job, so he wanted to stay. The next day, I took my kids and the money I had saved up, and we walked up the big, long hill near the construction site until we reached the highway. I carried Jonathan, and sometimes I carried Martin when he cried. I had a backpack full of food and water so I could stop to feed the kids when they were hungry and thirsty. We walked for a long time, maybe ten kilometres, before an old man and a woman in a truck gave us a ride. They dropped us off in Pancake Bay, where we caught a bus back to Thunder Bay.

JONATHAN'S DEATH

When we returned to Thunder Bay, I was twenty-three, Sarah was six, and Martin was five years old. Jonathan was only a few months old. I continued to drink too much alcohol, but I had hopes of getting a job and building a better life for me and my kids. I enrolled Sarah in kindergarten. I had enough money to rent an apartment in Jane's building, but no apartments were available. While we were waiting for one to open up, my three kids and I lived in one of Jane's basement rooms again. I slept with Jonathan on the bed, Sarah slept on some blankets on the floor, and Martin slept in a large crib. Jane said Jonathan looked a lot like me. He was a peaceful baby. When I fed him, I spoke to him in Ojibwe. He followed me with his eyes, as if he was really listening and understanding me.

Jonathan died when he was six months old. It happened on a day like any other day. I was at home, and I had not been drinking. I was looking after the kids and cleaning the house. Martin and Sarah were in the living room watching TV. I fed Jonathan, played with him for a little while, and laid him down for a nap. Afterward, I started vacuuming the floor outside the bedroom. As I was doing this, I thought I heard a voice say, "Ma-Nee?" I paused and then the voice said *"Miiweh"*—"That's it." I went to Karen's room to ask if she had said something, or heard anything, but she said she hadn't. Then I went to check on Jonathan. As I sat down on the bed, I expected him to wake up, because he was a light sleeper. But he didn't move. I grabbed him and picked him up, but he still didn't move. He wasn't breathing. I tried to breathe air into him, but it didn't work. I started to scream. People ran into the room. I told them something was wrong with Jonathan. I was crying and wailing, and Sarah and Martin started to cry too. Jane's mom pulled Jonathan away from me. We took him to the hospital, but when we got there, the staff told us he was gone. They said he had died of crib death, which today they call Sudden Infant Death Syndrome.

I lost my mind in grief after Jonathan died. I don't remember his funeral. In fact, I can't recall much about the next year. I just have bits and pieces of memories from that time. After Jonathan died, doctors gave me tranquilizers and told Jane to keep giving them to me regularly, and then to refill the bottle when the pills ran out. They told her it would keep me from going over the edge. I stayed on tranquilizers for several months, and during that period I felt like I was in a never-ending fog. I didn't recognize people and I often got lost. I also drank heavily, which made the situation worse. Every time I thought about Jonathan dying, I wanted to get drunk. I continued to drink in bars and sometimes I drank secretly with Karen at home. Jane, as always, was a huge help to me. She took much of the responsibility for looking after Sarah and Martin.

At some point in those months after Jonathan's death, Sarah, Martin, and I moved out of Jane's apartment and into a set of rooms in a basement in a different house. My brother Andy came from Sault Ste. Marie to live with us. He re-enrolled in school in Thunder Bay and helped me with Sarah and Martin. But Andy was not content, and he missed his girlfriend, so soon he returned to Sault Ste. Marie. In the new apartment, I continued drinking with my landlady, who lived upstairs. After her husband went to work each morning, a truck arrived and delivered beer for us, and then we drank right through the day.

That didn't last long. One morning in December 1974, about three months after Jonathan died, I woke up to find that my apartment had been cleared out, the drawers were empty, and Martin and Sarah were gone. The landlord told me that the Children's Aid Society, the governmental child protection agency, had taken away my kids. He wanted me to get out of the apartment too.

I went straight to the Children's Aid office. I grabbed the woman at the front desk by her collar and yelled, "Where are my kids?" I was very angry and worked up. A social worker came out to talk to me. She said that Martin and Sarah had been taken into foster care. I could see them in a supervised visit for ten minutes the next day, but otherwise they would stay in foster care unless I got sober. She strongly encouraged me to join AA, saying that it would help me stop drinking.

I went back to my apartment, but the landlord had thrown all of my stuff out on the curb and locked me out. I became homeless. I did go back to the Children's Aid office to see my kids for that first supervised visit, but then I went on a drinking binge and I did not see them again for several months.

LIVING ON THE STREETS

After I lost my apartment, there were days when I sobered up and stayed with Jane or another friend, but mostly I lived on the streets. During the first months, I went by different hotels each evening until I found other drinkers I knew, so I could hang out with them through the night. I often was drunk, and sometimes I tried other drugs, depending on what was available or what was offered to me. At times I got high on marijuana or snorted pills, which people had crushed into a powder. Once in a while I visited Jane and stole rubbing alcohol or hairspray from her house. My friends and I drank the rubbing alcohol and soaked rags in the hairspray, so we could sniff the fumes in a bag. That stopped when Jane figured out what I was doing, and she hid those things when I visited.

I also snorted cocaine a few times. The first time I tried it, I was at the bar in the St. Louis Hotel drinking and watching TV with some people. A guy came downstairs and said, "Hey, Ma-Nee, we've got some good stuff upstairs. My cousin's going to show you how to use it." I said okay, and went upstairs to check it out, but the guy wanted me to give him a blow-job in exchange for the drug, so I refused. Then he said I could have it if I gave him five dollars, or something worth five dollars. So I gave him the ring I was wearing. It may have been the ring my grandmother gave me before she died, but I'm not certain. He let me into a room where other people were snorting cocaine. I acted cocky, like I knew what I was doing, and I sniffed some of the cocaine. Not much later, I felt like I had grown wings, and I could fly. I went up to the third floor of the hotel and looked out the window. On the street below, I saw someone I knew, one of the guys who had been friends with me, Hank, and Shiigohbii in Ombabika. I waved to him, but he didn't wave back. I decided to fly. I climbed out of the window, leapt off the building, and fell three stories to the ground below. I don't know why I didn't die. I don't know why I didn't even break any bones. An ambulance rushed me to the hospital emergency room. The medical staff pumped my stomach and checked me for injuries, but then they said that I was fine. They asked me why I had tried to commit suicide. I explained that I had been trying to fly, not to kill myself. I used cocaine again a few times after that. I had one other bad episode while on it, and then I never took it again.

I experienced a lot of violence when I was homeless. Once, when I was in a hotel room drinking with Angela, I told her that I was tired of drinking and tired of what it did to me, so I was going to go to Jane's house to get sober. As I started to leave, she grabbed me and said, "Where do you think you're going? Nobody is going anywhere!" She slammed the door shut so I couldn't leave. I managed to slip away a while later, but when I was getting close to Jane's house, Angela caught up with me. She started to beat me up right there on the sidewalk, hitting me and kicking me. Jane ran out of her house, saying, "Hey, hey, hey! That's enough!" She convinced Angela to stop hitting me and leave.

Another time when I was homeless, some men caught me in the Current River Greenway and raped me. I was drunk and I had difficulty fighting them off. I kicked and I screamed, but I was not able to stop them. I never reported any attacks I experienced to the police. There were times when the police themselves assaulted me. One day, for example, I was walking on a sidewalk when two white policemen pulled up alongside me in their cruiser. They said they were going to take me to jail to sober up. I asked them to let me go, but they told me to get in the backseat, so I did. They drove me to Simpson Street and parked in an isolated spot. They insulted me, calling me mean names in English. Then they used a police baton to break the buttons off my shirt, and started pulling it off of me. Luckily, a homeless guy knocked on the window at that moment and asked the cops if they would light his cigarette. Maybe he had seen that I was in the car and he was trying to help me, or maybe it was just a coincidence. In any case, the policemen gave him a light and then asked him if he could help me get home. He agreed, so they let me go.

After my first couple of months of living on the streets, I met an old man named Harry who lived in a dingy boxcar down by the train tracks. He was a good-natured guy who didn't take advantage of people, sexually or otherwise. Harry looked like he might be part white and part Anishinaabe, but he only spoke English. He had such a thick, grey beard that I could hardly see his mouth move when he talked. It was winter, so he wore a hat and rough, layered clothing. Harry was a short, skinny man, no taller than me, but somehow he won people's respect enough that nobody messed with him. He allowed me and some other non-violent drinkers and drug users to stay with him in his boxcar, and we helped each other. Harry was careful about who he invited into the boxcar. If mean-spirited people showed up, he somehow had a way of making them leave. He did not put up with violence in his "house" or his "yard." So the boxcar was a safe place for those of us who stayed there. We kept it a secret, because we didn't want the police to find out about it and kick us out.

I lived in the boxcar for several months. We had candles and a little metal tub where I made fires to give us warmth, because it was freezing cold sometimes. On most days I went out to get food for me and Harry, usually by shoplifting bread and canned meat in a convenience store. I stole things simply by picking them up and running right out the door when the clerk wasn't paying attention, or couldn't catch me. At the same time, Harry somehow got us a couple bottles of wine. I did not get to know the other people staying in the boxcar very well, because we didn't speak often. Now and then we talked about going to visit our kids or grandkids. One woman was kind of bossy, but I ignored her. Some people there had cuts and wounds that needed medical treatment. We all liked to know who was there when we went to sleep, and we were grateful to see the same people when we woke up. Every once in a while, the train authorities moved the boxcar we were using, but Harry always managed to find that out in advance, so we moved our stuff to a different boxcar beforehand.

While I was on the streets, I was caught in a terrible cycle emotionally, mentally, and physically. Every time I sobered up, I desperately wanted to see my kids and get them back. But I felt helpless and out of control. I didn't know how to manage my addiction. I was also haunted by memories of the traumas I had experienced in Ombabika and Thunder Bay. I drank to forget, and the cycle continued.

BECOMING SOBER

In June 1975, when I had been on the streets for about half a year, I made some attempts to get sober with the help of my friend, Jane. I joined her and her kids when they took a trip away from Thunder Bay. While we were away, I stopped drinking alcohol and started to experience tremors, night sweats, and other withdrawal symptoms. But when we came back to the city, I returned to the streets and started drinking again. Then one morning in July 1975, Jane called a hotel where I sometimes hung out, and she left an urgent message for me to call her. When I got the message, I was scared that something bad had happened to my kids. On the phone, Jane just told me to get in a cab and come to her house, because she needed to talk to me in person. Once I got there, she opened the door and greeted me as usual. When I came inside, she shut the door and slapped me on the face. "I am so angry at you!," she yelled. "You don't even know what's happening to your kids! Did you know they ran away from their foster home to look for you? One day those children will be taken away from you forever, and you'll never see them again!" What she said really frightened me. I told Jane how much I wanted to get my kids back, but that I didn't know how to stop drinking. I wanted to try. I asked her to help me.

Jane said we should go to an Alcoholics Anonymous meeting to find out how the program helped people become sober. I agreed and suggested we go that night. And we did. People at the meeting must have seen what bad shape I was in. They didn't just give me information, they told us that someone would come to Jane's house right afterward to talk more with me. Jane and I went back home and waited. In the end, two women and a man arrived, including an Anishinaabe woman who became one of my AA sponsors. They talked to me about my wanting to become sober. Jane mostly listened. Given that I had been drinking heavily and doing other drugs on the streets, they didn't know what I would experience during withdrawal. They said there were no options for hospitalization, but that I should have a nurse or doctor to assist me through the worst of it. Then they asked Jane if she could help, since she was a nurse. She agreed. Two of the AA members said that they would move into the house to support her. I listened to them, but I did not yet take what they were saying very seriously. I kind of laughed to myself, thinking, "What, am I suddenly going to turn into a monster and need three people to take care of me?" I still didn't know how hard it was going to be.

Jane took a week off of work and stayed home to watch over me. The next day, she asked how I was feeling, and I said I really needed to go out and get a drink. She said, "Well, you can't. You can have tea or a cigarette, but we're going to stay with you when you go outside to smoke, to make sure you don't run off." And sure enough, both of the AA members came with me when I had a cigarette outside. I remember my hands were shaking as I lit the cigarette, and I kept thinking I needed to get a drink to calm my nerves.

On the third day it got worse and I started experiencing full body sweats. Then for several days after that my withdrawal symptoms became more intense. I was feverish, agitated, disoriented, and confused. I had terrifying nightmares and hallucinations. Sometime during that period, Jane and the others locked me in a room, with one of them staying with me at all times. Jane came in regularly to check my temperature and blood pressure. At one point I thought people or monsters were crawling out of the walls. I became horrified that something alien was moving inside of my feet. I felt like committing suicide. I tried to figure out how I could kill myself in the bathtub when they weren't watching me, but it didn't work, because they never let me out of their sight. Even when I locked the bathroom door, Jane managed to get through it in seconds. I don't know how she did that, but she did.

The worst of my detoxification symptoms lasted one week, maybe two. Slowly, my body started to return to normal. With the help of my best friend and some kind strangers, I had made it through withdrawal from the alcohol I had depended on for many years. My mind still felt like it was in a fog, and I still had a lot of work to do long-term. But those first difficult steps were behind me, and I was sober.

CHAPTER SEVEN

SOBRIETY AND SINGLE-PARENTING IN THUNDER BAY (1975–1980)

Overcoming my body's dependence on alcohol was only the first stage of my recovery from addiction. As soon as I was well enough to leave the house, I started attending daily AA meetings to strengthen my ability to be sober, both emotionally and socially. Children's Aid allowed me to visit my kids, first for thirty minutes at a time, and then for longer periods. I started building a new life with the assistance of a kind Children's Aid social worker who went well beyond what was expected of her job. Sometime earlier, Jane's brother Nick and their mother Karen had moved out of the house they shared with Jane and into a new one in a different neighbourhood. My social worker helped me to get an apartment next door to Nick and Karen. She also gave me sheets, blankets, and curtains from her own home to furnish my new place. Soon after I moved into that apartment, though, I was offered a much nicer one in another part of town, so I moved there with my kids.

MY FIRST MONTHS OF SOBRIETY

Participating in AA was key to my sobriety in those early days. AA provides different kinds of assistance, including: supportive meetings run by and for alcoholics; individual sponsorship; a "Big Book" that explains AA principles; and a twelve-step program. At speaker meetings, one or two members tell their stories, while at discussion meetings the broader group contributes. A sponsor is an experienced member who helps an inexperienced one understand and follow the program. From the start, I always tried to have two sponsors, so if one was unavailable, I still could get help from the other one. The AA principles encourage alcoholics to do several things: to admit that they cannot control their addiction; to recognize a higher power that can give them strength; to examine past errors with the help of a sponsor; to make amends for those errors; to learn to live a new life with new behaviour; and to help others who suffer from the same addiction.

FIGURE 7. SITTING IN A PARK DURING MY FIRST YEAR OF SOBRIETY IN THUNDER BAY (TWENTY-FIVE YEARS OLD, 1975). THIS PHOTOGRAPH WAS PROBABLY TAKEN BY ANGELA.

Three months after I got sober, I had a rough day and night when I experienced some withdrawal symptoms again, but they weren't as severe as they had been when I first stopped drinking. Soon afterward, I began to feel more energized and alert, as if I was coming out of a fog. I felt very grateful to be alive and sober (Figure 7). Until then, I had been attending different AA meetings on a day-to-day basis, without a long-term commitment to the program. On 17 September 1975, though, when I was at a meeting with the central AA group, I decided to sign up to be a group member. Making that commitment was a turning point for me. It was an important moment when I felt newly positive and hopeful about my future, so I always celebrate that date as the anniversary of my sobriety, even though I had already given up drinking a few months before.

During my first year of sobriety, I learned that Boxcar Harry, the man who had been my friend when I was homeless, had died on the streets. I never learned the details of how he passed away; I just felt sad at the loss of a good man. After I joined the central AA group, I also had a very bad experience with an AA member. He offered to drive me home one night. Once I was in his car, he locked the doors and drove me far outside of the city to an isolated place in the bush. Then he attacked me, and forced me to perform sex acts on him. He ripped off my clothes and was trying to rape me when I managed to get the door open and escape. I rolled down a hill and ran deep into the woods to hide. He called out to me in the darkness, saying he would just drive me home if I came back. I stayed hidden, and finally he drove away.

I started walking back to Thunder Bay along the highway. I was half-naked, bruised, and bleeding. After some time, a car pulled up behind me and I could hear a woman calling me. She and her husband took me to McKellar Hospital. The doctors there took care of me and called the police. A policewoman asked me who had tried to rape me, but I did not tell her the man's name. I was probably still in shock. Also, I was frightened and confused to have been assaulted by a long-time AA member. Being at a very early stage of my recovery, I was trying to trust and follow what I was told by more experienced program members. I was supposed to be grateful to AA for my sobriety, to recognize my powerlessness and how my life had become unmanageable, and to protect the anonymity of other AA members. Besides, I doubted that anyone would believe my word over that of a man who had been sober for so long. The policewoman gave me her name and number and told me I could call her if there was ever anything else I wanted to tell her, but I never did.

HOSPITALIZATION WITH TUBERCULOSIS

In early 1976, there were times when I coughed up blood, but I did not think much about it. I attended AA meetings almost every evening, usually bringing my children with me since I didn't have a babysitter. In the spring of that year, I was asked to chair a meeting. This meant that I would start the meeting, read from the Big Book, and then open the discussion up to the group. As I began to lead the meeting, I suddenly was covered in sweat and passed out—I just dropped to the floor. AA members called an ambulance and I was taken to McKellar Hospital. I only have a few memories of that night as I came in and out of consciousness: someone wrapping me in a blanket at the meeting; the flashing lights of the ambulance; and then a white man speaking to me in Ojibwe when I woke up at the hospital. When I heard him speak, I thought I was hallucinating, and passed out again. But when I came to, he was still speaking Ojibwe to me. It turned out that this doctor had worked in northern Ontario and learned my language there. He told me I was very, very ill, and he was not sure whether I would survive. He asked me, "In case we can't keep you alive, is there anyone you want us to contact, or any messages you want us to pass on?" I talked to him as the nurse took notes. I told the doctor to tell my brother that I loved him, and that I wanted him to take care of my children if I died. I thanked Jane for all she had done for me. And I told my children that I loved them dearly.

Soon after that, the machines around me started beeping and flashing wildly, and the doctor and nurses worked on me urgently. At one point I was lying on my side or my stomach, and I saw a priest's black shoes on the floor. I heard him say that he was going to give me last rites. I tried to say, "No, no, I don't want that water on me!" but I couldn't speak. One of them said, "I think she's gone." I felt a kind of acceptance then, like I had tried my best and it had not worked, so it was time for me to leave. I had a vision of a beautiful woman reaching out to me with her arms outstretched. There was a blue sky, a few clouds, and sun rays behind her. I ran towards her and tried to catch the woman's hands, but I couldn't. At that moment I woke up. The nurse was starting to cover my body and face with a sheet, as if I was dead. I wiggled my hand and she called, "Doctor!" The doctor came running back into the room, and they turned the machines back on. When I talked to him later, he told me that I had been dead for a short time.

I was diagnosed with tuberculosis and double pneumonia. The illnesses had gone far too long without treatment, which is why I became so sick. Once I had recovered enough, I was moved from critical care to a regular hospital floor. I stayed there for a week. Then they transferred me to the tuberculosis sanatorium by ambulance. Tuberculosis patients were required by law to stay there until they had fully recovered and could no longer infect anyone else. That is how, in the spring of 1976, I came to live in the same tuberculosis sanatorium where I had been born twenty-five years earlier. I ended up staying there for half a year.

I was very weak when I arrived at the sanatorium. I was still spitting blood, but I was starting to get better. At first the nurses gave me a shot once every day, which I hated. After a while they switched me to pills. During my first months there, I couldn't have visitors unless we all wore masks. Jane worked in the children's wing, so she dropped in to see me regularly. My friends in AA were also a big support. One kind white woman offered to take care of my children until I was released, so Children's Aid did not put them in foster care. She looked after them at her house and brought them to see me regularly. Some other friends also came to see me often. When I was allowed to meet visitors without masks, I asked for permission to hold AA meetings in the sanatorium, and the staff agreed. Most people who attended those meetings were AA members who came from outside of the sanatorium, but a few patients also joined us.

The sanatorium, which most people call "the San," was not a bad place to stay. The staff and patients were a friendly mix of Anishinaabe and white people. There were four patients in every room. We each had a bed with a curtain that could be pulled around it for privacy. Our biggest challenge was managing boredom as we waited to get well enough to leave. I made friends with three women and we got into mischief together. I had a crush on a certain French nurse, and sometimes I played pranks to get her attention. Once one of my friends and I took a wheelchair into a long hallway near the nurse's station. My friend sat down in it, and I pushed her and ran behind her until we had enough speed. Then I jumped on the back so we flew down the hallway together, with my hospital robe flowing behind us like a cape. The hallway was dimly lit, because the lights were turned off at 8:00 p.m. The French nurse and the others came out to see what was going on. They had a good laugh watching us, and then they sent us back to bed. Once in a while, I also played tricks on the nurse who gave me injections. A few times I piled all of my clothes under my covers in the shape of a body, and then hid under the bed or climbed up over the door until she found me.

There also were times when my three friends and I tried to escape from the San. In one attempt we asked another patient if we could tie her to a chair. She agreed, so we tied her up gently, but with a lot of knots. When the nurses came to untie her, we took off through the main meeting room and down the road to Victoria Street. A police cruiser caught up with us pretty quickly and brought us straight back. Another time, the four of us tried to get out through the basement, because we had heard about tunnels which led off the property. It was dark in the basement, and we quickly lost our way. Then we heard the night guard coming, so we hid behind the nearest door. As we crowded into the dark room together, one of my friends whispered, "I feel something cold!" She looked down and saw it was a man's foot. She started to scream, but I covered her mouth. We realized we had crammed ourselves into the morgue to hide. There were dead bodies all around us with tags on their toes. We managed to slip back into the hallway before the security guard found us.

I had my twenty-sixth birthday in the sanatorium. They threw a party for me and baked a big cake to celebrate the fact that I had been born there twenty-five years earlier. There was even an older nurse on staff who had been working when I was born. She said that my mother's labour happened very fast, so they did not have time to transfer her to the hospital. She also remembered that I was a very small baby, weighing only four and a half pounds (2 kilograms).

While I was living in the San, I got a message from Phillip, the man who may have been my biological father. He was ill and dying. One of Phillip's sons came to tell me that Phillip was my father, and that he wanted to see me before he died. I was not allowed to leave the sanatorium yet, so I couldn't travel to see him. Phillip died soon afterward. His family sent me a telegram to let me know. Later, they wrote me a letter telling me what he had been like, and sent me a photograph of him and his sons. There wasn't much

I could learn about Phillip from the photo. I just saw a skinny man who was somewhat taller than his sons. His face seemed a bit scruffy, like he had some facial hair. And he wore a baseball cap on his head, just like his sons.

THE TWELVE STEPS

In the fall of 1976 I was allowed to leave the tuberculosis sanatorium. The government provided me with enough social assistance to pay my rent, so I moved back into my old apartment with my kids. Sarah and Martin went to the local grade school, and my brother Andy, who was about eighteen years old at the time, moved back from Sault Ste. Marie to live with me. I continued to go to AA meetings regularly, but staying sober was not easy. My sponsor suggested that I participate in a twenty-eight-day residential treatment program focused on the twelve AA steps. She said it might help me understand AA on a deeper level. I agreed, and entered the treatment program at the Sister Margaret Smith Centre, which most people call the Smith Clinic.

When I first joined the residential program, I was struggling with an idea that is central to AA, which is having faith in a power greater than myself. Several of the twelve AA steps focus on that spiritual belief. They include: coming to believe that a power greater than ourselves can restore us to sanity; deciding to turn our lives over to the care of that power; admitting to our higher power, ourselves, and others the exact nature of our wrongs; asking this greater power to remove our shortcomings; and seeking an on-going, conscious contact with our higher power through prayer and meditation. Until I entered the twenty-eight-day program, I had just gone along with what other AA members said about their God, Higher Power, or Great Spirit, but I did not have a similar belief myself.

I had a breakthrough during the program, when I was sitting on the ground outside of the clinic, looking at the Sleeping Giant across the water. The Sleeping Giant is a land formation on the north shore of Lake Superior that—if seen from Thunder Bay—looks like an gigantic person lying on its back, sleeping. I asked the woman sitting next to me if she could tell me in plain English what AA members mean when they talk about a higher power. She said a higher power is a greater being that you can't see or touch, but you still believe exists. As she spoke, I felt a little tickle on my hand, and I looked down to see an ant crawling on me. I swept it away, and then I studied part of a root that I could see in the ground beside me. That root had a large, healthy plant growing out of it, even though it was in a bare spot where it probably did not get much water. The image reminded me of something my grandmother once told me. She always said that *Gitchi Manitou* lives within us and all around us. She believed that the Great Spirit is neither a man nor a woman, but both, because it draws on both beings from within itself to create men and women. My *kokum* told me that, if I didn't believe in the Great Spirit, then I should find a tree growing on a wide, flat rock and ask myself who made it grow there. That day in 1976, as I looked around me at the ant, the root, and the Sleeping Giant, I began to have faith in a higher power that created and sustains the world. Today I believe in a Great Spirit as my grandmother explained it to me, which is a gentle, loving, and healing creator who lives within us and all around us, and is neither man nor woman, but both. Over the years, the AA program has helped me to be sober and to live a healthy, balanced life, but my faith in a higher power has been even more important.

TRAINING AND WORKING AS AN ALCOHOLISM COUNSELLOR

In 1977, not long after I left the residential treatment program, I met an Anishinaabe man named Herbert who was arranging for the AA Big Book to be translated into Ojibwe and Cree. Herbert was very tall man with a gentle manner. He approached me to ask whether I would like to work as a part-time translator for two dollars an hour. I agreed and began the job right away, working together with another Anishinaabe woman. She and I went through the Big Book sentence by sentence, translating each one out loud for a cassette recording. I used a mix of Ojibwe and Cree, depending on what sounded like the best translation to me. Herbert planned to have my recordings typed up and printed for Native readers. I thought it also would be helpful if I just copied the cassettes and sent them to Anishinaabe communities around Ontario. The Big Book had been very helpful to me in my sobriety, so I wanted to share it with other Anishinaabeg in more isolated areas. I researched addresses for community centres and churches on reserves and in other Native communities, and personally sent cassette copies to many distant places, including Webequie, Lansdowne, Summer Beaver, Fort Hope, Pickle Lake, Sioux Lookout, Marathon, Heron Bay, Moose Factory, and Mobert.

Then, in the summer of 1977, Herbert asked me if I wanted to participate in a year-long training course to become an alcoholism counsellor. He
was coordinating the program, but I needed to apply for it through the
employment office. As it turned out, the employment officer, a Mr. Percy,
quickly turned down my application. He told me that I was "unteachable,"
because I only had a fourth-grade education and I had not really learned
to read, write, or speak English until I moved to Thunder Bay as an adult.
I remember that Mr. Percy had black, slicked-back hair and wore a bur-
gundy suit and tie as he sat behind his desk and told me I would waste my
time, and others', if I tried to do the training program.

I asked people in AA meetings what the employment officer meant when
he said I was unteachable. They explained that he believed that I was not able
to learn anything, and that anyone who tried to teach me would fail. That
really made me angry. I had had very little opportunity to go to school as
a child, and my experience at school had been difficult. But I knew I could
learn. I also knew I could be a very good counsellor. So I begged Herbert
to let me join the program, even though the employment office had turned
down my application. Luckily, somebody withdrew from the program at the
last minute and Herbert let me participate instead. He told me that it would
take the government at least six months to sort out the red tape and realize
that my application had been rejected. By then it would be too late for them
to kick me out. And he was right. By the time the authorities caught on, I
was earning high marks in all of my coursework, and they let me complete
the program.

I began studying in the Native alcoholism counselling program at
the Confederation College in the fall of 1977. Over the next year I worked
incredibly hard. I got up at 6:00 a.m. to get my kids ready for school. Then I
took a bus across town to participate in classes at the college. If my children
did not have school that day, they came with me. Between classes, I studied
in the library or outside under the trees. I often asked librarians to assist
me, not just when I needed to find particular books, but even to explain
unfamiliar English words in difficult texts. The library staff were very patient and helpful. In fact, I asked them for assistance so often that the head
librarian assigned a student employee to assist me whenever I came to the
library. In the evenings, I took my kids with me to AA meetings and then
back home for dinner, baths, and bedtime. Afterward I studied late into the

night. My friends in AA supported me in many ways that year. Herbert, for example, gave me money to pay babysitters once in a while. At other times he left me groceries.

A lot of people in my training program did not seem very motivated. Some just hung out at the college, flirting and socializing when they weren't in class. But I was very serious about the program and driven to succeed, for several reasons. I wanted to help other people to overcome alcoholism the way that others had helped me. I also knew counselling would give me a good salary, so I would be able to support my family long-term. And I wanted to prove that I was smart, and that I could learn, if I was given a chance.

In the summer of 1978, I graduated from the program with a certificate in alcoholism counselling. Soon afterward, I returned to the employment office and asked to speak with Mr. Percy. When we met, I reminded him that he had told me that I was unteachable. Then I showed him my certificate and asked him to help me find a job as an alcoholism counsellor. He was embarrassed, and suggested that it would be better if I worked with a different employment officer. I agreed. The Smith Clinic manager had already told me he wanted to hire me when I finished my course, and the second employment officer helped me apply for that job.

That fall, I started working ten-hour night shifts in the Smith Clinic's alcohol and drug detoxification unit, mostly speaking with Ojibwa and Cree patients who did not understand English. It was hard to know when an interpreter would be needed, because it depended on how many people had been admitted on a given night. I needed to stay awake all night, so I found ways to keep myself busy during slow shifts, for example by cooking bannock for the staff and patients. Often I also worked twelve-hour day shifts in the general clinic further down the hill at St. Joseph's Hospital. Usually my work there involved translating materials, working with patients directly, or interpreting for staff who did not speak Ojibwe or Cree.

While I was working as an alcoholism counsellor at the Smith Clinic, I had a heart-warming experience when an old man who had listened to my cassette translations of the AA Big Book came looking for me to say *miigwetch* (thank you). He had listened to the cassettes up north and said that they had helped him to get sober. When I met him, the man was surprised that I was only twenty-nine years old. Not many people of my generation spoke Ojibwe or Cree well, so he had assumed I was much older. He also thought that I had made up everything on the tapes myself, but I explained that I had only translated a book that already existed. He told me that the twelve steps had been very helpful to him, especially the step of admitting he was powerless over alcohol.

Around the same time, I began volunteering in a program for street youth. It targeted all high-risk youth, not just young Anishinaabeg, or those who were already in AA. We worked with any youths who lived on the streets, or any who spent their days engaged in high-risk activities. The rates of suicide among street youth were high, so the goal was to make contact with them, support them, and inform them about available social services. I started a regular youth support group in the basement of St. Andrew's Church. The first few times I scheduled it, no one came, so I sat in the church for hours on my own. Then I began doing street outreach, talking to kids I met until I convinced them to attend the meeting. Once they did and they liked it, they brought their friends too. After that, I didn't have any problems with group attendance.

In 1979, some AA members in Thunder Bay arranged to hold AA meetings at Ontario reserves where alcoholism was a problem and AA had not yet been introduced. They wanted to have Ojibwa and Cree AA members lead the meetings, so they asked me and another Anishinaabe speaker to go. The other AA member and I ended up introducing the Alcoholics Anonymous program to many different northern communities, including Webequie, Lansdowne, Summer Beaver, Fort Hope, Pickle Lake, and Pikangikum. We travelled by plane. Several of the people I met on those reserves had already listened to my tape cassette translation of the Big Book. It was the first time I ever visited Fort Hope, the reserve where my grandmother had been a band member. Phillip, the man who possibly was my biological father, also had lived in Fort Hope with his family until he died in 1976. None of his family members were at the reserve when I visited in 1979, so I did not get a chance to meet them then.

SUPPORTING A LARGE HOUSEHOLD

During my first five years of sobriety, I managed a large household on my own. After I was discharged from the San, Sarah and Martin always lived with me. Usually, they were happy and content kids. They enjoyed school, even though Martin sometimes found it difficult to keep up with his classmates. Once in a while, they got into mischief together. For example, one day in 1976, when Sarah was about nine years old and Martin about seven, they cut each other's hair without my permission. Until then, Sarah wore her hair in two long, straight brown pigtails, and Martin, whose hair had never been cut, had a long, wavy black ponytail. That day, when I called them down for dinner, I discovered that Sarah was missing one pigtail and Martin's hair was very short and jagged at the back. So that night I trimmed their hair as best I could, until they both had short, even cuts.

In addition to raising my two children, I took in my cousin Angela's daughter for several years. While I had been getting sober in the mid-1970s, Angela had moved away from Thunder Bay and later returned with a baby girl named Sabrina. Angela tried to raise Sabrina on her own, but she had difficulty doing that, because she was still drinking heavily. Angela asked me if I would take care of Sabrina for her, and I agreed. I raised Sabrina from the time she was about one year old until she was five. She was a sweet, skinny little girl, with long, straight black hair. I loved her like my own kids, but it was not easy having a baby and then a toddler in the house again, given all the work involved in caring for a child that young.

There were times when Angela got sober and took Sabrina with her for weeks or months, but she always brought her back. In the end, Angela became very ill and was hospitalized. She was diagnosed with cirrhosis of the liver. Her doctors told her that there was nothing they could do to treat or reverse it. She managed to stay sober for nine months after that, but then she went on a drinking binge. Again she became very sick and needed hospitalization. She suffered horribly, and never recovered. I stayed with Angela during her final days in the hospital. I held her in my arms when she died. Sabrina continued to live with me for some time after Angela's death, until I moved away from Thunder Bay in 1980. Then Sabrina was taken in by one of my cousins who wanted to legally foster her.

During those years, I also took in family members, friends, and friends of friends when they came to Thunder Bay and needed a place to stay. For example, Edith, the widow of Phillip, who may have been my father, asked to stay with me in 1977 when she came to Thunder Bay to attend the Canadian Lakehead Exhibition. It was the first time I met her. She was a petite woman, maybe only five feet tall. She wore large glasses and a flower-patterned kerchief around her hair. She was missing several teeth, and she had a big, bright smile. Edith told me that Phillip had dearly wanted to meet me at the end of his life, but that he had understood that I could not leave the tuberculosis sanatorium to visit him. At some point in their years together, he had told her that I was his daughter. She said she did not understand how that was possible, because she had had a daughter with him about the same time I was born. It was not clear to me whether she believed he was my biological father, or she believed he had claimed to be my father so I would not be considered a bastard. But she had come to accept that I was his daughter, and she had encouraged him to make contact with me. I did not really care whether Phillip was my father, because I had not known him and I had never felt a need to discover my father's identity. But I was happy to welcome Phillip's family and to hear what they had to say.

While I was working and single-parenting in the late 1970s, I sometimes also sheltered homeless teenagers who I met on my way to or from AA meetings. I worried about them being assaulted or freezing to death while sleeping outside on winter nights, so I started offering them a place to stay. Teenage girls were harder to convince than teenage boys. When I saw them, they usually were standing by the side of the road, waiting for men to pick them up and pay them for sex. They also had pimps who drove up and down the street keeping an eye on their activity. I did not understand their relationships with those men at first, but some girls in their early teens explained it to me when they visited me at home. Those girls did not want to stay at my place, but they came home with me to see where I lived, so they could return if they ever wanted to do so later. Now and then homeless teens who had stayed with me before returned with other kids, and once my brother Andy brought home street kids who he thought needed a safe place to stay.

I also found some of my young relatives living on the streets, so they came to live with me too. At that time, Angela's older brother, Gilbert, was institutionalized in a long-term psychiatric unit in Thunder Bay. Gilbert was the adult cousin who had beaten me badly when I was a child. His wife had died years earlier in Ombabika, and most of their children had ended up on the streets of Thunder Bay. In the end, one daughter and five of their sons stayed at my house. Gilbert's oldest daughter, Barbara, lived in Vancouver, British Columbia. One by one, those kids left my home in Thunder Bay to go live with her.

Our apartment building had a big, empty basement, so I had enough space to house many kids. Each child had his or her own blanket, and they just slept on the floor. I liked that they stayed with me. I taught them how to play rummy, and I was glad to hear them laugh as they talked and played cards. I fried huge quantities of bannock or donuts to feed them. They all called me "mum," just like my brother and my own kids. Sometimes they also called me "Columbo," after the police detective on TV, because I wore a long trench coat like he did.

There were days when I felt exhausted by having all of those young people staying with me, on top of my other responsibilities, but I still enjoyed it. Most of the teenagers were drinking and doing drugs on the streets, but I never had a problem with that in my house. One time they did rob the corner store, though. That day I came home and I could tell something was up by the way they were all sitting at the kitchen table smiling at me. They told me to look in the refrigerator, where I found a large bag and a card with the words "Happy Big Day" on it. The bag contained salami, a cake, two cartons of cigarettes, a bottle of Coca Cola, and many Wintario lottery tickets. I asked them where they got all that stuff, and they told me that I didn't need to worry about it. Then they pointed to a garbage bag on the floor, where I found more cigarette cartons and lottery tickets. I said, "Oh my God, you robbed the corner store, didn't you?" And they admitted that they had, and they had brought me the things to thank me.

I explained to them that it was not a burden for them to stay with me, because I liked their company and I loved knowing that they were safe at night. The best way they could thank me, I said, was to keep my home clean and safe. And I told them that we would have to return all of the things they had stolen. At first they were afraid that they would be put in jail, but I assured them that I would take care of it. I called a friendly police constable that I knew and explained what had happened. He agreed to meet me and the kids at the corner store. We returned everything unopened, and the store owner did not file charges. Then the constable gave the kids a good talking to, telling them that if they ever robbed a store again they would indeed go to jail. That seemed to frighten them a bit. I hoped it would stop them from stealing in the future.

MANAGING CHALLENGES IN MY PERSONAL LIFE

There were several important changes in my life between 1978 and 1980. Some of them were positive new developments for me or for someone I cared about, like Jane, who moved to Sault Ste. Marie to live with a man she had been involved with for some time. But other experiences were very challenging. My vision had been limited since childhood, but it was steadily getting worse. Almost every year I needed to get stronger prescription eyeglasses. In 1978, my eye doctor decided to perform a series of tests on me, to identify what different factors might be causing my vision problems. Midway through the tests, though, he needed to take a few months' leave, so in his absence he asked me to follow up with another eye doctor, a Dr. Boyle.

Dr. Boyle sexually assaulted me during my only appointment with him. The day I went to see him, I was his last scheduled patient. I recognized him as an older white man from AA meetings, and I remembered he had been sober for many years. As I entered the exam room, I heard him tell his secretary that she could leave for the day. He had me sit in an examination chair and then moved his equipment into position around my head. The machine locked my head in place, so when Dr. Boyle sat a few inches in front of me, he could look through the equipment directly into my eyes as he tested them. My other doctor had examined my eyes in the same way before.

Unlike my other doctor, though, Dr. Boyle told me that I had a very serious eye problem and to understand it he needed to examine my breasts. I refused, telling him he could not do that, but he forced himself on me. I struggled and fought him as he touched my breasts and roughly tried to take off my shirt, breaking off one of my buttons as he did it. I yelled at him to stop, but he just kept saying I needed to calm down so he could assess my condition. Then he tried to unzip my pants. I kicked and kneed him with all my strength. I guess I hurt him or the equipment enough to make him stop, because he finally let me go. I shot out of the chair and ran for the door. Dr. Boyle said, "No one is going to believe you if you tell them about this. You have a lot of problems, and it's your word against mine." I was shaking as I left his office. When I got home, I avoided all of the children, because I did not want them to see me so upset. I just showered and got into bed. Still, the kids came into my room and asked me what was the matter. I told them that I was sick, and that I felt like drinking. They begged me not to start drinking again, and I didn't.

Days later, I tried to talk about what had happened in an AA meeting, but I couldn't say it. I only started crying. I saw Dr. Boyle at AA meetings again after that. Each time, he stared at me until I left. One of my sponsors asked me why I kept leaving meetings early, but I didn't tell her. I believed Dr. Boyle. I didn't think that anyone would take my word as a recently sober, Native woman with little formal education over the word of a white doctor with many years of sobriety.

After two long-time AA members sexually assaulted me in my first years of sobriety, I realized that some men are predators who use AA to target vulnerable women. Women who have only recently stopped using alcohol or drugs may have little confidence and ability to stand up for themselves. They are in a fragile place where a bad experience can easily set them back in their recovery. Even if they stay sober and have the courage to speak out against abuse, others may not believe what they say, if someone with more status, authority, and long-term sobriety denies it. Those men may especially target newly-recovered Native women who are poor and have limited education, because those women have very little power in our society. As a result, whenever I sponsor a woman who is new to AA, I warn her to be cautious around the men in the program. I try to give her practical tips, like to avoid being alone with a male AA member, and not to accept rides from one.

Another challenge I faced during the late 1970s was looking after my stepsister and stepfather, who both were drinking heavily and needed a place to live. At that point, my kids and I had moved into an apartment closer to where I worked. First Matilda and her boyfriend showed up on my doorstep, and I agreed that they could stay with me for a few nights until they found another place to stay. Matilda caused some real trouble during that visit. One day when I was away at work, she rummaged through the boxes that were stored in my basement and found my journals. I had a few books full of drawings of Ombabika, including maps I drew of our neighbourhood and trapping grounds. I also had several journals that I had filled after I came to Thunder Bay, when I was learning to read and write. Matilda took all of my journals, piled them in the bathtub, and set them on fire. When I returned later that day, I smelled the smoke as soon as

I entered the house. I asked Sarah what had happened, and she explained that auntie had burnt papers in the bathroom. I found all of my journals destroyed, and Matilda was gone.

Despite the harm she had done, Matilda returned a few weeks later and begged me to let her, her three sons, and my stepdad move in with me. Her sons were all close in age to Sarah and Martin, and I did not want any of them living on the streets, so I let them stay. While living with me, my stepdad talked about my mom a lot. He missed her very much. I asked him why he had left Ombabika after she died, and he couldn't give me an answer. I told him that nobody had been there to help me after he left, and that Gus and his mother had abused me terribly. My stepdad apologized for leaving me, but he was drunk when he said it, so I don't know if it was sincere. Still, I forgave him, and I tried to help him, but I found it very difficult to live with him and my stepsister when they were drinking so much. My stepdad never considered quitting, but Matilda was trying to become sober, and it wasn't working. One day she left the house and didn't come back for months. I kept taking care of her sons in her absence.

Once in a while, my stepdad and other friends told me it was strange that I was a single woman raising so many kids on my own. They encouraged me to date men, with the hope that I would marry one in the end. I didn't have much awareness about my sexuality at the time. I thought that maybe they were right, that after years of working hard on my own, I should find a man to help me. I agreed to date a security guard I met at an event at my college. Very quickly—too quickly—we decided to live together. We bought a house, and I moved in with him, my kids, and Angela's daughter Sabrina, who I was still raising. Looking back, I realize that I was probably trying to escape the drunkenness that my stepdad and stepsister had brought into my home, but that was not clear to me then. I only lived with that man for a short time. He started acting in disturbing ways toward both me and Sabrina, so the kids and I moved out. He only paid me $2,000 for my part of the house, which was a small amount compared to what I had put into it. But I wanted to be rid of him, so I did not care.

Next I found a three-storey house that I thought would comfortably house many people, because my stepdad and stepsister still wanted to live with me. I made a space for myself in the small third-floor attic, which had a bedroom, a kitchenette, and a bathroom. My stepdad lived on the second floor. When my stepsister was with us, she lived with all of the kids on the large ground floor. Finally, my brother Andy lived in the basement. I paid the $350 monthly rent with my salary from the Smith Clinic. The others chipped in small amounts of cash toward their expenses.

DECIDING TO GET MARRIED

During this period, I met a French Canadian named Nate. Nate was a trim man who was a little bit taller than me. He had curly red hair and blue eyes. He was several years older than me and, like me, he was a recovering alcoholic. Nate had been sober for one year and was living in a halfway house. He often came by my house to visit and play cards with my family. For a while I tried to fix him up with Matilda. They didn't hit it off, but I got along well with Nate. We both liked to joke and laugh. He was very patient, and he did not seem like he would ever be a violent man, compared to many other men I had known. We also had similar life stories, because his dad had been abusive toward him the way my mom had been toward me. Nate had been a mill worker, but he had suffered a work injury that made it difficult for him to continue in his position, so he had lost his job.

While I was getting to know Nate, my stepdad continued to pressure me to get married. I thought about it and wondered whether I would be happier if I had someone to keep me company and share my responsibilities. I was tired of working so hard and being a single mom. I didn't think about sex or my sexuality. I had never experienced romantic feelings or sexual desire for a man. At best, I felt sexually indifferent toward men, and, at worst, sickened by the idea of sex with them. The possibility of finding a female partner and experiencing happiness in a lesbian relationship was not something I even imagined at the time. In Thunder Bay in the late 1970s, there was no visible lesbian or gay community. I believed my crushes and attractions for women were my own unique, strange burden to bear. I had learned to suppress those feelings long ago.

Having only experienced an abusive, arranged marriage, I decided to try marriage to a man who I chose myself. So one day, on the spur of the moment, I asked Nate whether he would marry me. We were playing cards at the time, and Nate was so shocked that he fell off the corner of the bed where he was sitting. He nervously said that no one had ever asked him to marry her before. And then he told me he had to leave and quickly left. I did not see him again for a week, and even then he didn't give me an answer.

FIGURE 8. IN MY WEDDING DRESS ON THE DAY I MARRIED NATE IN THUNDER BAY (TWENTY-NINE YEARS OLD, 1979).

Three weeks after my proposal, though, he came up to me and said, "Okay, I've never been married. Let's give it a try."

Before we got married, Nate and I travelled to Quebec to meet his family. His mother was a kind and a beautiful woman. She welcomed me into their family home, taught me some good recipes, and gave me a quilt she had made herself. She seemed truly happy that Nate was marrying me. Nate's sister, who had Down syndrome, was also sweet and friendly. In addition, I spent a fair bit of time during that visit with Nate's brother's wife. She only spoke French, so we had to communicate through sign language. When I met Nate's dad, I was sad to see that he was as mean-spirited as Nate had told me. I witnessed first-hand how hard he was on Nate.

In the spring of 1980, Nate and I had a small wedding at the Wesley United Church in Thunder Bay, where non-members were allowed to marry for free (Figure 8). My stepdad, stepsister, brother, and kids were all there, as well as Nate's mother and sister. My co-workers and our friends from AA also attended. We had a nice meal and a party afterward. Nate was unemployed when we got married, so I continued supporting the family on my salary alone. He and I moved into a new house with Sarah and Martin, but we did not stay there long. Soon after we got married, Nate told me he was going to Winnipeg to visit his brother. He left and I did not see him for some time. Then he called and told me that he had found a job working as a handyman in Winnipeg. He said that the kids and I should move there to live with him. Nate's new job only paid six dollars an hour, which was much less than what I earned as an alcoholism counsellor. I also liked my work and did not want to give it up, so I was frustrated by this sudden turn of events. But I understood that people expected wives to adapt to their husbands more than the other way around. Whether that was fair or not, I wanted to give the marriage a good try. So I quit my job, and the kids and I moved 600 kilometres west, to Winnipeg, Manitoba.

CHAPTER EIGHT

WORKING WITH ADDICTED MOTHERS AND RAISING FOSTER KIDS WITH NATE IN WINNIPEG (1980–1987)

Sarah, Martin, and I arrived in Winnipeg in the fall of 1980. At that point the city had a population of about half a million, which was several times larger than Thunder Bay. Nate had rented a small apartment where we all lived at the beginning. Around the same time, my brother Andy moved to Winnipeg with his new girlfriend, Lori, so I was happy to have some family in the area. I enrolled Martin and Sarah, who were eleven and twelve years old, in a French school where they learned both English and French.

Over the following years, Sarah did well in school, and she was happy to participate in after-school activities like ballet. As a teenager, she volunteered as a candy striper at a hospital and was very proud of her work there. Martin continued to struggle in school, so Sarah and I helped him a lot at home. He was a visual learner. Martin understood when people explained things to him in simple English, but he still was not able to read and write. His teachers knew that he was slower than his classmates, but they felt it was good for him to be with kids of the same age, as long as he was learning at his own pace. If Martin were in the school system today, he probably would have been assessed as having a developmental delay and then received special educational services, but that wasn't the practice in 1980.

Nate and I got in the habit of sharing household and work responsibilities. We both cooked and cleaned the house. We also did mechanical work together, like maintaining and fixing our radios and kitchen appliances.

We often played board games or cards with the kids. Sometimes we went out for walks with them to explore the area. As the kids got to know their classmates, they started bringing friends home. I liked it when they were all in the apartment, because it was easier to keep track of what they were doing. Nate also was supportive when Sarah and Martin got sick. One time Sarah became very ill and I had to stay up taking care of her for twenty-four hours. The next night she was still sick and I was exhausted, so Nate watched over her instead. Another night when Martin was ill, Nate stayed up with him.

Not long after we arrived in Winnipeg, I found a larger apartment for us in a huge, block-long building on Portage Avenue. I made a deal with the landlord to do basic renovations and paint walls when tenants moved out of units. That was steady work for about six months, because there were always apartments in need of painting. When Martin wasn't in school, he helped me. Once I explained to him how to do a task like that, he was very thorough and did a good job.

One day while I was breaking down an old wall to expand a room in an empty apartment, I found a brown paper bag inside the wall space. Someone must have made a hole in the wall and then completely covered it up, because I couldn't see any other way that the bag could have been placed there. It was full of money—maybe $3,000 to $4,000 in small bills. I didn't know what to do with it. At first I just I shoved the bag into a different wall space and left it there. Later, I realized that the person who put the bag in between those walls was probably long gone, and possibly even dead. The apartment and walls were old, and the bag looked like it had been there for years. So before new tenants moved in, I took the bag and hid it at home. I didn't consider using the cash for a long time, not until after I had started a new job, moved houses, and begun raising foster kids. I never felt comfortable with the idea of spending that money on myself. In the end, I used it to buy new bicycles for my kids and foster kids. Also, I secretly gave cash to friends and neighbours who were in financial trouble, including a poor Anishinaabe family who moved in across the street from us, and some of the families of my foster kids. I never told them who gave them the money. I just left it in envelopes for them in their mailboxes.

During our first years in Winnipeg, Nate offered to adopt my kids. He and Sarah got along well, and Sarah wanted him to adopt her, so we started that process. Nate and Martin did not connect as much, and Martin did not want Nate to adopt him. Instead, Martin told me he really wanted to go and see his father in Auden. Martin had not seen Gus since Gus kidnapped him ten years earlier. I told Martin that Gus had been abusive to me, so I would be worried if Martin went to see him. But Martin insisted, saying it was important for him to meet his dad after so many recent changes in his life, what with me marrying Nate and all of us moving to Winnipeg. I decided to let him visit Gus. I contacted Gus in Auden and he agreed, but before I put Martin on the train, I gave him names of people who he could ask for help if he had problems with his dad. And I gave him enough money to return to Winnipeg when he wanted.

Martin's visit to Gus did not go well. After a short time, Martin called me and said his dad was being very mean to him, so he was coming back to Winnipeg. I also talked to Gus, who just said, "Your son's got a lot of problems." Until then, Gus did not know that Martin was slower than other kids. I doubt Gus ever understood that Martin's condition was probably the result of his premature birth, which was caused by Gus beating me when I was seven months pregnant. When Martin came back to Winnipeg, he told me that he never wanted to see his father again. In fact, when Gus contacted Sarah and Martin many years later, Sarah agreed to meet him, but Martin refused.

STREET OUTREACH WITH ADDICTED PREGNANT WOMEN

In Winnipeg in 1982, there were three nurse's stations which provided free or low-cost health care in poor inner-city communities. That year those nurse's stations started a joint multicultural outreach program to improve services for pregnant women and new mothers who were living on the streets. I was one of six women hired to do street work for the program. All of us spoke at least one language other than English that was common in the inner city. We were trained in street outreach and maternal and child health. I started working downtown in the north end of Winnipeg. To record details about the women who I met and the outcomes of our conversations, I carried a clipboard. I had check-in meetings with my supervisor at the nurse's station each morning, to update her on my work and get more supplies.

Over my four years of doing street outreach, I mostly worked with homeless pregnant teenagers. Many of them were injecting or using other illegal drugs, not alcohol. To meet new clients, I simply walked the streets of the inner city and approached pregnant women who looked like they might be homeless. I spoke with them about available food, health, social, housing, and addiction services. I had a backpack full of brochures and pamphlets that provided referral options, as well as pregnancy and infant care information. If the woman was standing in a larger group, and it was a tough, gang-like situation, then I just handed out my business cards to everyone. Once I made contact with a woman, I tried to check in on her regularly to see how she was doing, either through follow-up appointments in coffee shops, or just by finding her in the area where she told me she stayed on the streets. If a woman was in a relationship and her partner wanted to participate, I also worked with him to help them both get needed services.

Usually the women most eager to talk with me and to access these services were those near the end of their pregnancies, because at that point they often felt frightened and desperate. I tried to motivate them to cut down on their drug use. I also made sure they knew where to go to get food and obstetric services. If they were ready to get off the streets, I helped them access social assistance, enter a halfway house, get affordable housing, and buy the things they needed, like groceries and baby supplies. Once in a while I made follow-up home visits with a program nurse, especially if the nurse was new and inexperienced. The nurses were all white and did not speak any Anishinaabe languages. The new ones sometimes offended clients without meaning to. For example, when one young nurse visited the home of one of my clients, she went straight to the cupboards to check what was inside, without asking permission first. I visited the client later, and she complained that the nurse had not been polite and had not respected her privacy. She said she already felt badly about her situation, so when the nurse criticized her food choices, she only felt worse. I persuaded the client to let the nurse come back by promising to be there the next time she dropped by. Working with our clients could be a tricky process, because many did not care whether we visited them at home, and they could easily shut us out.

I had some wonderful experiences on that job, including helping to deliver a few babies. A lot of our clients were teenage runaways who did not want any contact with their families. Some also did not have boyfriends to go with them to the hospital. I gave my clients my home number, so if they went into labour, they could call me and I would meet them at the hospital for the delivery. Seeing those babies come into the world was a gift. Still, the job was stressful and took an emotional toll on me. Conditions in the downtown area were grim and sometimes unsafe. People I met on the streets were often in very bad shape, both mentally and physically. I understood street life and the desperation that people experienced when they were addicted and homeless, because I had known it myself. But some of the people I met were aggressive toward me, and I had to be cautious and on my guard at all times.

HOME-BASED COUNSELLING WITH MOTHERS IN RECOVERY

In late 1985, I was offered a position with Child and Family Services and I decided to accept it. In my new job, I made home visits to mothers who were recovering alcoholics and addicts, and I assisted them when they tried to regain custody of their children in foster care. I had a large client load from the start, because I replaced someone who had left suddenly. Many of my new clients were single mothers who lived in isolated places outside of the city, so I needed a driver's licence and a private vehicle to work. That was not a problem, since I had learned how to drive and got my licence soon after I moved to Winnipeg. I had my own car, a second-hand red-and-white Dodge Duster that I loved.

Usually I met with a client many times over several weeks or months. Sometimes I met with her one-on-one, and now and then with her adult family members, or her children who were in foster care. I facilitated referrals to counselling and treatment centres, and supported women in AA or Narcotics Anonymous programs. If my clients were trying to regain custody of their children, I went with them to court. I helped them solve practical problems like getting jobs, housing, or furniture. I did my own research on where to buy cheap groceries locally and which private or public services offered free meals, to help my clients and their kids get enough to eat.

Once in a while I went with social workers when they took custody of children whose parents were negligent or abusive. That was a very sad process. I also worked with young grandmothers, women in their early thirties who were struggling to raise their grandchildren. A lot of my interactions with both mothers and grandmothers focused on parenting skills and discipline. Many of them had grown up in places where children were disciplined by being shouted at, spanked, or hit. Most of the women understood that that was not acceptable, but few knew of other ways to discipline their kids. When some of them felt overwhelmed, they just let their kids do as they pleased, whatever their behaviour. At that time, Child and Family Services and a few other agencies offered parenting programs, but there weren't enough spaces available to meet the needs of so many parents and grandparents. As a result, in addition to my direct counselling work, I spent a lot of time researching the availability of parenting programs and arranging participation for my clients.

BEING A FOSTER PARENT

After I got my job doing street outreach work in 1982, I began earning enough money to get a home loan. Nate was not eligible for one, so the house and mortgage were in my name only. I bought a four-bedroom house with a front and a backyard on the outskirts of Winnipeg. At that point, Nate and I were still getting along and working well together, but I did not enjoy having sex with him. I told him I wanted to have a separate bedroom, and he agreed. I made a bedroom for myself in the basement, and he took the master bedroom upstairs.

Not long after we moved into that house, I was working with a woman from Child and Family Services one day and she asked me if I would like to become a foster parent. She explained that I could take in children around my own kids' ages, and it could be short-term or long-term, depending on our needs. I told her about my experience taking in homeless kids in Thunder Bay. She pointed out that I would have a lot more support in the formal foster care system. I discussed the idea with Nate, and we decided to try it. I applied to be the primary foster parent, so I held the licence, but as my husband, Nate also needed to be interviewed and accepted by the agency in a supportive role. We were surprised by how quickly our application was accepted and children were placed with us.

My first foster child was a nine-year-old boy. He was a good-hearted child, but he had issues that made it challenging to foster him. He often was very agitated, and stayed up late into the night. He got into other people's things, scrounging around like he was looking for something that he couldn't find. Then he started carrying knives. When I realized that, I told him it was not allowed, but one night I still found him with a table knife in bed. That frightened me. For a few nights after I tried to stay up to watch him until morning, but I was still going to work during the daytime, so soon I was exhausted. After two weeks, I told Child and Family Services that I couldn't take care of him anymore. I recommended that they place him in twenty-four-hour care, or a home where the foster parent did not have other kids or an outside job.

Later, most of the foster children who lived with us were older and stayed with us for years. Of course, we were open to taking in foster kids of any race or background, but it turned out that all of those placed with us were Anishinaabe. Two of the boys who we took in during the early years were twelve and fourteen when they arrived. Afterward I also cared for three siblings—two girls and a boy—who were eight to eleven years old when they first came to stay with us. All of them got along with Sarah and Martin. Over the years, some other children were placed with us for shorter periods, like a baby girl who just stayed for a few nights. But those five older children stayed with us for several years. There always were at least seven kids living in the house. Sometimes, we also took in other kids for weeks or months. For example, some of Sarah's and Martin's friends stayed with us when their parents were away.

I found teenagers easier to foster than young children, because they were very independent. Each Saturday and Sunday, I chopped, cooked, and froze many meals—usually casseroles, stews, soups, potatoes, and other vegetables. Then on weekdays, when the first older child got home from school, he or she took a meal out of the freezer and put it in the oven. We also ate a lot of hamburgers, grilled cheese sandwiches, and bannock (Figure 9). I liked to cook spinach, broccoli, and carrots into bannock, because the kids usually weren't willing to eat those vegetables in any other way. I also often made blueberry or raisin bannock.

All of my foster kids came from troubled homes. They struggled to understand what had happened to them. Some had been taken away from single moms who were drinking heavily and doing drugs. Many felt rejected by their mothers, as if their moms had chosen addiction over them. I spoke openly with them about my own experience of losing my children and living on the streets, to explain to them that their mothers probably

FIGURE 9. MAKING BANNOCK TO FEED MY KIDS AND FOSTER KIDS IN WINNIPEG (THIRTY-SEVEN YEARS OLD, 1987).

loved them greatly, but had not yet figured out how to manage their addictions. Several of my foster kids didn't have much confidence and they craved affection. I tried to listen to them, to give them positive feedback, and just to show them that I loved them every day.

GROWING AWARENESS OF MY SEXUALITY

In the early 1980s, I had never met an openly gay man or woman. Once, though, when I was doing street outreach with pregnant women, I came across two men kissing. Another time I saw two women walking arm-in-arm, and then holding hands. I was fascinated and drawn to them, although I did not approach them. By then I also had seen a few gay and lesbian characters on television programs. I decided to ask some friends in AA what they thought about homosexuals. I raised the topic with questions like, "Have you ever heard of a woman going with a woman? I saw it once on TV. Does that happen in real life?" All of them were very negative, describing gays and lesbians as awful or disgusting. I did not raise the topic with them again.

Despite those reactions, I was beginning to understand that I was romantically and sexually attracted to women. There were moments when I met a woman who I was so drawn to that my heart raced with excitement. I had experienced such feelings at different times throughout my life, but I did not have the words to express them until then. And apart from Shi-igohbii, Bonnie, and Angela, I had not imagined that there were any other people like me. I was very busy with work and raising children during that period, but I tried to find time to get away on my own to think through the problems in my life. One of my favourite ways to do this was to go to the symphony. I loved hearing classical music performed live in a concert hall. Whenever I could, I bought a ticket and listened to a performance while reflecting on what was worrying me. Sometimes I also packed up my kids and foster kids and took them camping outside of Winnipeg. Nate and I had bought an old, ten-passenger van so we could carry all of them together. I got the time I needed to think when the kids and I were outside of the city, sleeping in the woods under the stars (Figure 10).

Now and then, when I had privacy at home, I sketched images that represented my feelings, and I even painted. I remember carefully sketching a bird in black, grey, and red colours on a twelve-by-sixteen-inch sheet

FIGURE 10. ON A CAMPING TRIP WITH MY KIDS AND FOSTER KIDS OUTSIDE OF WINNIPEG (THIRTY-THREE YEARS OLD, 1983).

of paper. In my mind's eye, that bird was carrying my soul away from my day-to-day life and the troubles I knew. I kept some of my sketches, and others I gave away.

One day in the mid-1980s, I learned there was a regular AA meeting for lesbians and gays. I decided to slip away from my usual life to attend it. When I got there, it felt like I had come home to my real family. These men and women had stories just like mine, and they were kind and welcoming. I secretly attended that group's meetings a few more times in 1986. I was grateful and excited to have found the group, but I also felt scared. I was unhappily married to a man. I could not imagine any of my friends, family, or co-workers responding positively if I told them I was a lesbian. I couldn't see how I could come out and still live in Winnipeg.

On Labour Day weekend in 1986, a large women's music and cultural festival was held at Kildonan Park in Winnipeg. I told Nate and the kids that I was going to the festival and that they could join me if they wanted. There were some other big events happening that same weekend, and Nate wanted to go to a carnival that had amusement park rides instead. Most of the children chose to go with him, but two of our foster kids—a teenage boy and his younger sister—chose to come with me. At the festival, my foster daughter wanted to play in the child care tent, so her brother and I left her there and we wandered around listening to music together. We polka danced in one tent, and I taught him how to jig in another. Then we came upon a performance where the attendance was restricted to women only, so he went to listen to music in another tent while I joined the audience there.

The women-only performance was mainly attended by lesbians, but I did not realize that at the time. At first I just sat and listened to the musician, whose songs drew me in right away. Listening to her, I felt like I was coming alive in ways I had not felt for a long time. Then she asked everyone in the audience to come to the centre, to hold hands, and to sing in a circle, which we did. I could not see the women around me very well, but the energy of the group was wonderful. It was powerfully moving for me. I felt like I was no longer alone, because there were many others who were similar to me. I didn't know it then, but there were several women in that circle who one day would become my close friends, and one who would become my lover.

LOSING MY VISION AND MY JOB

During the early 1980s, my vision continued to worsen. It was a slow but steady process. Ever since I had been sexually assaulted by the eye doctor in Thunder Bay, I hated having my eyes examined. When I needed to make an appointment, I requested to have a woman doctor. If that wasn't possible, I asked Nate or a female nurse to go with me into the examination room, although I never told Nate why I did this. Still, I sometimes panicked when large equipment was used to examine my eyes. In those moments I had difficulty concentrating and answering questions doctors asked me about my vision. When I did get new lenses, they never fully corrected my poor eyesight.

Over time, I figured out ways to compensate when I couldn't see things well, even though I wasn't always aware I was doing it. Looking back I realize that I was probably compensating even when I took my practical driver's licence examination in the early 1980s. I remember I got out of my car and studied the road very carefully before parallel parking during the exam. I felt proud when the examiner told me it was one of the best examples of parallel parking he had ever seen. After I started my new job in 1985 and bought a car, I took my daughter Sarah with me to help guide me, especially when I had to drive on unfamiliar roads. I asked her to read signs or tell me the colour of traffic lights when I couldn't see them at intersections. Today, I am grateful I never hurt anyone while driving in that condition, but at the time I was in denial about how I might put others at risk when I could not see well.

By 1986, my vision had become so bad that I was hit by a car while walking across a street, not only once, but twice. Both times I had looked up and down the street before stepping off the sidewalk, but I still had not seen the cars coming toward me. I was not badly hurt, but after each incident I was taken to the hospital. After my second hospital visit, the medical staff suggested that I have my vision checked. They thought I just needed a prescription for new glasses to adequately correct my vision, and so did I. I knew I was having more and more difficulty reading and writing. I could see print on paper if I studied it closely and used a magnifying glass, but my eyes usually tired after only five or ten minutes, so I had to stop.

I went to see another eye doctor to get a new prescription, and he told me that I was legally blind. He explained that, even with new lenses, my vision was so impaired that I needed to give up my driver's licence. He said he was required to inform the motor vehicle licence office, but I could go there myself to have my eyes re-examined, if it would help me believe his assessment. I did as he suggested and I completely failed the test, so I handed in my licence. My job with Child and Family Services required me to drive all over Winnipeg to visit rural clients in areas where there was no public transportation. When I informed my supervisors that I could not drive anymore, they said I could continue long enough to train my replacement and to say goodbye to my clients, but then they would have to let me go.

After I lost my licence and my job, I went through a very dark period. I fell apart. I stayed in my room in the basement for weeks, just sleeping and crying. My work had been very important to me. I had loved everything about it—helping other Anishinaabe families, earning a good salary, and financially supporting my family. Being unable to drive or read and write easily, I feared that I would never get a good job again. I worried that I would not be able to support my family, and we would lose the life I had worked so hard to build. I felt like suddenly I was losing my identity, my hard-won independence, and my financial security, all in one go.

During that difficult period, my kids and my foster kids were the main reason I didn't drink. I didn't want to let them down, and I wanted to make sure they were okay. By that time, Sarah and Martin were young adults with increasing independence. At five feet and nine inches and at six feet tall, Sarah and Martin were both much taller than me. Sarah was nineteen and still lived at home with me, but she had finished school and was working as an aide in a hospital, where she once had been a volunteer candy-striper. Martin was almost eighteen years old, and he had already moved out of the house and was sharing an apartment with a friend. A year or two earlier, I had helped Martin to get a job in a nice restaurant. I had approached the owner, explained Martin's situation, and outlined the strengths he could bring to the work. The owner had agreed to interview Martin and then offered him the job. As I started to come out of my depression, my immediate focus was on my foster children, who were all younger and more dependent on me than Martin and Sarah. I contacted Children's Aid and told them that I no longer could be a foster parent. They started the process of finding other homes for those kids.

While I had shut myself away in the basement, representatives of the Canadian National Institute for the Blind (CNIB) repeatedly came to the house and tried to speak to me. Each time I refused to meet them. After living in the basement for about six weeks, I finally agreed to meet with one persistent social worker. She explained that there were a lot of services available for visually impaired people. She took me to the CNIB offices, and I participated in a training course on managing daily life with visual impairment. That course made me realize how much I already had been compensating for my poor vision. I did very well in all of the activities that relied on touch, like being blindfolded, feeling an apple, and then identifying it in a bowl of similar apples. It was easy for me to do those kinds of exercises. The CNIB workers also helped me sign up for disability assistance, so I started to get a small income.

ENDING MY MARRIAGE

My breakdown was prompted by the loss of my vision, my driver's licence, and my job, but I had also been miserable in my marriage for a long time. I became more aware of that as I started to rebuild my life. At its best, my marriage to Nate had been a partnership, with the two of us working on shared tasks of raising kids and running a household together. For years, though, it hadn't even been that. Nate and I had slept in separate bedrooms almost since the beginning of our marriage. I had known for some time that he was seeing another woman. On one level that disturbed me, but, on another, I understood and felt relieved, because it meant he did not expect anything from me sexually.

What concerned me more was that Nate often became angry and mean when he talked to me. He never physically abused me, but he swore at me and put me down. More and more, he insulted Martin too. As a young adult, Martin had a child-like quality that related to his developmental delay, but Nate did not seem to understand Martin or sympathize with him. Where I saw Martin as careful and thorough, Nate saw him as slow and lazy. Nate even started insulting me and Martin in racist ways. He called us "lazy, dirty Indians." I asked him why he married me if he didn't like Anishinaabeg, and who he was to say that I was either lazy or dirty when I worked harder and I was cleaner than him, and probably anyone he knew. He denied that he was racist, but his words spoke otherwise.

In May 1987, I heard there was going to be an AA Round-up in Thunder Bay. Round-ups are large annual gatherings where AA members come together to share their experiences, to participate in different program activities, and to celebrate their sobriety together. I decided to go to the round-up in Thunder Bay that year. While I was there, I met some of my old friends, and they encouraged me to move back. I felt like I needed a fresh start away from Winnipeg. I was also struck by how much more at home I felt in Thunder Bay. I went back to Winnipeg and told Nate that I was leaving him. He did not mind that I wanted a divorce, but he was concerned about what would happen to the house when I left. I told him he could keep it. He asked me who would pay the mortgage. I said he could pay for it himself, or sell the house and keep the money. I didn't care. I did not understand at the time that Nate couldn't sell the house, because the mortgage was in my name. I just asked him to give all of my furniture to Sarah whenever she moved out.

In the fall of 1987, I moved to Thunder Bay. Nate contacted a lawyer to start the divorce process, and his lawyer told me that I needed to get a divorce lawyer for myself. I was able to get free legal assistance through Legal Aid Ontario. I signed the papers to process the divorce and to sell the house, and I received a total of $17,000 in return. Over the following year, I used the money to buy furniture for my new apartment and presents for friends. I shared most of the money with others I met who were struggling financially. My divorce was finalized in 1988.

CHAPTER NINE

COMING OUT, FALLING IN LOVE, AND LIVING WITH LEAH IN THUNDER BAY AND BOSTON (1987–1991)

In the fall of 1987, at the age of thirty-seven, I moved back to Thunder Bay. It was the only time in almost twenty years that I had not had children with me during such a big transition. At first I stayed in a friend's apartment, and I started attending local AA meetings. Then I found an apartment on Algoma Street. A male AA member helped transport my things to my new place, but afterward he tried to force himself on me. He threw me on the bed, kissed me, and tried to take my pants down. I shouted at him and hit and kicked him until he got off of me. As he left, he said he would come back later to finish what he had started. I told him that if he did, I would tell everyone we knew in AA about it.

After that experience, I fell into a depression. I felt like no matter how many obstacles I overcame, I just kept meeting new ones. I had lost my car, my job, and my financial independence. I was trying to adjust to being blind. Then as I was struggling to start a new life by myself, someone tried to assault me again. I felt doomed, like maybe I really was a devil's child, as some people had said back in Ombabika. I stayed in that apartment for days. I thought about suicide. I imagined hanging myself from a beautiful old tree that stood just outside my bedroom window. Its branches reached right up to the house. At one point, I took a white sheet off of the bed and stood at the open window, thinking about crawling out on to the tree, tying the sheet around my neck and the branch, and jumping. In the end, though, I pulled myself out of my depression. I went to the Thunder Bay CNIB office and met with a social worker named Charlotte. She ended up being a very big support to me. Charlotte arranged for me to get legal aid and housing assistance. Then she put me on a waiting list for a much better apartment, and helped me move into it once I got it.

Charlotte also arranged for me to get my first treaty status card. That was not a simple process, because I had been trying to get one for over fifteen years. When I first arrived in Thunder Bay in the early 1970s, government officials could not find any record of my birth, possibly because I was born in the tuberculosis sanatorium and then was adopted right afterward. There was no government record of "Ma-Nee," the name my grandmother had given me, or of "Chacaby," my grandfather's family name. In the end, I found several different combinations of first and last names for me on record. One of the family names was my stepfather's, and the other one belonged to my first husband, Gus. One of the first names was a nickname from my childhood, and another was a Christian name that I may have been given by the Department of Indian Affairs, or maybe by the French family that adopted me in my early years.

When I tried to obtain treaty status in Winnipeg in the early 1980s, again I did not succeed. Officials there also could not find any record of my birth, but they found the name "Shacaby" in the Métis records, so they gave me a Métis status card. In fact, my grandmother always pronounced "Chacaby" with a "sh" rather than a "ch," a pronunciation I continue to use today. It was only when I returned to Thunder Bay in the late 1980s that I was able to find my birth certificate with the assistance of my CNIB social worker, Charlotte. On it, both my mother and Phillip were recorded as my biological parents. Given that my mother was eligible to be a Fort Hope band member through my grandmother, and Phillip was already a band member there, I also became officially linked to that reserve and finally received my status card.

In Thunder Bay I met up again with my older cousin, Flora, who was sober and living there at that time. She and her husband Ethan had divorced many years earlier. I often visited Flora in her apartment, where we had tea and talked about the old days. Flora teased me, telling me that I was starting to look like my grandmother, which I was glad to hear. She also told me some family secrets, for instance that Andy was not my mother's and stepfather's biological son. I thought that Andy had a right to know, especially because his biological mother had had several other children, and he might want to meet those siblings. So I called Andy in Manitoba to tell him what Flora had said, but he was not very happy about it.

Not long after I returned to Thunder Bay, I collapsed in pain on the street one day and was rushed to the hospital. After examining me, the doctors told me that I had endometriosis, which I learned is a fairly common condition. It happens when special cells from the womb grow outside of the womb. In many cases, endometriosis does not cause much harm, but in mine it had damaged some of my internal organs. The doctors recommended that they entirely remove my uterus and both of my ovaries. I was in such great pain that I agreed right away. After the procedure, I needed to go on hormone therapy, and my symptoms stopped.

Around that same time, I met a man from the Grassy Narrows Reserve who told me he was sick with AIDS, the Acquired Immune Deficiency Syndrome. In Ojibwe he called it a deadly disease that came out in 1985, which is what a lot of Native people called AIDS then. The Human Immunodeficiency Virus (HIV), the virus that causes AIDS, weakens a person's ability to fight infections, and in the end those infections can kill the person. Today people living with HIV can take medicines which help them live long, healthy lives, but that treatment was not available in 1988. The man's doctors had told him that he did not have long to live. He asked if I knew any Anishinaabe elders who could treat him with traditional medicines. I explained to him where he could get cedar and other sacred plants down by the river, and how to prepare them himself. But I honestly said that I was not sure whether traditional medicines would help him. I told him that during hard times in my life, it had helped me emotionally to rediscover my spirituality, and also to join a support group, like AA, to be with others who were experiencing the same thing. I encouraged him to spend time in the bush, to focus on his connection to the Great Spirit, and to join a support group for people with AIDS, if there were any. That was my first experience meeting a person living with AIDS. Later I learned more about how the disease was causing great harm to many gay men and Anishinaabeg.

FINDING A LESBIAN COMMUNITY

I met a number of old friends during my first months back in Thunder Bay, including a French Canadian woman named Tracey, who was about ten years older than me. Tracey had gone with me to the hospital when I fell ill with tuberculosis in 1976. Afterward, she visited me in the sanatorium. I developed a crush on her then, but I didn't speak of it. When I first returned to Thunder Bay in 1987, she and I often met in coffee shops, where we drank coffee, smoked, talked, and laughed together a lot. Tracey was about my height but she had a fuller figure, and she had permed her hair and dyed it a strawberry-blonde colour. I was drawn to her friendliness and humour. I told her I was a lesbian, and she accepted me without judgment, unlike other AA members. She told me that she had other gay and lesbian friends, and she introduced me to some of them.

I was attracted to Tracey, and I told her how I felt. That was the beginning of an unhealthy relationship that lasted for several months. Tracey flirted with me and encouraged me in my feelings for her. She had a boyfriend, but she said that she was planning to break up with him. She told me that she was in love with me, and that she wanted to be my lover. Tracey made many promises to me, but she always broke them. I bought her gifts, and, more than once, I made her a romantic dinner with candlelight and soft music, but she did not show up or even call to cancel. Still, she was very possessive of me. She always wanted to know where I was going and who I was seeing. She accused me of betraying her if she saw me with other men or women. Tracey and I never became lovers. In the end, I realized that she did not truly share my feelings and instead was using me, so I stayed away from her.

I had one other experience of dating a woman during my first year in Thunder Bay. A gay man I met introduced me to a lesbian who worked in a coffee shop. She was sociable and made it clear from the start that she liked me a lot. She asked me out to dinner, and I decided to give it a try. When we went out, she tried to hug me and kiss me on the lips right away, and that made me uncomfortable. Throughout dinner she stared at me intensely while we talked. She came on too strong and I did not feel attracted to her, so we never had a second date.

During those months, I sometimes went to public gatherings about causes that interested or concerned me, like demonstrations for women's rights. At these events I mostly listened and observed without talking to anyone. At one of those meetings, though, a friendly woman named Paige approached me and introduced herself. She was white and a few years younger than me, with short brown hair and a bright smile. She worked in the forestry department at the university. While we were talking, Paige mentioned that she was a lesbian. She said that her partner, Tabitha, worked in construction out in the bush. I was very curious to hear about her and Tabitha. It sounded like they were living the life I had always wanted. Paige also told me about the Northwestern Ontario Women's Centre, explaining that it was a warm, safe place where I could meet other women like us.

One day not much later, I went to the women's centre. The woman on staff welcomed me kindly and offered me tea. She told me a little bit about the services, and said that I could spend time there whenever I wanted. After that, I started hanging out there regularly. The women who used the centre were interested in women's rights and creating a community together. They were a mix of lesbians, bisexuals, and heterosexuals. They held many potluck suppers, which I loved because there always was good food and a feeling of celebration in the air. The potlucks reminded me of feasts I experienced as a child in Ombabika. I also started attending gay and lesbian socials which were held monthly at a local church. A mix of women went to those dances—mostly white, but also a few Anishinaabe women who were not out as lesbians anywhere else. I did not get a chance to speak with them much, because the place was loud and dark, and some of the women were drinking and getting drunk. So I kept a distance, but I was very happy to dance on my own.

Different images come to my mind when I remember my experience of coming out. Some days I felt like I was unzipping a layer of unwanted skin, and shedding it from my body like a snake, so I could move freely for the first time. Other days I felt as if I was coming out of a dark prison cell into sunlight. And then there were days I saw myself as a piece of a jigsaw puzzle that, until then, had been forced into the wrong spaces, even into the wrong puzzle. But at last I had found the right puzzle, and I fit very well (Figure 11).

FIGURE 11. HAPPY TO BE SINGLE AND COMING OUT IN THUNDER
BAY (THIRTY-EIGHT YEARS OLD, 1988).

COMING OUT PUBLICLY

During my first months in Thunder Bay, I did not tell most of my old friends and family that I was a lesbian. Then I told my daughter, Sarah, when she visited me. She was surprised. She did not know much about lesbians and had not thought about them much, negatively or positively. It had never occurred to her that I might be a lesbian, but once she considered it more, she said it made sense. She knew that I had not shared a bedroom with Nate since our first year of marriage, and that I had been unhappy with him for a long time. She asked me if I had a girlfriend. I told her not yet, because I was still getting the hang of it. Sarah told me she did not really care if I was a lesbian, because she loved me either way.

Not long after I arrived in Thunder Bay, I started attending a regular lesbian and gay AA meeting. It was the first meeting of its kind in the area. In July 1988, we wanted to celebrate the group's one-year anniversary by renting a local tour boat called the "Welcome Ship" on Lake Superior. Our request was refused, because we were an openly gay and lesbian group. We organized a public protest in response. At that protest, I was interviewed by a reporter from a local TV news station. I was worried, because I knew people might give me a hard time about it later, but I was tired of hiding. I believed that we needed to speak out against the injustices we faced. My grandmother had told me that I would face many difficulties in life. She had said that I would have to meet them with courage, like a warrior. I kept her words close to my heart when I participated in that television interview.

Still, I was not prepared for the hostility I experienced after the interview aired. Before 1988, very few people had come out publicly in Thunder Bay, and none of them were Anishinaabe. Afterward, a lot of people recognized me on the streets, in the mall, and in coffee shops. Some turned and walked away when they saw me, while others spit on the sidewalk when I went by. A number of people at regular AA meetings were mean to me and rejected me. Someone left threatening messages on my answering machine. The police came to investigate them, but they couldn't identify the caller, or make the person stop.

Most people in my family also shunned me. Several of my extended family members refused to talk to me when they saw me in public places, including my cousin Flora, who was usually pretty easygoing. A few of my relatives yelled and swore at me. Sometimes their rejection came from Christian beliefs about homosexuality being evil. Others were mad because Anishinaabeg already were struggling with prejudice, and they thought that I was making it worse by leading white people to believe that Native people were gay too. It was like they thought I had changed in a deep, horrible way. They didn't understand that I was the same old Ma-Nee, but that I had become more self-aware and open.

At that time, my stepfather was living with my stepsister Matilda in Timmins, about 600 kilometres east of Thunder Bay (Figure 2). Matilda had become sober and was trying to keep my stepdad from drinking, but he still drank secretly when he could. I called my stepdad to come out to him directly. He told me I shouldn't be a lesbian, because it was a sin. I think he would have listened to me and discussed it in a more open-minded way if Matilda hadn't taken the phone away from him. She yelled at me, saying, "My dad's not your real dad anyway, so why do you need to tell him about the evil things you do?" She said that I didn't deserve him in my life, and that I should never call him again. Then she hung up. I didn't speak to either of them again for a long time.

In the months following my TV interview, I was attacked three times when people recognized me on the streets of Thunder Bay. I don't know if any of the assaulters had been drinking or not. The first time I was targeted by a group of white women that I didn't know on St. Paul Street. They were led by a heavy, red-haired woman who came up behind me, grabbed me around the chest, and threw me up against a wall. I saw her angry expression close-up just before she hit me in the face, and tried to smash my head against the wall. I managed to push her away and duck down to the ground. I rolled up in a ball, covering my head with my arms to protect myself. The red-headed woman shouted at me, calling me all kinds of racist, sexist, and homophobic insults as she kicked me. The people who were with her started to beat me too. I thought I was going to die, but a taxi driver saw what was happening, stopped his car, and pulled me out of the group. Then he took me to St. Joseph's Hospital. My face was swollen, my nose was bleeding, my ribs ached, and I was very bruised all over my body, but at least they did not break any of my bones. The nurses at the hospital patched me up and talked about admitting me to the hospital overnight. They also wanted me to speak with the police. I just wanted to go home, so I snuck out of the hospital and spent the next few days alone in my apartment. I did not tell anybody else what had happened, and I did not open the door for anyone.

The second time I was assaulted, the group was led by one of my female relatives. I was walking down a sidewalk when out of nowhere she grabbed me and started hitting me and calling me names. Again, I dropped to the ground and rolled up in a ball to protect myself. She was with four Anishinaabe men and women who also beat and kicked me. The whole time, she shouted at me, saying that I was ruining life for other Native people by being a lesbian. Once again, the beating only stopped when a taxi driver came to help me and managed to pull me into his car. He rescued me soon after the attack began, so they did not injure me as much as the first group had, although I still had bruises all over my body. That taxi driver was a white man, like the first one. I don't remember ever seeing any Anishinaabe men or any women driving taxis in Thunder Bay in the 1980s. He later told me that he witnessed many drunken fights on the streets, and he usually avoided them, but he could tell something was different about the way they were assaulting me. He saw that I was not fighting back, and he thought they might kill me. Like the first taxi driver, he wanted to take me to the hospital, but I asked him to drop me off at the women's centre instead. He did, and my friends there took care of me.

The relative who attacked me on the sidewalk was the same person who came after me the third time. That time, I saw her before she reached me, and I ran away. She and another Native woman chased after me. I tripped and fell. Then I heard one of them say, "Give me that knife," as they approached me. I jumped up and took off, running as fast as I could. I was terrified! I crossed a road in front of traffic to get to the women's centre, which was not far away. A few cars honked at me, but I made it there before my relative and her friend caught me.

Once I realized how many people had seen my interview—and how aggressive some of them were with me—I was pretty scared. I did not understand why certain people seemed so threatened by me, as if I had some great power that could harm them. I became much more careful. I stayed home a lot. When I did go somewhere on foot, I always found someone to walk with me, and I did not go very far. Instead, I went to two or three nearby places that I considered safe. I stopped going to the inner city unless I had at least two other people with me. There were a few kind people outside of the lesbian and gay community who supported me during that time. Charlotte, my CNIB social worker, was one of them. She didn't care if I was gay, she just wanted me to get proper help when I needed it. When Charlotte found out that I had been beaten up because people recognized me from the television news, she called the police and tried to get me some protection, but nothing came of it.

FALLING IN LOVE WITH LEAH

In December 1988, Paige and Tabitha had a winter solstice party at their big log cabin in the woods outside of Thunder Bay. That night there was a full moon and the party was very festive. There was good food inside of the house, a bonfire and sauna outside, and some women were sledding and making angels in the snow. I was watching all of the different people in the house when I noticed a young white woman who I had never seen before. She was slim and a bit taller than me. She wore a sweater and a long skirt, and her light brown hair fell partway down her back. Later, when I was outside chopping wood for the firepit, she approached me. She introduced herself as Leah, and said she was visiting from Boston for a month. We talked a little about the party, and while we were chatting, I started to light a cigarette. Leah said something like, "You know, those aren't good for you." I thought, "Hmm, she's one of those women. I'm not going to bother with her, because she doesn't like me smoking." We did not talk much more. Afterward, when we were inside of the house again, I continued to watch her. Tabitha came over and whispered to me that I should ask Leah out. She teased me, saying that I always talked about all of the women I liked, but I never was brave enough to actually approach any of them.

The next day I decided to take up Tabitha's challenge. I went to look for Leah at the women's centre, because I had heard she was working there on a computer. I asked her to go out for coffee, and she agreed. At the coffee shop, she asked me many questions about my life. I didn't know how to answer some of them, but she was interested in what I had to say, and I found it very easy to talk to her. She had kind eyes and a gentle spirit. I asked her about her life and where Boston was in the U.S. She told me it was on the coast of the Atlantic Ocean, explaining that the ocean is like Lake Superior, but much larger and salty. That fascinated me, because I had never been to an ocean, and I always thought that oceans were made of fresh water, like lakes. When we left the coffee shop, I gave Leah my phone number. She called me the next day, and we talked more on the phone.

I saw Leah again soon afterward at a party. I only knew a few of the women who were there, so I kept to myself and quietly observed everything going on around me. I saw her sitting across from me, and we smiled and waved to each other silently. Later, we spoke and decided to leave the party. We walked back to my apartment, talking the whole time. In fact, we talked most of the night. I told her a lot about my life, and she told me many things about hers. I was surprised to learn that she was only twenty-two years old, because she had had very interesting experiences and seemed wise beyond her years. She had recently finished university, where she had worked in a library and volunteered as a rape crisis counsellor. She also had participated in her college's lesbian, gay, and bisexual group for four years. Leah had been that group's coordinator during her final year there. Like me, she had only dated a couple of women, and she had never had a female lover. The two of us talked, kissed, and held each other that night, and then we fell asleep.

FIGURE 12. MAKING A SNOW ANGEL DURING A WALK WITH LEAH, NOT LONG AFTER WE MET IN THUNDER BAY (THIRTY-EIGHT YEARS OLD, 1988).

The next day, after Leah left, I felt excited and scared. My heart raced and my body ached in ways I had not felt before. I called Tabitha and exclaimed, "Oh my God, something's happening to me!" She asked, "What happened? Are you hurt?" I said, "No, I met this person I really like, and I think I'm having a heart attack!" I told her about my night with Leah and the symptoms I was having. She listened and then she laughed. She explained that what I was feeling was normal, and that many women experience those sensations when they are strongly attracted to someone. I was scared of what might happen to my body if I went further with Leah, but Tabitha assured me that it would not kill me. She encouraged me to relax and let go the next time I was with Leah.

And I did. Leah stayed in Thunder Bay for a couple more weeks, and we were together for most of that time. We went for a lot of walks in the snow (Figure 12), and we spent a lot of time in bed. I discovered sexual pleasure for the first time. There were moments when I felt like I had walked up the side of a great mountain and then joyfully fell off the other side, dropping right off the planet into blissful nothingness. It was a wonderful, exploratory time for both of us. I started to understand that this was what my grandmother had talked about when she told me that, one day, I would become close to a special person, and we would experience deep pleasure and happiness together.

When it came time for Leah to leave Thunder Bay, we agreed that I would visit her the next month in the U.S., and while I was there, I would see an eye specialist. My eye doctors in Thunder Bay were having a hard time categorizing my blindness and identifying all of the factors that might be causing it. There was an eye institute in Boston where Leah arranged for me to see a specialist, and CNIB agreed to pay for my trip. As it turned out, my medical examinations in the U.S. did not add much to what the doctors in Thunder Bay already knew about my visual impairment. But I was happy to visit Leah in her home for a few weeks. At that point, she was sharing an apartment with three other women outside of Boston. We took many walks and I got to know some of her friends. We also went to the ocean. The first time I saw the Atlantic, I could not contain myself. When I caught a glimpse of the waves ahead of me beyond the dunes, I took off running, leaving Leah and her friends behind. I danced on the beach and laid down in the cold water. I was wearing my big northern parka, so I did not get too cold, even though I ended up dripping wet.

By the end of our visit, Leah and I agreed that I would return to Canada to make arrangements for my apartment and other things, and then I would come back to the United States to live with her. As a treaty Indian, I did not need special permission to live or work in the U.S. Leah had applied and been accepted for a year-long position in Europe, but she postponed taking it for one year when I decided to move to Massachusetts. In March 1989, I returned to Canada and went to see my kids in Winnipeg, to let them know my plans. Then I packed, gave away, or sold my things, and moved out of my apartment in Thunder Bay. My friends threw a nice going-away party for me. Many people said that they were going to miss me, and that I shouldn't go, but I told them that I needed to follow my heart.

LIVING IN MASSACHUSETTS

When I returned to Massachusetts, Leah and I continued living with her roommates outside of Boston. She had started working as a health educator and a counsellor in a housing project clinic in the city, so each morning I saw her off at the train station when she went to work. During the day, I explored the surrounding area on my own. It was hard for me to get around, because I did not know the roads and couldn't read street signs. Leah encouraged me to use a cane I had been given by CNIB. I tried walking with it a couple of times, but I didn't feel comfortable with it. I decided to just use my old approach of walking carefully and slowly, asking for directions when needed, and stopping when my vision became too poor. Usually I could see a limited distance in front of me, but there were times when my vision completely clouded over for an hour or two. When that happened, I just sat down wherever I was, and I waited until my sight returned. That could be a frustrating, vulnerable, and frightening experience, especially because I never knew exactly when my vision would come back. So when I was on my own during those first months, I mostly travelled on foot in a small area around our house—to AA meetings, coffee shops, and a nearby cemetery, where I ate lunch by the river under maple and oak trees.

One day I was feeling bored, and on the spur of the moment I decided to find a gay and lesbian AA meeting in Boston that I had heard about. I had met a few lesbians and gay men at a local AA meeting, and one of them had explained to me how to reach the group in Boston using public transportation. I took the train into the city and quickly got lost, but I asked for directions and found the place in the end. I walked to the building down a long, narrow street made of cobblestone. I remember singing as I walked, enjoying the sound my feet made on the stones as I passed over them. Some people I met at the AA meeting that day invited me to go with them to a party. They took me to a gay bar where each room was lit up in a different neon colour, like green or pink. It looked amazing to me, because I had never seen anything like it before. Many of the men at the bar were wearing leather clothes, and were only half-dressed, which shocked me at first. But they all were very friendly and welcoming, and quickly put me at ease. After a while, my new friends introduced me to a woman who was driving in the direction of my house, so she dropped me off. I returned home after dark to find Leah very worried, because I had not left a note when I went out. She was relieved to see me come home safely. The next week, we had a good laugh when we picked up a gay paper and saw a series of photographs of local nightlife, including one of me in my big winter coat talking to some of the half-naked men at the leather bar.

A few months later, Leah and I rented a large, sunny third-floor apartment that was closer to Boston and her work. Our new home had smooth hardwood floors, a big, bright kitchen, and many books and plants. When we were there together, we talked, played music, danced, and worked on our different projects. We both enjoyed photography, and I kept a journal and painted carefully when my eyesight would allow it. Mostly I painted birds and animals to express my dreams, visions, and feelings. At the time, I was thinking a lot about who I was and where I was in the world, so I also started painting self-portraits.

Being with Leah, I became aware of how much I smoked and how it was affecting my health, so I tried to cut down. I didn't smoke in the apartment. Over time that helped me to reduce from three packs to one pack of cigarettes a day. I continued to walk Leah to work each morning, and then during the day, on my own, I explored the streets, cafés, parks, and train tracks near our new apartment. In public and at work, Leah and I were careful about our relationship, not bringing it up, but also not denying it. Sometimes we held hands when we went for a walk together. Once on the sidewalk near our house, some teenagers called us names. Leah told them that they should mind their own business. I was frightened, because I had been beaten up before when I was recognized on the streets as a lesbian. We continued on our way, and luckily nothing else happened.

WORKING IN A HALFWAY HOUSE
WITH PREGNANT WOMEN IN RECOVERY

In the summer of 1989, I learned of a nearby job opening for a counsel-lor, to work with pregnant women recovering from addiction to alcohol and other drugs. I applied and was happy when they offered me the job. During my interview, I was open about my visual impairment. My new supervisor and other colleagues were very supportive and changed some of the program procedures when I was hired, so that it was easier for me to write and review notes. At the beginning of shifts, my co-workers gave me an update and read recent log entries aloud to me. At the end of my shifts, I told the program secretary everything I wanted recorded in the log, and she wrote it down for me. I also spoke into a small tape recorder during the day, and used it to record training sessions and meetings, so I could remember details about them later.

The halfway house where I worked usually took in women, as well as some of their newborn babies. Most of them were in their late teens or early twenties. They came from diverse racial and ethnic backgrounds—African American, Latina, white, and Native American. Many of them had been homeless right before they entered the program. All of them only became sober after learning that they were pregnant, so they were still in very early stages of their recovery. As counsellors, we were responsible for working with all of the women, but we were also assigned particular clients to work with more closely. The women stayed in the house for nine months. During their first months, they worked on staying sober, building their life skills, taking care of their pregnancies, and preparing for delivery. The other counsellors and I went with them to AA or Narcotics Anonymous meetings, prenatal visits, and the supermarket. After their deliveries, we focused on infant care and household management, and later we helped them to find housing.

In the year that I worked at the halfway house, five women asked me to be with them while they delivered their babies. Each of those births was a wonderful, moving experience for me. One of the babies was born in an ambulance right outside of the halfway house, because the woman had such a fast delivery. I was sad when one baby was born addicted to cocaine, with foam coming out of his mouth and his whole body shaking with tremors. The mother had gone through her withdrawal during her pregnancy, but the baby needed to do it all over again after he was born.

Seeing that infant go through terrible symptoms like the ones that I experienced during alcohol withdrawal was heartbreaking.

My job working with pregnant women in recovery was emotionally challenging sometimes, but it was also very rewarding. Most of the women that I worked with were determined to stay sober. They were interesting people too, some fierce and humorous, and others quiet and gentle. I learned a lot about other cultures while I was working in the halfway house. I did not come out as a lesbian to the house residents, but once in a while they guessed and I did not confirm or deny it. By the time they had guessed I was gay, we usually had a close enough relationship that they did not seem to care, even if they still had some prejudices against homosexuals.

SOCIAL, POLITICAL, AND FAMILY GATHERINGS

On weekends, Leah and I often went to gay and lesbian clubs and events where we danced for hours. I also continued going to gay and lesbian AA meetings, even though, at that stage of my life, I had already been sober for fifteen years. When I contributed at AA meetings, I tended to focus on recent experiences and positive lessons, rather than discussing my drinking history. I especially enjoyed the huge annual Boston gay and lesbian AA roundups, where there were many interesting speakers and activities. Sometimes Leah joined me for AA meetings when they were open to people who were not alcoholics. She herself did not drink or use other drugs. Leah had grown up with an alcoholic parent, so she understood AA's importance to me.

One of my favourite events in Boston was the annual gay pride parade (Figure 13). It was the largest gay and lesbian event that I have ever attended, with tens of thousands, if not hundreds of thousands, of participants. I was moved by how many people were there, and the huge variety of gay, lesbian, bisexual, and transgender people walking and dancing in the streets. Leah and I always tried to see as much of the parade as we could. We liked to walk backward through it, and sometimes we climbed trees to get a better view. I remember once getting stuck in a tree and not being able to get down again until a kind man came out of the parade to help me.

Almost all of the participants in the gay pride parades looked like anyone else that I saw walking down a city street in summertime, but they were there to celebrate and it was like a festival. A small number of people were dressed in ways that shocked me, like couples wearing sadomasochist

FIGURE 13. WALKING IN THE BOSTON GAY PRIDE PARADE (THIRTY-NINE YEARS OLD, 1989).

gear, with one person leading the other around by a chain on a dog collar. Someone explained to me that those couples were only dressing up, and that both partners found that kind of role-playing erotic. I understood that people were diverse in what they desired and how they expressed themselves, and that as long as they were not hurting anyone, it was their right to be the way they wanted to be. But having experienced real abuse and torture, I could not understand why anyone would enjoy acting it out, and it disturbed me to see it.

A couple of times, Leah and I also travelled to Washington, DC with friends to participate in national demonstrations. In April 1989, we took part in the National March for Women's Equality, which focused on increasing women's reproductive freedom. Again I was surprised by the size of the demonstration, because hundreds of thousands of people gathered together for it. I was also fascinated to see so many famous buildings and memorials around me as we marched. When I was a child in Ombabika, my schoolteachers had shown my class photographs of the White House, the Lincoln Memorial, and other important buildings in the U.S. capital city. My cousin Paula and I had talked about going to Washington, DC to see them one day, so to actually find myself there, thirty years later, was exciting for me.

In October 1989, Leah and I returned to Washington, DC to join tens of thousands of people who were protesting the national shortage of decent, affordable housing. That day we also saw the AIDS Memorial Quilt, because it was being displayed in a large open area at the park near the White House (Figure 14). The quilt was made out of thousands of three-by-six-foot panels, each uniquely designed in the memory of a person who had died of AIDS. The size of the quilt amazed and saddened me at the same time. I was moved to see such a beautiful, heartfelt tribute to all of the people who had died of AIDS. Looking at the quilt, I also thought about the countless Anishinaabeg who died in smallpox and measles epidemics after Europeans colonized the Americas. I wondered what a quilt for them would look like.

In late 1989, Leah and I flew to Winnipeg to visit Martin and Sarah. I had not yet told Martin that I was a lesbian, so first I called him to let him know. He told me that he had always heard people say that homosexuality was wrong, but he personally did not seem bothered by me coming out

FIGURE 14. PART OF THE AIDS QUILT DISPLAYED IN FRONT
OF THE WHITE HOUSE IN WASHINGTON, DC (THIRTY-NINE YEARS
OLD, 1989).

to him. When we visited Winnipeg, Leah and I stayed in a motel. At that time, Sarah was living with an Anishinaabe man named Ken and helping him to raise his two daughters from a previous relationship. Ken was a stocky, broad-shouldered man about the same height as Sarah. He wore his hair short in the front and shoulder-length at the back. In the past, I had heard Ken say insulting things about gay people, but he was polite to me and Leah when we visited them. During our visit, Sarah was in the seventh month of her first pregnancy. She was tired but in good spirits. After Sarah and Martin met Leah, they both told me they liked her and how she treated me, especially because they knew how unhappy I had been in my previous relationships.

Leah and I returned to Boston by train so we could visit friends and family in Thunder Bay and Sault Ste. Marie along the way. In Sault Ste. Marie we saw my old friend Jane. During that visit, I didn't hide that I was a lesbian or that Leah was my partner, but I don't remember if Jane and I spoke about it openly. I saw Jane again a year later, and I know we talked more about it then. At that time Jane asked me when and how I first knew that I was a lesbian. I explained that I had always been attracted to women, but for years I didn't tell her or anyone else, because I was afraid of how they would react. Jane said she did not mind that I was a lesbian. Then I told her that her cousin, Bonnie, and my cousin, Angela, also had been lesbians, or at least, they had been in a lesbian relationship together. Jane said she didn't believe me, and we stopped talking about it.

RETURNING TO THUNDER BAY

From the start of my relationship with Leah, some of my friends had warned me that our sixteen-year age difference would be a problem. For a long time, it wasn't. In the summer of 1990, though, it became clear that we were at very different stages of our lives and this would become a challenge for our relationship. That summer I turned forty, and Leah turned twenty-four. She had postponed taking a year-long position in Europe when she met me, so she had to decide whether to take it or give it up completely. The decision brought up bigger questions about any long-term future we might have together. I would have been happy to marry Leah and settle down with her for life, if it had been legal at the time. But I did not want to have any more children. I had spent most of my life raising my kids and foster kids, and I saw that as part of my past, not my future. Leah on the other hand was not yet ready to commit to me or to anyone else for the rest of her life. One thing she was certain about, though, was that she wanted to have children one day.

These were major differences, and we could not resolve them. Leah decided to take the position that she had been offered overseas. When she did, I gave notice at my job. I did not want to stay in Massachusetts alone. Giving up the loving home that we had made together and watching Leah pack her things and prepare to leave was very hard. We had not fought. We still loved each other. But we did not know if we were separating for a year or for good. Several of my friends in Massachusetts tried to convince me to stay. One of them, a subway conductor, offered to move in with me, share the rent, and help me get around when I needed transportation. I also thought about staying because I was afraid to return to Thunder Bay. Only a couple of years earlier, I had been beaten up on the streets for being a lesbian. I did not know if I would experience such harassment and violence there again. But Thunder Bay was my home, and I wanted to go back. I knew I had to have courage and be true to myself there, regardless of how others perceived me.

When I returned to Thunder Bay, Tabitha and Paige helped me move into a new apartment. Soon I was going by the women's centre and all of the other places I used to visit regularly. I felt very sad about separating from Leah, but my lesbian friends were sympathetic and supportive. Not long after I returned, I started volunteering for the local AIDS Committee, first helping them develop a brochure for Anishinaabeg, and then translating English to Ojibwe and Cree in HIV/AIDS education workshops. At the end of 1990, the AIDS Committee hired me to co-facilitate a series of workshops in more isolated areas of Ontario. HIV was on the rise in those places because of the number of people moving back and forth from cities, especially men who had sex with men, people who used intravenous drugs, and sex workers and their sexual partners. I was hired for fifteen weeks to help lead workshops in Kenora, Dryden, and Sioux Lookout and their nearby reserves, about 300–400 kilometres northwest of Thunder Bay (Figure 2). I carefully prepared my workshops (Figure 15). I was happy that they went well, especially because they focused on such a sensitive topic.

FIGURE 15. WRITING NOTES FOR AN HIV/AIDS EDUCATION
WORKSHOP IN NORTHERN ONTARIO (FORTY YEARS OLD, 1991).

When my work for the AIDS Committee ended, I was only one week short of the sixteen weeks needed to receive unemployment benefits. I tried to sign up for disability assistance again, but that was a difficult process. Social services staff explained to me that the system was not designed for people to go off of disability assistance when they found work. They told me that, the next time I took a job, I should make sure it was long-term and better paying than the support I was receiving from the government, because once I gave up that support, I would not get it again. At that point, I was receiving $700 a month in disability assistance. I had a large apartment that cost me $500, so I had the possibility of subletting one or two rooms if needed. Otherwise, I only had $200 left for utilities and groceries. It was challenging getting by on so little, so after some time CNIB arranged for me to receive an additional $200 a month. In the last twenty years, my social assistance package has only increased by another $100 per month.

Some of my family and others who knew me before I came out continued to be hostile toward me when I returned to Canada. Several of my cousins glared at me and refused to talk when they saw me in Thunder Bay. I also had an unpleasant experience when I travelled to Winnipeg to see my daughter Sarah and her baby girl, Valerie. It was just before Christmas in 1990, so I brought a turkey and presents for everyone. We had agreed that I would stay with Sarah and her boyfriend, Ken. On the first night, Ken became angry and shouted homophobic insults at me. He kicked me out of their apartment in the middle of that cold, winter night. I found a pay phone and called my brother, Andy, who still lived in Winnipeg with his girlfriend, Lori. I asked if I could stay with them for the rest of that night, and he agreed. While I was there, I explained why Ken had kicked me out, and I ended up coming out to Andy. Andy asked me why I had never told him that I was a lesbian when we lived together. I explained that I had been struggling with it myself at the time. During that visit, Andy acted like he was okay with me being a lesbian. Later, though, when I was back in Thunder Bay, he phoned me when he was drunk. He said that homosexuality was wrong and he did not accept it. I told him that we both would just have to live our lives the best way we knew how.

From my work with different social services organizations, I understood that young gays and lesbians had high rates of suicide. My own experiences with rejection, hostility, and violence when I came out helped me to understand why some young people became suicidal. But I did have one positive family experience during that time—a warm reunion with my step-father and stepsister in Timmins. I had spoken with them by phone while I was living in Massachusetts. On the phone, my stepdad was very loving to me, and Matilda told me that she was no longer angry at me for being lesbian. She also said that my stepdad missed me a lot and wanted to see me. So after I returned to Thunder Bay, I went to see them and we had a good visit.

For my first six months back in Thunder Bay, Leah and I continued to write to each other regularly. We also recorded tape cassettes which we sent by mail. Sometimes we talked on the phone, but that was very expensive, so our conversations didn't last long. At the beginning of 1991, she completed her work in Europe early and asked me if I wanted her to come to Thunder Bay. I agreed. We were cautious with each other when she arrived, at first sleeping in separate rooms in my apartment. But soon we became lovers again, and we settled into a new home life together. Leah tried to find work, but that was not easy. She was a U.S. citizen, and before hiring her, a Canadian employer would have had to prove there were no Canadians who could do the same job. Instead, she picked up a string of odd jobs under the table, like carpentry, babysitting, and modelling for an art class.

In February 1991, the Fort Hope Reserve chief heard that I had been conducting HIV/AIDS education workshops, so he invited me to hold a series of them in Fort Hope. Leah and I signed on to do that job together. It was winter and the roads were blocked by snow, so they flew us to the reserve by a small plane. After we arrived, the chief told us that he had changed his mind and no longer wanted us to do the workshops. He did not say why, but we got the impression that it was because he had heard or guessed that we were in a lesbian relationship. I decided to go door-to-door to talk to elders about the need for AIDS education on the reserve. During those visits, I again met Edith, the wife of Phillip, the man who may have been my biological father. She was very friendly and welcoming. Edith and her elder friends went to talk to the chief about allowing the workshops, and then he agreed to go ahead with it.

Leah and I facilitated our first workshop at midday, with all of the old women lined up in the front row, and a group of young people behind them. The elders had a good sense of humour and giggled among themselves when I explained some things in Ojibwe and Cree, like when I said they should think of a condom as a rain jacket for a penis. The workshop went very well. Afterward, Leah and I started to pack up our things, but then another group of ten or twelve people arrived and asked us to do it again. So we did. And that same pattern continued through the day and into the night, until we finished our last workshop at 2:00 a.m. Then Leah and I stayed at Fort Hope for a while longer visiting with Phillip's family. We cooked meals together, went ice fishing, and took snowmobile rides across the frozen lake. We also visited Phillip's grave (Figure 16). By the time we left, the chief had warmed up to us, and he took us around the reserve to show us the school and the clinic. I was happy to see that there were several regularly scheduled AA meetings, unlike twenty years earlier when I first visited Fort Hope and introduced the AA program.

Leah and I returned to Thunder Bay and continued going to the usual lesbian socials, potlucks, and dances. We spent time with Paige, Tabitha, and other long-time friends. We also made some new friends. They were mostly shy, young, lesbian and bisexual women, both Native and white, who liked to come by our house to visit. Sometimes we went hiking and camping outside of Thunder Bay. One night in April we camped with our friend Nancy near some rapids. The snow was still on the ground. The river was partially frozen over and it was a bitterly cold night, so we all huddled together in our tent to keep warm. Nancy was a single mother with five- and six-year-old daughters who Leah and I sometimes babysat. She was a kind, gentle person who was very loving with her kids. When she told us a few weeks later that she and her daughters needed a place to live, we agreed that they could move into our large apartment and help pay the rent.

THE END OF MY FIRST LESBIAN RELATIONSHIP

Leah continued to be frustrated that she could not get reliable work in Thunder Bay. In the end, she decided to leave and go back to the U.S. We separated for the second time in June 1991. Again, we did not fight, and again, there were many tears. I decided to go with her by train back to Boston, to stay with her for her first few weeks there. But she was very busy trying to set up a new life—sleeping on the floor of a friend's house while looking for work and an apartment—so I left earlier.

When I returned to Thunder Bay, I felt heartbroken and betrayed. I had thought that I could convince Leah to stay with me, and that we would

FIGURE 16. IN FORT HOPE, VISITING THE GRAVE OF PHILLIP, THE
MAN WHO MAY HAVE BEEN MY BIOLOGICAL FATHER (FORTY-ONE
YEARS OLD, 1991).

make our life together last long-term. I went through a hard time emotionally. Tabitha, Paige, and my other lesbian friends helped by talking with me and keeping me busy. They assured me that I would fall in love again, but I didn't believe them. I didn't regret my relationship with Leah. For the first time in my life, I had experienced romance, passion, and a mutually respectful partnership. I had come to know what a healthy relationship could be. I knew that, no matter what else happened, I would not settle for less in the future. Leah and I stayed in touch through letters and phone calls, but it was a long time before we could see each other again and not feel conflicted about our relationship. By then, we both were in long-term, committed relationships with other partners.

CHAPTER TEN

MEETING GRACE AND BUILDING A LIFE TOGETHER IN KAMINISTIQUIA (1991–2004)

In June 1991, I returned to Thunder Bay and to the apartment I was sharing with Nancy and her daughters. At that time, I was surprised to learn that Nancy had started her first lesbian relationship with a woman she met while I was away. Nancy was giddy and excited, and I would have been happy for her, except that I thought her new partner was not very nice. Even worse, the woman had moved into our apartment before I got back. Nancy's new girlfriend shouted and swore a lot. She verbally abused Nancy, calling her insulting names. Nancy had been in an abusive relationship with her daughters' father, and she did not seem to realize that she had fallen into a similar one with this woman. It was the first time that I saw that lesbian relationships, like heterosexual ones, were sometimes dysfunctional and even violent. I tried to talk to Nancy about it, but she was not yet in a place where she could hear my concerns.

To get away from that disturbing situation at home, I started staying overnight with friends. I also decided to do some travelling. That summer I knew a number of women who were going to different music festivals within a day's drive of Thunder Bay. I offered to join them and share gas and other costs. First, Paige and I went to a small women's event in Fort Frances, about 350 kilometres west of Thunder Bay. While I was there, I met a woman from Thunder Bay who wanted to become involved with me. I was not very attracted to her, but she seemed nice and I knew that I had to move on after my breakup with Leah. So I agreed to see her again once we returned to Thunder Bay. Over the following weeks, I visited her a few times and we became involved for a brief period. I quickly knew, though, that the relationship was not what I wanted, so I ended it.

FINDING LOVE WITH GRACE

In the second week of July 1991, I made a road trip with Tabitha and Paige to a folk music festival in Winnipeg. When I arrived there, I wandered from tent to tent on my own, listening to different acts and enjoying the music. A couple of times I passed a slender white woman of about my own height who wore her thick black hair in a long braid. She waved to me, so I waved back. The second time that happened, we stopped and chatted a bit about the festival. Then she asked me if I wanted to have a coffee with her. We ended up sitting on the grass, drinking coffee, and talking for hours.

The woman's name was Grace. She was thirty-four years old, and she worked in a tree nursery. She told me she lived in a cabin in the bush near Dryden, Ontario, about 300 kilometres northwest of Thunder Bay (Figure 2). I couldn't believe she lived all by herself in the wilderness. I had not met many women who, like me, were happy to live without electricity or running water, but the more we talked, the more I saw that we valued similar things. I told her that I was a lesbian, and that I had recently broken up with my first love. She said that she was interested in women, but the way she talked about her male boss made me think that they might be involved, so I assumed that she was not available. By the end of our conversation, I was very drawn to her and how grounded and peaceful she seemed to be. I was confident we would become good friends.

In the following weeks, Grace and I wrote letters to each other. We agreed I would come to Dryden to visit her at her cabin for a few nights in late July, to celebrate my forty-first birthday. When I arrived there, I discovered she really did live in the wilderness. Her house sat on 160 acres of land about a forty-five-minute drive from Dryden. We went for long walks through the woods and meadows on her property. She had built her own cabin, workshop, woodshed, and an outhouse. Each evening we sat outside of her cabin by a bonfire, and Grace played guitar and sang lovely songs which she had written herself, including one that she wrote for me. I also played one of her drums and sang songs to her in Ojibwe. At night, it was quiet and serene. The only sounds we heard were crickets, frogs, owls, and—once in a while—the calls of large animals.

Grace and I told each other our life stories during that visit. I learned that her grandparents were Old Order Mennonite, a religious group that avoids modern technology. They had used a horse and buggy rather than a car for transportation. When Grace's father grew up, he became a Mennonite minister. Grace also told me that she had adopted and raised a ten-year-old Ojibwa girl, Diana, who had already reached adulthood. Grace had been in a relationship with an abusive man for many years, and since then, she had been alone. She told me she was a lesbian, although she had never had a female lover. I was very attracted to Grace, both physically and emotionally. When I looked into her deep brown eyes or touched her hand, I felt a surge of energy as if I was coming alive again. But after my recent breakup with Leah, I was cautious, and Grace was also. We did not speak openly about our attraction for each other at that time.

FIGURE 17. AT THE ENTRANCE TO THE MICHIGAN WOMYN'S MUSIC FESTIVAL (FORTY-ONE YEARS OLD, 1991).

Earlier in the summer, I had made arrangements to go to a women's music festival in Michigan in August. From there I had planned to get a ride to the U.S. west coast, so I could visit friends in Seattle. I did go to Michigan as planned, and I enjoyed it very much (Figure 17). Afterward, though, I decided not to go on to the west coast. I wanted to see Grace again, sooner rather than later. When I returned to Thunder Bay, I found a lot of letters from Grace waiting for me at my house. I wrote to her, and she came to pick me up and take me back to Dryden for another visit.

Grace and I became lovers the second time I went to Dryden. I was excited that such a beautiful woman wanted me as much as I wanted her. To me, she seemed natural like the land itself. Grace had a wonderful mix of qualities. She was both serious and easygoing, both cautious and fearless. I stayed with her for a few days and then she drove me back to Thunder Bay, where she stayed with me for a few days. When it was time for her to go, we decided that I would go back up to Dryden with her again for a few days. We continued going back and forth together like that until October, when Grace decided to move in with me. She kept her property and her cabin, but she took a job that had opened up for a counsellor at a battered women's shelter near Thunder Bay. Luckily, Nancy and her girlfriend had already moved out of my apartment and into one of their own, so Grace and I had my place all to ourselves.

LOSING OUR GRANDSON

Not long after Grace and I started living together, her daughter Diana came to live with us, along with her Ojibwa boyfriend, Randy, and their one-year-old son, Quinn. Diana was a short young woman with straight black hair that fell to her shoulders. Randy was about six feet tall. Both he and Diana were members of the White Dog Reserve in northern Ontario. I liked Diana, and I could relate to her experiences and attitudes. Like me, she had lived through a very difficult childhood, which she had survived with a strong sense of humour. Also, like me, both Diana and Randy struggled with addiction.

Diana had not stopped drinking during her first pregnancy, so her son Quinn had the small eyes and other facial features often seen with fetal alcohol syndrome, a condition that causes physical defects and developmental delays in children. Diana had become pregnant again in 1991, so she moved in with us for the last few months of her pregnancy. We wanted to help her be sober and healthy, and also to assist her with Quinn. Grace was by Diana's side when Diana delivered her daughter, Abigail, at the hospital. I was outside the room, playing with Quinn in the hall. I remember that Quinn became excited when he heard his baby sister crying for the first time.

Diana and her family moved into their own apartment not long after Abigail was born, but they continued to have difficulties. Within a couple of months, Children's Aid took the two children into custody and placed them in foster care. Grace and I tried to keep in close contact with the children, Diana, and the agency during that time. Within one month, Diana and Randy were told they would get custody of Quinn and Abigail again. In early February 1992, though, on the night before the children were supposed to be returned to Diana and Randy, Quinn died while in foster care. We were told that he had died of Sudden Infant Death Syndrome. All of us were beside ourselves with grief.

Afterward, Diana, Randy, and Abigail drove back to the White Dog Reserve, 550 kilometres northwest of Thunder Bay, to prepare for the funeral. Grace and I borrowed a truck that could hold a coffin, and we followed them to the reserve in the freezing cold weather, carrying Quinn's body. A three-day wake was held in the home of Quinn's great-grandparents. It was heartbreaking to see him lying in the casket. We became even more upset when we saw that he had a large bruise on the side of his head. Already we had doubted that he had died of Sudden Infant Death Syndrome, because—at two years of age—he seemed too old for that. But seeing his head injury made us wonder whether he actually died of abuse or neglect in foster care. Several people at the wake told us stories of other children who had died in foster care.

After the funeral, Diana and Randy decided to stay and live on the reserve with Abigail. Grace and I returned to Thunder Bay and reported our concerns about Quinn's injury to Children's Aid. They said that there would be an investigation. A year later, they still did not have any new information about Quinn's death, so we asked a journalist friend to follow up on it. She had Quinn's autopsy report examined. In it, there was no mention of the bruise on Quinn's head. Instead the document simply stated there was no known cause of death. To this day, we do not know how Quinn died.

BUILDING A HOME TOGETHER

During our first year together, Grace and I were not content living in a city. We tried to go camping as often as possible. Grace had an old truck that we called "the Black Beast," because of its colour, size, and heavy use of fuel. She built a wooden frame on its back and covered it with tarps, so we could sleep in it when we were camping or when we went to music festivals. In the summer of 1992, we returned to the four-day Winnipeg folk festival where we had met the year before. Our vehicle was a funny sight parked next to all of the newer cars, campers, and vans we saw there. Sometime during this period, Grace, Paige, Tabitha, and I also talked about the 1986 Winnipeg music festival. We realized that we had all been there together during that moving moment when the audience joined hands and sang in a circle with the performer in the women-only tent.

In the summer of 1992, the four of us took a road trip to Ombabika and Auden. It had been twenty-two years since I left Auden, wounded and in pain, when I ran away from Gus with my brother and children. Not many people travelled to that area by car anymore, so the road was in a bad state. There were sections where we had difficulty getting through, even though it was summertime. Most of Ombabika and Auden had been abandoned, and all of the houses I remembered were fallen down and overgrown with bushes. In Ombabika, I was struck by the small size of some of the buildings I recognized from childhood. They seemed a lot bigger in my memories. I could not find my mom and stepdad's cabin where I thought it should be, and I had difficulty finding my favourite places in the bush, like the boulder with a hollow that had been my safe place as a child. In Auden, I found my mother-in-law's old house. After I entered it, I was shocked to find that there was a snake nest on the floor, and snakes were hanging off the doors and rafters. I took off like a shot, running right out of that house and not looking back.

When Grace and I returned to Thunder Bay, we started looking for ways that we could live outside of the city and stop spending our limited income on rent. In the end, Grace and two of our friends pooled their savings to come up with the $20,000 needed to buy a property. In October 1992, she and I moved onto a twenty-acre piece of land in Kaministiquia, forty kilometres outside of Thunder Bay. The property was made up of fields and wet meadows, but there also were some wooded patches. It did not have any buildings on it. Around the same time, we bought a bunk-house that had been used to house workers at an Abitibi Pulp and Paper Company camp in Savant Lake, which is about 200 kilometres west of Ombabika. Actually, we bought the first section of a much longer bunk-house that had been split into three pieces. Our piece was fifty-two feet long by twenty-four feet wide, and contained eight small bedrooms and four bathrooms. We decided to place it near an old bridge that connected the gravel roads on both sides of the Kaministiquia River. Before the house arrived, friends helped us lay weeping tiles and a foundation of wooden beams. To transport the building, it needed to be cut lengthwise into fifty-two-feet-by-twelve-feet wide sections, which we then reconnected after they were placed on the beams.

Grace and I put a lot of hard work into making our house livable. When it first arrived, it did not have a back wall where another part of the bunk house had been attached. We built a temporary wall and insulated it with tarps and blankets to prevent the house getting too cold in winter. Anyone—bear or human—could have easily gotten through that wall if they had wanted to, so we were glad that no one ever tried. In October, we covered most of the interior with tarps for insulation and moved in. We created a little cocoon of warmth around a wood stove in the living room, where we slept and stayed when we weren't working on the other parts of the house.

Throughout our first couple of years in Kaministiquia, Grace and I used gas or oil lamps for light and wood stoves for heating. We did not yet have plumbing, so we built an outhouse nearby and hauled water that we kept in our bathtub. We filled large buckets with water at our friends' houses in town, and brought them back to our house in Grace's truck. In our second year, we tried to dig a well. We didn't know where to place one, and we didn't find water in the first spot where we dug for it. I prayed and slept on it. After smudging myself, I dreamt that we would find water underneath an old truck that had been abandoned on the property. When we brought a bulldozer in to dig for water on that spot, we found it. We built a well there that worked fine for twenty years. In the second year of living in that house, we also built a back wall onto it. That was a large task, because we needed to replace a lot of flooring in the area before we built the wall. Over the following years, we broke down and rebuilt the interior walls

FIGURE 18. THE HOME THAT GRACE AND I BUILT IN KAMINISTIQUIA (FORTY-EIGHT YEARS OLD, 1998). THE SHED WHERE WE STORED WOOD FOR WINTER HEATING IS ON THE LEFT OF THE PHOTO.

FIGURE 19. *THE GATHERING AT HARVEST TIME*, 1997 WATERCOLOUR.

to create a large bedroom, two smaller rooms, a living room, a kitchen, a laundry area, and one bathroom. We also constructed a big woodshed and a workshop, starting from the ground up by laying beams for the foundations, and then by building the floors, the walls, and the roofs.

Grace was very skilled in construction even before we started our work on the property, so she guided our efforts to improve the house. She and I worked well together. We thought through projects in a similar way, so we only needed to check in briefly at the beginning of each day to decide who was doing what job. Then we worked independently, calling on each other when we needed assistance. We both were patient and did not rush things. Grace did much of the woodwork, while I often did the heavier labour, like breaking down walls, or digging ditches for electrical wires, telephone lines, and underground pipes. We did all of our own plumbing and electrical wiring. Sometimes friends helped us in those efforts. One day I asked a friend to test whether there were any live wires in the walls before I did some electrical work. She checked with a circuit tester, and said there were none. That tester wasn't working properly, though. When I touched the wire with a screwdriver, I got an electric shock so powerful that it threw me across the room, as if I were as light as a feather. Afterward, my heart raced and my arms were numb, but I was very lucky to recover without any long-term problems. Over time, Grace and I succeeded in making a warm, comfortable home that we loved (Figure 18).

ENJOYING LIFE IN THE BUSH

Throughout this period, Grace continued to work full-time at the women's shelter, and I worked on the house while she was gone. Once in a while I rode into Thunder Bay with her in the morning, and then I spent the day in the city running errands and visiting friends until she was ready to drive back home. Sometimes we went to women's parties and potlucks, and now and then we hosted them ourselves. These still reminded me of the feasts I had participated in as a child in Ombabika, so I painted some of those positive memories in watercolour (Figure 19). The lesbian community in Thunder Bay was not very large at that time, so we all got to know each other and each other's families pretty well. Some couples we knew split up during those years. Nancy and her girlfriend separated after a couple of years, and so did Paige and Tabitha after almost ten years together. Most of those who broke up later found new partners but stayed at least loosely connected to their exes, because they were co-parenting together, or just continued to run into each other at social events.

Grace and I never experienced much prejudice or homophobia during our time living in the country. We got along well with our neighbours. Some of them were lesbian, and some weren't. We helped them with projects on their properties, and they did the same for us. Our neighbours often said they liked to visit our home, because it was such a peaceful place. We usually did not come across anybody else in the country, and we hardly went to Thunder Bay together, except to shop for groceries. Strangers we met in the city probably did not realize that we were a lesbian couple, so we did not experience discrimination there either.

Over our years together, Grace and I took many car trips, some as far as the Pacific and the Atlantic Ocean. Mostly, though, we liked to stay close to home. On weekends and vacations, we often hiked and camped in nearby forests, sleeping overnight by the river at Crooked Rapids or Silver Falls. I had begun to develop arthritis, which made it difficult for me to have a fast pace. I also needed to be careful on the paths because of my limited vision. I enjoyed going slowly so I could explore things around me, studying and smelling plants, pools, and rocks along the way. Grace was patient and did not mind my pace. At some point in our hikes, we always stopped to make a campfire and have a cup of cedar tea. We also took longer annual trips to Pukaskwa National Park, 350 kilometres to the east on the shore of Lake Superior. Few people went to that park, so the beaches did not feel crowded like at some other places. At that time, we didn't have lightweight, modern camping gear. Instead, we used an old-fashioned tent and backpacks, but there was a good network of trails and bridges that made it manageable to hike to isolated campsites.

Early on in Kaministiquia, Grace and I tried canoeing and kayaking together. At first I was not comfortable with boats, because they reminded me too much of the canoe accident I had experienced as a child, when people were injured and died. After a while, I overcame my fears. I realized that I liked kayaking more than canoeing, and over time I grew to love it. At first, I couldn't kayak far from shore, because I couldn't see very well and I didn't know how to swim. That inspired me to learn to swim, though, and Grace and other friends taught me how to do so over a couple of years. I succeeded one day in my mid-forties, when we were enjoying ourselves on a sandbar just below Little Dog Lake. I swam all the way across Dog River with my dog Shkiizhig by my side. Shkiizhig knew I was scared, so she stayed close to me. We did not take our eyes off each other the whole time I swam. Grace and my friends also swam nearby, looking out for me and cheering me on. After that, I was able to take longer trips in my kayak, *Wanamikiikwe* (Thunder Flight Woman), but I didn't join Grace and the others for long trips. My arthritis made it too painful for me to sit in the kayak for long. Also, my limited vision meant that I needed people close by to guide me, and made it difficult for them to help me return to land in bad conditions.

Once or twice a year Grace went on a long kayaking trip with friends, and during that period I sometimes took buses out west as far as Vancouver or Seattle, or to the east as far as Toronto or Boston, visiting different friends and family along the way. I never flew in a plane, even when I could get a cheap ticket or someone offered to buy me one, because I was very scared of flying. When I was younger and I had to fly for my work, I always managed to overcome my fear, but I preferred riding on the ground and seeing the different sights along the way. Grace and I enjoyed our trips together and alone, which made for a good balance in our relationship. We were content companions and didn't argue very much. When we did, we resolved our conflicts peacefully, without yelling or harsh words. We had different ways of managing our anger, though. When I got cranky, Grace told me to go and talk to the river about it. I usually did just that, letting everything out at the riverbank, and then I returned home in a cheerful mood. Grace could stew for longer. When that happened, she just took more time to herself until she came back around.

In Kaministiquia, Grace and I lived with several smart and loyal animals who became part of our family. We had a grey cat named Shadrack who thought he was a dog. Shadrack went with me and one of our dogs whenever we took a long walk, striding along beside us the whole way. He lived for nineteen years, which is a long life for a cat, especially one that spent a lot of time in the bush. We also had two dogs—first Nichi, which means "friend" in Ojibwe, and then Shkiizhig, which means "my eyes." They both were beautiful, loving dogs with some Labrador blood in them. Nichi had white paws and a white chest that made him look like he was wearing a tuxedo. Shkiizhig was almost entirely black, except for her white tail. I started training both of them soon after they were born. They understood that I did not see very well, so they guided me when I needed help. For example, when I suddenly lost my vision while on a long walk on the property, I was able to find my way home by telling my dogs to lead me and by holding on to their fur. There also were times when someone dropped me off on the road on the other side of the river, after dark. My dogs knew to meet me and guide me over the bridge, even making sure that I missed the mud puddles.

Both of our dogs protected us. Nichi once saved me and Grace from a fire in the middle of the night. It happened after I poured ash from our wood stove in the hole of our outhouse one afternoon, to reduce the smell. We often did that after the ash had cooled, but that time it must not have cooled enough. The fire probably burned slowly underground, because we did not notice any smoke during the evening. By 2:00 a.m., though, the outhouse was on fire. We would not have realized it, except that Nichi banged on our bedroom window until we woke up. Once awake, we couldn't stop the fire, but we called a neighbour for help and worked through the night to stop it from spreading to the woodshed or the house.

Shkiizhig protected me in other ways. She was a very good "bear dog." Once, when I was coming home after dark, she found a bear in our driveway and chased it into a tree. Then she kept guard over it there until I made it safely into the house. She also kept her nose to the ground when we went for walks, and several times she warned me away from a nest of bees in the grass. One time she fought off bees when they started swarming around me as I sat outside the house. The bees might have been drawn by flowering plants nearby. All I knew was that, suddenly, there were many agitated bees right in front of me. Shkiizhig immediately came between me and the bees and started snapping and swiping at them. My allergy to bee stings would have put me in great danger if she had not protected me. Shkiizhig was stung herself, but she recovered quickly.

WORKING ON MY WELL-BEING

While living in Kaministiquia, I returned to the daily and seasonal spiritual practices that my grandmother had taught me. I collected plants to use when smudging myself and talking each day with my Higher Power. I made my own drums and drumsticks from wood, birchbark, and animal hide. I used my drums when I was singing, dancing, praying, and giving thanks to the Great Spirit. Once or twice a year, I also built a sweat lodge. I made it by bending long saplings into a round, beehive-like structure in the traditional way, except I covered it with canvas material rather than birchbark or rush mats. When I wanted to have a sweat, I fasted for a few days and then heated the rocks to bring inside of the lodge. Usually I spent several hours inside, singing, drumming, and talking to *Gitchi Manitou*. All of those practices helped cleanse and sustain me, and brought me back to a better balance, both emotionally and spiritually. Sometimes I did my sweats alone, and other times I invited Grace or friends to join me.

After I returned from the U.S., I started smoking heavily again, until I was up to three packs a day. In 1994, I saw a doctor who told me that, if I continued at that rate, he expected to see me back in his office with lung cancer in a couple of years. I had known for a long time that smoking was bad for my health, but for some reason his warning helped me decide to stop. When I got home that day, I started thinking of ways to reduce my smoking to the point that I might quit completely. Grace was also a smoker, but we followed a strict rule to only smoke outside of our house. That meant we did not smoke as much in wintertime, because we did not want to dress up warmly and stand in the cold every time we craved a cigarette. But even then we did not quit completely.

I decided to reduce my cigarette use gradually, so that each time I wanted a cigarette I only smoked enough to soothe the craving and left the rest for later. Over a year, I went down to smoking only one cigarette a day. I just took a puff every couple of hours throughout the day. I stopped completely in February 1995. I became very ill afterward. For four days after I stopped, I was feverish, nauseous, and exhausted, but I refused to see a doctor. On the fourth night I became delirious. While I looked out of my window, I thought I saw a white wolf come to visit me. I reached out to the wolf and tried to touch it, but my hand slipped, and then the wolf was gone. When I woke up the next morning, my fever had broken and I was extremely hungry. I saw the little stub of a cigarette that I had left for myself five days earlier. I had told myself that I would smoke it if I really felt a need for it, but I never did. I have not smoked in the nineteen years since then.

FIGURE 20. *THE LETTING GO*, 1998 WATERCOLOUR.

FIGURE 21. PAINTING A PLASTER MOULD OF MY FACE TO MAKE A
MASK (FORTY-FIVE YEARS OLD, 1995).

My spiritual work helped me to stop smoking and to stay sober during difficult periods while I was living in Kaministiquia. During that time, I stopped attending AA meetings regularly, partly because I didn't feel a need to go as often, and partly because it was difficult to make it to meetings in the city in the evenings. In 1994, though, I joined a support group for survivors of sexual abuse. I had told Grace about my experiences of sexual violence, and she thought the group would help me in my healing. Through that group, I was referred to a social worker for individual counselling. I continued meeting with a counsellor and the support group for many years. I also continued to write and paint (Figure 20), and I explored new ways to express my feelings through art. When I had attended the Michigan Womyn's Music Festival in 1991, I learned how to make a plaster cast of my face, which I could paint and decorate with feathers, beads, and other objects to make an artistic but true-to-life mask. After I returned to Ontario, I continued to use plaster as a new way of making self-portraits. I found that the process of creating a mask, like painting a picture, helped me to work through and let go of difficult emotions (Figure 21).

For most of the years we lived in Kaministiquia, Grace worked as a sexual abuse counsellor, first for a women's shelter and then for a children's centre. She was too close to me to formally counsel me, which is why she suggested I join the support group. Grace usually did not tell me much about her job, because it upset me and reminded me of my own experiences. When her co-workers visited, they sometimes talked about their jobs in general ways, without betraying their clients' confidentiality. I could not bear, though, to hear about sexual abuse in the safe space of my home, so I always left the room when they began those discussions.

ADOPTING MY DAUGHTER TALIA
Grace and I sometimes invited women to stay with us if they needed a safe place to live for a few days or weeks. Usually they were battered wives who were escaping abusive husbands. They were not women who Grace met through her work, but others who I met in town, or who were brought to us by friends. Around 1993, a friend approached me and Grace about a runaway girl named Talia. The friend thought she would benefit from meeting us. Talia was about seventeen years old at that time and she was living on the streets. We invited her to come visit us. She stayed with us for

several days and loved being in our home and the surrounding bush. She explained that she had run away from a very harmful home environment. She also said that she was a lesbian, and appreciated being able to experience the peaceful life that Grace and I had created for ourselves as a lesbian couple. We invited her to come back whenever she wanted. Talia stayed with us again for several weekends over the following months. When we first met Talia, she did not speak any Ojibwe, but she was very interested in learning it. I enjoyed teaching Ojibwe to her and found that she was a fast learner. Soon she was calling me "mum," and I didn't mind.

Talia was determined to build a better life for herself. Before long she moved to Toronto, where she got a job working at a martial arts centre and went back to school. She wrote to me and Grace regularly, and came back to visit us when she got a chance. Over time, her appearance changed. When we first met her, she had dyed-red hair that she wore in dreadlocks, but later she grew her fine brown hair out and wore it in a long braid. On one of her visits to Kaministiquia, Talia asked me if I would legally adopt her. I didn't think she was serious at first, but she was, and I was happy to agree. She arranged all of the paperwork, we signed the forms, and she officially took my family name. Talia continued to speak Ojibwe with me and later concentrated her university study on First Nations languages and cultures. She worked hard at it, and as a result is a very good Ojibwe speaker today.

HELPING TO RAISE OUR GRANDDAUGHTERS

For many years, Grace and I also helped to raise our three granddaughters. In 1991, when my daughter Sarah was still living in Winnipeg with Ken and her daughter Valerie, she had a second girl named Susannah. In 1994, Sarah left Ken and moved back to Thunder Bay with the girls, so Grace and I began to see them regularly. Often, we brought Valerie and Susannah home for the weekend at our house. Once in a while, the girls lived with us for several weeks or months. When they stayed with us, they called it "Kokum's Boot Camp," because we liked to take them out into the bush.

Grace's daughter, Diana, continued to live on the White Dog Reserve with Randy and Abigail, so we tried to support them long distance, calling and visiting them when we could. It was a very difficult time for them. In addition to losing Quinn, Diana's father froze to death on his porch that winter, and one of her sisters committed suicide. Diana and Randy continued to struggle with addiction. In the end, they lost custody of Abigail again. At that time we were contacted by a Native Child and Family Service agency and asked if we would consider raising Abigail. The alternative was that Abigail would be placed in a foster family or an adoptive family that we did not know. Like Grace, I already loved Abigail as one of my granddaughters. Both Grace and I could not bear to think that Diana—and we—might never have contact with Abigail again. We were also scared because of what had happened to Quinn. We could not trust that Abigail would be placed in a safe home, so we agreed that Abigail would come and live with us. The Native Child and Family Service agency interviewed us on the phone, and we went through a series of supervised visits with Abigail. We were matter-of-fact about being lesbian partners, and the agency never made an issue of it. Grace already was legally recognized as Abigail's grandmother, so she was officially awarded "customary care" of her, but both of us signed papers taking responsibility for her. The agency gave us some transitional funding, but we did not receive any other financial assistance during the fourteen years that we raised Abigail.

Abigail came to live with us in Kaministiquia in 1996, when she was almost four years old. She was a sweet, cheerful girl (Figure 22). She had just lost her front teeth and had a bright gap-toothed smile. Abigail looked like her mother, Diana. She had similarly beautiful dark skin and pure black hair, and like her mom she joked and laughed a lot. Grace was working full-time, so I became the main person responsible for Abigail and her needs. Although Abigail called me *kokum* like my other granddaughters, in many ways I became more like a parent than a grandparent to her. I got her meals ready, cleaned up after her, and educated and played with her every day.

Before Abigail arrived, she already spoke and understood Ojibwe, because she had grown up speaking it with her parents on the reserve. I tried to only speak Ojibwe with her as well. Once she started school, she began to confuse Ojibwe and English, and in the end she only answered me in English. I continued to speak to her only in Ojibwe, though, so she did not lose her understanding of it. Often I took her out to a teepee I had built on the property (Figure 23), where I explained to her how to survive in the bush and I told her stories about my grandmother and the old ways of life that she had taught me. When I wasn't teaching Abigail in my teepee, I

FIGURE 22. WITH MY FOSTER DAUGHTER, ABIGAIL (FIFTY YEARS OLD, 2000).

FIGURE 23. THE FRAME OF A TEEPEE THAT I USED FOR MANY YEARS IN KAMINISTIQUIA (2000).

liked to use it as a private, personal space where I could take time to myself and reflect.

Abigail was a gentle, loving child, so she was not difficult to parent. She was patient and easygoing. For many years, I followed a schedule of getting her ready for school each morning and then working on construction tasks and household chores while she and Grace were away. Sometimes I also painted and wrote in my journal. The days went by quickly, though, and usually I did not have much time before Abigail returned home and I needed to take care of her and prepare dinner for all of us. There was only one year when I was not able to parent her, because I began to have great pain in my legs. My condition became so bad that it was difficult for me to get out of bed and move around. During that period, Sarah agreed to care for Abigail at her house in Thunder Bay. I was diagnosed with osteoporosis, arthritis, and other bone problems. My doctor put me on medication for several months. Once I had recovered enough, Abigail came back to live with me and Grace.

As Abigail was growing up, Grace and I tried to arrange for her to see Diana when it was possible. Several times we took Abigail to the White Dog Reserve to see her mom, and they had good reunions. We invited Diana to come see Abigail at our house too, and we offered to pay her transportation, but that usually did not work out. We also continued to have Valerie and Susannah stay with us off and on. Both girls were quite different from each other. We helped Sarah get them involved in activities that interested them, like dance and soccer for Valerie, and art and design for Susannah. Helping to raise our three granddaughters was an important part of Grace's and my life during that time. Sometimes I made that the subject of my paintings (Figure 24).

REUNIONS AND LOSS IN EXTENDED FAMILIES

Grace had come out to her parents before she met me, but they had never seen her with a female partner, so her being a lesbian did not seem real to them. Her parents lived a two-day drive away from us, in Cambridge, Ontario, so I did not meet them in the first years that Grace and I lived together. Early on, Grace told her parents that I was her partner, and that she wanted them to meet me. She also said she wanted them to accept and welcome me in the same way they had welcomed her husband. The next Christmas, her parents invited Grace to a large family dinner at their house,

FIGURE 24. *THE GRANDMOTHER AND HER GRANDCHILDREN*, 2002. WATERCOLOUR.

but they did not invite me, so Grace refused to go. The year after that, they invited us both. From the first night that I met her parents, they were kind and respectful toward me. They were curious to know more about me and my background. I learned that the family had a tradition of singing songs together, and after dinner I enjoyed listening to how beautifully they all sang together. After that first visit, I often went with Grace when she went to family gatherings. I always found them warm and spirited. Over time, her parents embraced me as a family member, even asking me to join them in their formal family portraits.

Martin and Sarah had both met Grace early in our relationship, and they got along very well with her. Like Sarah, Martin had come to live in Thunder Bay not long after Grace and I started living together. Over time, Grace became like a second mother to both of them, helping them with medical appointments, child-rearing, and other important activities. In 1994, Grace also met my stepfather and stepsister. That summer, Matilda and her boyfriend wanted to have some time to themselves. My stepdad said he missed me and the bush, so he came to live with us. He probably was in his late seventies or early eighties at the time. He did not want to stay in our house, so instead Grace and I set up a tent for him in our yard. We laid down electrical wires from the house to his tent, so he could plug in a light and a radio. He was very content once he settled in there. He often sat peacefully outside of his tent, listening to the radio, playing cards, and looking off into the fields.

That visit was the first time my stepdad saw me living with a female partner. When he met Grace, he called her my wife, saying, "So, this is your *wiidigewaagan*?" When I said yes, he said, "Tell me, can your wife take me for a canoe ride?" He wanted to go upriver to camp by the rapids, but he knew that I was blind, so I couldn't take him myself. Grace agreed, and they had a good trip together. After he returned, he told me that he liked Grace a lot. He thought that she was a very nice wife.

My stepdad and I had some good talks that summer. He told me that I had had a harder life than anyone he knew, and he was very happy that I had come through it alright. He said, "Look at you, you're such a strong person now. You survived so much, and you don't drink. You've built a home and a good life for yourself. Your grandmother would be very proud of you." My stepfather never stopped drinking alcohol, but he did not drink heavily during those later years. Once Matilda became sober, she didn't allow alcohol in her house, and she worked hard to keep it from him. This often seemed to make him miserable, and usually he found ways to get alcohol anyway. When he came to stay with us, Grace and I compromised with him and bought him a limited amount of light beer. After he drank one, he relaxed and sang songs, but he did not get drunk.

A few years later, my stepdad became seriously ill and was hospitalized in Thunder Bay. The hospital staff said he was dying. When I first went to see him, the nurse told me he had a restless day and night. They did not know how to calm him. I noticed that his hospital bed faced the west. In our tradition, someone preparing for a journey—including death—should face the sunrise, even if it is in the middle of the night. I explained and asked the nurse to help me move my stepdad's bed so that he faced eastward, and she agreed. He seemed to become more relaxed and at peace then. Matilda and I both stayed with him in his last hours. I held his hand and sang songs to him in Ojibwe and Cree, right up until the moment he left us.

A number of Grace's and my other relatives died in 1998 and 1999, around the time that my stepfather died. It was a very sad period for both of us. Sometimes it felt like we were surrounded by death. We spent days or weeks at someone's side in a hospital, and mourned them at a funeral, only to go back to the hospital to start the whole process over again with someone else. It wore us down. Grace lost her mother, then her aunt, and then a brother in a short period of time. I lost several elders and cousins, including Flora. She had rejected me when I first came out as a lesbian, but later reconciled with me. Flora came to understand that I was still the same person I had always been. After we started talking again, she told me, "I changed your diapers when you were little, so you can't be mad at me!" She had a good sense of humour. In later years, we often talked about my grandmother, appreciating how well she had raised me in hard times.

Flora died of cirrhosis, the same way my cousin Angela had died many years earlier. Like Angela, Flora experienced a terrible, painful death. As she was dying, she became swollen and her skin leaked blood and other fluids from puncture holes and wounds all over her body. I tried to stop the leakage with cloths and paper towels, asking nurses for help, but there was not much that could be done. In the middle of that horrible time, I remember seeing myself in a bathroom mirror and realizing that I had Flora's blood and body fluids all over my shirt and pants. It looked like I had been in a war zone. I did everything I could to try to make her passing peaceful. I held her and sang to her until the end, as I have tried to do with all the other friends and family who I have kept company as they died.

During those years, I sometimes visited Victoria, my friend Bonnie's mother, who was one of my mother's good friends in Ombabika. Victoria did not speak much English, so she was happy when we spoke Ojibwe together. As she got older, she needed more assistance. Victoria had never gotten over losing her daughter Adrienne and one of her sons to adoption. She asked me to help her find them, so I approached friends, librarians, and Children's Aid social workers to get information. They searched records on the Internet, in libraries, and in government offices. In the end, we discovered that the two children had been placed with a French Canadian family that had moved to Vancouver. We contacted Adrienne and her brother, and they agreed to have Victoria come visit them. I helped her pack her things, including wrapping her $10,000 in cash savings in a bundle. I tied that bundle over her stretchy black pants, so she could carry it safely under her big sweater on her bus trip.

Sometime later, in 2004, I got a chance to visit Victoria and Adrienne when I took a bus to the west coast to comfort a friend whose partner had recently died. While I was in Vancouver, I met Adrienne for the first time since we were small children in Ombabika, fifty years earlier. She was about my height and looked like her mother. Because her adoptive parents had been French speakers, she spoke French with her children. Adrienne told me that she did not have many memories of Ombabika. In fact, she knew very little about her biological family until I contacted her. By that time, Victoria had been living in a home for elderly people on Vancouver Island for years. I went to see her. The staff told me that I may have been the only visitor she had ever had. When I first went in, Victoria did not recognize me. With my short hair, pants, and jacket, she thought that I was a man. But then I sang her a song and she recognized my voice and said my name. I stayed with her for a long time.

MOVING BACK TO THE CITY

In September 2004, on my way back to Thunder Bay from Vancouver, I had a life-changing experience. I was sleeping on the bus in the middle of the night when I awoke to the smell of smoke. I was sitting just behind the driver, so I leaned forward to ask him about it. He said that it was probably only exhaust, because we had just climbed a steep slope in the mountains. At that point, we had crossed from British Columbia into Alberta and were not far from Banff. A little while later, the driver decided to stop the bus at a fork in the road, because there was not enough space to pull off to the side. He explained that he was going to go check something in the back, but he returned right away, shouting that the bus was on fire. He said that he was going to find the nearest place to pull off the road, and then everyone would have to get off. Another passenger and I quickly started waking everyone else up. Many people were disoriented and became panicked when they heard the news. Very soon the bus driver pulled over and we all got out safely onto the road. I helped unload the luggage, and then we all stood back and watched as the bus went up in flames. We waited several hours until a new bus came to pick us up.

As usual, I did well during the crisis. I felt very calm. But it triggered something emotional in me afterward. As I sat on the second bus, I heard a voice in my head clearly ask, "Ma-Nee, is this what you want from your life?" I started to have flashbacks of a house on fire in Ombabika—I didn't know exactly when or where—and memories of my mother grabbing me and hitting me. When I returned home, I had other flashbacks of traumatic experiences—painful memories of beatings and sexual abuse that I had not thought much about for many years. These images came to me suddenly and randomly at different times of the day and night.

I began to feel out of control. I had difficulty functioning and concentrating on the tasks that I needed to do to care for Abigail. When she was at school, I tried to work through my feelings by painting or writing in my journal, but it didn't help. Grace tried to talk to me and support me, but I wasn't able to speak to her about the pain that I was feeling. I started thinking about smoking and drinking again. Grace smoked and drank beer once in a while, so she kept cigarettes and alcohol in the kitchen. Until then, that had not been a problem for me, but it was starting to bother me, and I was feeling tempted by them. I felt like everything was caving in on me, and I couldn't stay in our house anymore. The only solution that I could see was to leave. I decided to move out. I asked some friends to help me find an apartment in Thunder Bay. We were surprised to find one very fast. That is how, in October 2004, I left the home that I had shared with Grace for twelve years.

CHAPTER ELEVEN

RECOVERING FROM POST-TRAUMATIC STRESS DISORDER AND BECOMING AN ELDER IN THUNDER BAY (2004–2014)

During all of the time that I had been in counselling, I had told my counsellors about individual assaults that I had experienced, but I did not reveal the full extent of the abuse. For most of my life, I had carried the pain of many acts of violence in my body and spirit. Bearing those traumas in silence meant that I did not confront them and I had difficulty getting beyond them. Suddenly, after experiencing the bus fire in late 2004, I couldn't stop the flood of memories I had of being beaten, tortured, and raped. I started to talk about all of it in my counselling sessions. At first my counsellor increased our sessions to twice a week. As I told her more of my history and the flashbacks I was experiencing, she became worried that I would start drinking again. She explained that she had never worked with someone who had lived through so many traumatic experiences. She thought it would be best for me to enter a more intensive treatment program for post-traumatic stress disorder. In February 2005, I began a six-week, in-patient program involving individual and group therapy focused on sexual abuse, alcoholism, and post-traumatic stress disorder. I was lucky to get a place in that program, because some people waited years to get into it. At times, participating in the therapy was very difficult, but in the end it helped me to work through much of my trauma and regain my ability to function. After I left the program, I continued seeing my counsellor once a week for several years, until I was in a healthy place and no longer having flashbacks.

I don't know how I would get by today if I had not had those years of counselling and therapy. I certainly would not have been able to tell about all of my experiences of violence in this book. I will never be completely at peace with those experiences. There are days when I feel shame, regret, or anger with myself and others, and nights when I struggle to sleep. Those happened more often while I was working on this book. When I had to revisit some of the most terrible experiences in detail, I became weary and exhausted. My body ached for days, as if someone were trampling on my head, neck, and shoulders. At some points I needed to take a break from working on the book, so I could sleep and recover.

Today I know how to help myself get through difficult times positively. I drum, sing, and smudge myself daily. I focus on love and forgiveness, for myself and others. I talk to the Great Spirit, sometimes at home, and at other times by a river in town, or in the bush outside of Thunder Bay. I walk long distances every day. I take pleasure in whatever nature there is around me, whether I am in the city or in the country. I drink cedar teas and other Anishinaabe medicines that I learned to make from my grandmother. At least once or twice a year, I cleanse myself in a sweat lodge. My faith and spiritual practices help me stay centred, healthy, and sober, even during hard times. I don't attend AA meetings very often anymore, but I do when I feel a need for extra support. I still sponsor younger AA members, and, when I am asked to assist, I help those going through detoxification. As of this writing, I have been sober for thirty-eight years.

I also continue to paint to let go of my pain and to focus on my healing (Figure 25). This requires a lot of concentration. Usually I can't paint for more than ten or fifteen minutes before my eyes begin to ache and my vision becomes too blurred, so I have to stop. It can take me several weeks or months to complete one painting. The themes of my artwork come to me as visions when I am awake, and dreams when I am sleeping. For example, I have seen a spirit bear talking to a woman, a wolf standing tensely in confrontation, and a woman and an eagle making an offering to the Great Spirit. There are times I feel a physical ache when I see such things. The images in my dreams can be so powerful that I wake up, turn on the lights, and sketch pictures to remember them better later.

FIGURE 25. *THE CHILD WITHIN*, 2006 WATERCOLOUR.

I still keep a journal that I use now and then to work through my feelings, and I participate in a writers' group. While I lived in Kaministiquia, Grace and I started a women's writers' group, and it has continued in the ten years since then. Members are friends and neighbours who meet weekly or monthly, depending on the season. We might have as few as two participants or as many as ten attend a meeting. At each one, someone proposes a topic, from the simple and everyday (like "socks") to more meaningful ideas and feelings (like "resentment"). Then we each write about it for twenty minutes before sharing what we have written with each other. That process has helped me to better understand my feelings. It has also improved my English vocabulary, and my ability to express myself in English.

TRANSITION FROM LOVERS TO FAMILY

Grace was very hurt when I moved out of our house. She knew I was going through great difficulties, and she tried to be understanding and supportive, even helping me with moving tasks. We continued to be in frequent contact about practical issues. At that time, we were still parenting Abigail, who was only twelve years old. Grace and I always put her needs first, even though there were unresolved issues in our relationship. We agreed that Abigail would continue living with Grace and would attend school in Kaministiquia during the week. Then she would come to stay with me on the weekends.

For a long time, Grace and I did not talk about what our separation meant for us as a couple. After I completed my in-patient treatment for post-traumatic stress disorder, neither of us brought up the question of whether I should move back to Kaministiquia. I am not sure why we didn't talk about it, but we didn't. Several years went by like that, with the two of us sharing responsibility for Abigail and managing the house and property together. I often went out to Kaministiquia to help Grace with construction projects, to house-sit when she travelled, and to take care of Abigail when I was needed. But when I stayed there, Grace and I did not share a bed, and we no longer were lovers.

FIGURE 26. *TWO-SPIRIT BEAVER LOOKING FOR ANSWERS*, 2007 WATERCOLOUR.

I felt conflicted and uncertain about my relationship with Grace, and these feelings came out in some of my paintings at the time (Figure 26). In 2007 I finally asked Grace to talk about our relationship and whether we might become lovers and partners again. I felt very guilty for having walked out on her. A number of times we sat down together to talk about it, but each time our discussions ended in arguments. Finally, in 2008, we met with a marriage counsellor several times. In those sessions we discussed how we both had issues with trust and betrayal. Each of us also acknowledged that we had become comfortable, and even content, living on our own. Through that counselling, we finally came to accept that we could be friends and family, but we would not be lovers again.

Grace and I continue to play an important role in each other's lives. We share responsibilities as parents, grandparents, and great-grandparents. My daughter Sarah and my son Martin, for instance, still call Grace "mum," and Sarah's children call her "*kokum.*" If my kids are not able to reach me in a crisis, Grace is the one they call, and she helps them in whatever way they need.

My first lover, Leah, also has become like family to me. Since we broke up in 1991, we have visited each other in the U.S. or Canada every two to three years (Figure 27). We talk by phone or send letters regularly. Leah and I celebrate each other's achievements, and we support each other through difficult times. Over the years, we have gotten to know and care for each other's partners and families, and I love spending time with her children.

MY GROWING AND CHANGING FAMILY

Abigail was not happy when Grace and I separated in 2004. Grace was Abigail's legal guardian, but throughout her childhood Grace had worked a full-time job, so I had been the main parent at home. Abigail wanted to continue living with both of us. If she couldn't do that, she wanted to live with me most of the time, but that was not possible in my little apartment in Thunder Bay. We also did not want her to leave her school in Kaministiquia, because the staff there were very understanding and supportive of her. Abigail had always been slower than most of her peers in school, but her teachers knew her well and gave her assignments to fit her learning needs. In ninth grade, she was assessed and found to have learning difficulties related to fetal alcohol syndrome. This condition had not been identified earlier, because she did not have any of the physical signs of the

FIGURE 27. AT A BEAVER POND IN MASSACHUSETTS (FIFTY-EIGHT YEARS OLD, 2008).

syndrome. After that, she was placed in a special program that helped her develop her strengths and interests and successfully complete grade twelve.

At around the same time, my granddaughters Valerie and Susannah also finished high school. At five feet and nine inches, Valerie had become tall like her mom, while Susannah stayed nearer to my height of five feet and three inches. During their teen years, the two girls stopped spending weekends with me, but they still visited me a lot. My son Martin and daughter Sarah have also continued to live in Thunder Bay, so I see them pretty often. Their father, Gus, came to Thunder Bay about six years ago and asked to meet with them. He would have been in his mid- to late seventies at the time. Martin refused to see him, but Sarah and her fiancé agreed to have dinner with him and one of his other daughters, a younger half-sister. They never actually ate the meal, because before they sat down, Gus referred to Sarah as his daughter, and Sarah's anger toward him boiled over. She told him off for abusing me, rejecting her, and never contributing to our family in a positive way. She told him that I had been both her mother and her father, and he was only a sperm donor. Sarah had not planned to confront him, but it just happened that way. Then she and her fiancé left.

A couple of days later, Sarah and I were on a city bus together. After we got off, she told me that Gus had been sitting at the back of the bus. In that moment, I was glad to be visually impaired, so I did not see him or know that he was there. Over time, I have come to forgive Gus. Of all the abuse I experienced in my life, his was the worst, but holding on to my anger and hatred of him would only make me suffer. It is not my place to judge or to punish anyone else. And despite the horrible things that he did to me, I walked away from him with two beautiful children, my daughter Sarah and my son Martin. I am left today with love for them, not hatred for him. None of us ever saw Gus again after that day on the bus. He died a few years later.

Once in a while I see members of my extended family, or other people I knew during my childhood up north. Recently I ran into my cousin Justin's son, Mitchell, who was the breech baby that I helped Helene to deliver in Ombabika in 1966. The day I bumped into him, I had gone to a casino with a friend and was sitting, watching her play, when Mitchell approached me. He greeted me and shook my hand. He recognized me because Justin had once introduced us in the 1980s. At that time, Justin told his son that

I was the one who helped Helene during Mitchell's difficult birth. Today Mitchell is a handsome, tall, fit man who works in railway construction. He told me he is building a cabin back in Ombabika, so he can take his family to hunt there.

All of my extended family and friends seem to know that I am a lesbian, although I don't discuss it with them unless they raise it. None of them treat me with hostility as some once did, when I first came out. Most of my contact with them is pleasant and polite. Usually, Anishinaabe men seem to have less of a problem with me being lesbian, so we might hang out together and talk and laugh over tea. Many of the Anishinaabe women I know believe that my lesbianism conflicts too much with their Christian faith, so we greet each other, but we don't talk much beyond that.

Now and then I speak with my brother Andy, who lives with his wife Lori on her Cree reserve in Manitoba. I reached out to him a few years ago, when the government was making financial settlements for the damages done to First Nation survivors of residential schools. I encouraged Andy to apply, and he did, successfully. Andy and I have never talked about me being a lesbian since that night twenty-five years ago, when he told me on the phone that he did not accept it. But he is still my little brother, and I am still the woman he calls "mum."

Phillip's children, who are all in their sixties now, are kind and warm to me when I see them. They have accepted me as Phillip's daughter, even though none of us are certain whether he really was my biological father. Recently one of Phillip's other daughters passed away after she became ill with the flu here in Thunder Bay. I visited her when she was in the hospital, and I helped the doctors to explain her condition to her family. At that time I met many of Phillip's children, grandchildren, and extended family members who I had never met before. I was touched that I was respectfully introduced as a sister or an aunt. Afterward, the family asked me to lead a ceremony at my half-sister's funeral, which I did.

I have been at the side of a number of other, older relatives when they were ill and passed away in Thunder Bay in recent years, including my stepsister, Matilda. I have also experienced the tragic deaths of several of my young relatives and friends. One of the most painful events that my family and I have faced was the loss of my granddaughter Valerie's fiancé, Matthew, in 2009. Only a year before he died, Matthew and Valerie had

had a beautiful baby girl, my first great-grandchild, Namiid, who I helped deliver (Figure 28).

Matthew was a tall, thin, good-hearted Anishinaabe who loved Valerie and Namiid a lot. He had been unemployed for some time, so he was very

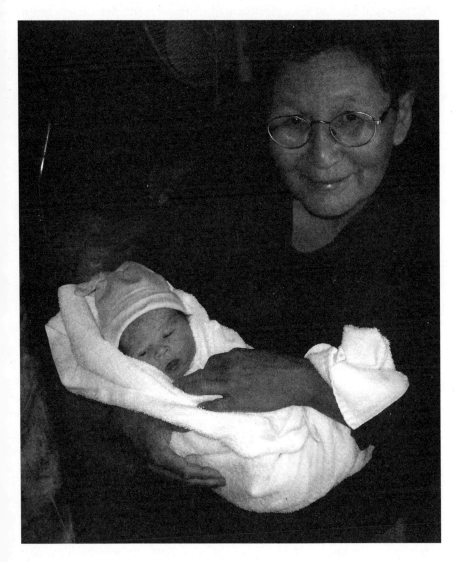

FIGURE 28. WITH MY GREAT-GRANDDAUGHTER, NAMIID (FIFTY-EIGHT YEARS OLD, 2008).

happy the day that he and his father got roofing jobs together. That night, Matthew told me on the phone how proud he felt that soon he would be earning an income and supporting his family. After his first paycheque, he planned to take Valerie and Namiid out for a nice meal, and then throw a big first birthday party for Namiid. But on their second day on the job, Matthew and his dad were electrocuted in an accident. Matthew was still alive when I got to the hospital, but he was in terrible condition. Soon afterward his heart stopped. Valerie was beside herself with grief and could not believe that he was gone. Grace and I did our best to comfort her and Matthew's mother and siblings. I held a ceremony in the intensive care unit to mark Matthew's passage to the spirit world.

Losing Matthew affected me deeply. It brought up memories of when my son Jonathan died in 1974. I thought about how he would have been a grown man today, if he had lived. After Jonathan died, I lost myself in alcohol and other drugs for months, so I never properly grieved for him. When I mourned Matthew thirty-five years later, I was also grieving for Jonathan.

Today I am blessed to have a large family of individuals who are related to me by blood, adoption, and fostering. My family has continued to grow over the last ten years, and we have a new generation of young children. Several years ago, my daughter Talia and her partner adopted two Anishinaabe boys, Darrius and Noah, who are now five and seven years old. I enjoy babysitting them when I get a chance to visit the family in Toronto. I appreciate how the boys are being raised with some of our traditions, like the beautiful way that they wear their hair in long braids down their backs. Abigail and her partner also recently had a son named William, so now I have both a great-grandson and a great-granddaughter. I try to help my daughters and granddaughters with their young children as much as I can. I love to get down on the ground to play with the little ones. I am grateful that most of my family lives near me in Thunder Bay, and several times a year Talia and her family come to visit me, or I go to visit them.

Each one of my children, grandchildren, and great-grandchildren has had her or his own unique journey in life. Like me, they have experienced many joys, including warm friendships, passionate love, and birthing, fostering, and adopting children. I wish I could say that none of them have experienced the kinds of trauma and suffering I have known, but I cannot.

Their stories are theirs to tell, though, not mine, so I will not write more about them here.

LIVING A SIMPLE LIFE IN THE CITY

At the age of sixty-three, I still enjoy new experiences, exploring unfamiliar places, and having adventures, but most of the time my life is very simple. Each year I learn to tolerate and manage new aches and pains. I am lucky to have access to good medical and social services, which have helped reduce the challenges I experience with arthritis, visual impairment, sleep problems, and other conditions. I try to do my part in taking care of my health by walking a lot and eating a balanced diet. That is not always easy on a limited budget. As I write this in early 2014, I receive a total of $1,000 a month in disability assistance and social supplements, which is

FIGURE 29. *JOURNEY OF A GOOSE WOMAN LEAVING*, 2010

about half of the monthly minimum-wage income in Canada. Half of my income goes toward rent for my apartment, which has one bedroom, a living room, a half-kitchen, and a bathroom. I use the remaining $500 each month to pay for water, electricity, heating, phone, Internet, and groceries. Some Anishinaabe reserves provide their band members with additional income, but I have never received anything from Fort Hope.

I get my disability assistance cheque at the beginning of each month, so at that time I stock up on groceries, mostly buying things on sale. I never buy red meat, but I eat it when someone offers it to me, and once in a while I buy turkey, chicken, or pork to have at home. I often make dishes out of rice, tofu, and nuts. I drink a lot of water and herbal teas. I stopped drinking coffee, Coca Cola, and other forms of caffeine when I entered the post-traumatic stress disorder treatment program in 2005, because they required that, and I have continued to avoid caffeine since. I love fresh produce and I eat many salads. Usually I buy as much produce as possible at the start of the month, and then store what I can in a cupboard, or chop it up and freeze it to use later. Still, by the end of the month, my freezer, refrigerator, and cupboards are usually pretty bare. I try to take advantage of opportunities to get additional quality food for free or at a reduced price. Sometimes I buy a "Good Food Box" for only twenty dollars when the women's centre provides large containers of fruit and vegetables to local people on a limited income. At Christmas time, a Thunder Bay charity also provides free food hampers to people in need, so I stand in line in the cold with other poor people to receive one of those. It especially helps to get extra food at that time of the year, because I receive my January disability assistance and social supplements in mid-December, before social service staff go on vacation. After buying a few small Christmas presents for my grandchildren and great-grandchildren, it can be difficult to make it all the way to the end of January on what remains.

Even on my limited income, I still sometimes give money to friends or family members who are struggling more than I am. There are days when I am completely broke, so some of my friends help me out in the same way, by giving me a little cash or food, like a bag of apples. I do not have a lot of clothing or other belongings. The things I value most are my art supplies and my artwork (Figure 29). Now and then I sell one of my paintings, but otherwise I keep them or give them to loved ones, or to people who have helped me. I enjoy using my computer for communicating with people. I am lucky that CNIB has given me a computer that is specially designed for visually impaired people. It reads out my e-mails when I can't see them. CNIB also gave me magnifiers and other visual aids which help me when I work on my art.

If everything else were equal, I would prefer to live in the bush, but given my visual impairment, living in the city is much more manageable today. When I lived in Kaministiquia, I couldn't get beyond our property very easily, because I had to depend on others for rides. In Thunder Bay I am much more independent. I walk ten kilometres or more on most days. The streets and public transportation routes are all very familiar to me. Despite my limited vision, I can go to stores, friends' houses, the women's centre, and anywhere else I want to go on foot or by bus. My arthritis symptoms have reduced since I moved back to Thunder Bay, probably because I get more exercise in the city than I did when I was living in the country. When I want to be closer to nature, I can walk fifteen or twenty minutes from my apartment to a nearby river. There has been increased violence in that area recently, so I am cautious.

My vision problems still challenge me today. I am scheduled to have cataract and glaucoma surgeries soon. I hope these procedures will make it a bit easier for me to see. I use a number of strategies to get by on my own with limited vision. I keep my home very neat and well-organized. If I know the exact location of furniture and other household items, I am less likely to bang into them or break them. When my children and grand-children visit, they know they need to leave everything exactly in place, so I don't become confused. At night, when I have difficulty sleeping and everything is pitch black, I sometimes practise making my way through my apartment just by touch or with a cane. I even do chores in the middle of the night, like washing and putting away dishes and utensils in complete darkness. I believe those kinds of activities strengthen my spatial skills, which may become more important if my eyesight gets even worse.

These days I like to have a certain amount of solitude, but I also enjoy spending time with friends, talking and laughing together. Recently, after ten years of being single, I have decided to start dating again. In the last year, I have gone out with two women. Neither of those relationships has developed into a long-term partnership, but I am still hopeful about falling in love again. In the meantime, I have a lot of fun with my friends. I love a good joke and shared silliness. My sense of humour helped me to survive at the worst times in my life, and it kept me grounded and gave me pleasure at other times. These days, when I get together with some of my friends, we drink tea and play marathon Scrabble or card games for hours. Sometimes several of us go out to the bush for a day of hiking up the river to one of our favourite waterfalls. Now and then a few of us go on overnight kayaking trips (Figures 30 and 31).

My friends and I enjoy having big social events too. For the last six years, Grace and I have held an annual "snowshoe baseball" party on her property. We build a firepit and host a potluck, and about twenty women have a day of fun in the snow together. We really do play baseball while wearing our snowshoes, walking or running from base to base as best we can. Most of the people in our community are white lesbians and bisexual women in their forties or older, but there are a few Anishinaabe women as well. Some of my closest friends are Ojibwa or Cree lesbians and bisexual women who keep their sexual orientation secret. They are very afraid of discrimination and rejection if they come out to their families and communities.

Living in a Canadian city as an older Anishinaabe lesbian is some-times difficult. I keep my hair short on the sides and long down my back. I wear comfortable clothing, like T-shirts, flannel shirts, sweatshirts, jeans, and tennis shoes. I don't think of those clothes as specifically male, but now and then people mistake me for a man, and call me "sir." I don't mind when they do. A couple of times young people at bus stops have even called me "faggot." I guess they didn't only confuse me for a man but for a gay man, given their word choice. When that happened, I replied, "Thank you," which surprised them, and afterward they left me alone.

I have less tolerance for racism, and I experience it far too often. It can be as simple as how white cashiers treat Native customers, whether it is in an expensive specialty camping store, or in a large chain supermarket. At my local Safeway store, for example, I often see white clerks cheerfully greet white customers and then ignore me or other Anishinaabe custom-ers once we get to the front of the line. They also treat our groceries more roughly and sometimes act like we aren't there, and instead help a white customer behind us. When this happens, I usually make a joke about it, saying, "What am I, chopped liver?" I have appreciated when people in

FIGURE 30. ON THE SOUTHERN SHORE OF LAKE NIPIGON IN MY KAYAK, WANAMIKIIKWE (FIFTY-SEVEN YEARS OLD, 2007).

FIGURE 31. CAMPING ON A KAYAKING TRIP (FIFTY-EIGHT YEARS OLD, 2008).

line behind me, both Native and white, have laughed and supported me. At their worst, supermarket cashiers have actually refused to let me buy certain items because I am Native. Twice store clerks have picked a bottle of Listerine out of my groceries and told me that they didn't know if they were allowed to sell it to me. I think they were afraid that I would go outside and drink the mouthwash for its alcohol content, and they saw it as their job to take it away. Both of the times that this happened, I made a formal complaint to the store manager and then I was able to buy the mouthwash. Afterward, I completed and mailed in complaint forms to the supermarket's headquarters, but whether that made any difference, I don't know.

BEING AN ELDER

Over the past decade, I have volunteered for a number of organizations and causes, but most of my work with people has taken place less formally. Some ask for my help when they are struggling with emotional challenges, especially recovery from abuse or alcoholism. Others seek me out while they are managing difficult medical conditions, or when they want to deepen their understanding and connection to their sacred power or being. I listen and refer them to other services, if I think someone else can help them too. Every person and situation is different. I lead a lot of drumming-singing circles and smudging ceremonies using sage, tobacco, cedar, and sweetgrass. I teach people how to build and use sweat lodges to cleanse and heal themselves, physically and spiritually. With the help of friends, I recently constructed a new sweat lodge on Grace's property. I still plan to build a structure over the lodge to protect it from bad weather, so it will last and we can use it for a long time. I also make medicine bundles out of leather, beads, and sacred items that people can wear around their necks. Inside, I place some sacred herbs and things that are special to that individual and his or her spiritual journey. I perform naming, clan, marriage, and bundling ceremonies. A bundling ceremony is a healing act that involves wrapping a person up as if they were in a cradle. No one pays me for those services, although some people provide me with a lift to events, give me tobacco to use in my spiritual practices, or assist me with my projects. For example, I have been helping a man with HIV on his spiritual journey for several years now, and he, in turn, has helped me build my sweat lodge.

In my work I follow the practices that my grandmother taught me, but I also have adopted or created some new ones. For example, I make dream catchers by bending a small willow branch into a hoop, weaving a web of string inside, and decorating it with beads and feathers. When someone is asleep, dream catchers are meant to filter out bad dreams and only allow good ones to remain. I especially like to make them for the children in my life, to help them feel safe and protected as they sleep at night. When I work with an adult over several days, we sometimes make a plaster mask together. This is an intimate process that requires the person to be calm and relaxed as I mould the plaster to his or her face. It helps that person focus and let go of pain or tension. I later paint the mask and go "shopping" in the bush for ways to decorate it with bone, feather, or fur. Then I mount it on a plaque, so the person has a unique, peaceful self-image to take home with them.

These days I continue to spend a lot of time working with young people informally. In my wanderings through the city, I often meet teenagers and young adults and end up sitting down and talking to them for a while. Now and then I'm approached at the mall or the bus stop by former classmates of my granddaughters, or students who I have taught about Ojibwa culture at the high school. They usually offer to buy me a cup of tea and have a chat, and I try to make time for them. Street youth also continue to be a part of my life, although I don't bring them home to live with me like I did in my thirties and forties. Sometimes they approach me first, especially gay, lesbian, bisexual, and transgender youth. They recognize me from gay pride events, or from seeing me in the newspaper or in the television coverage of those events. They hug me and hang out with me for a while. Often they are homeless runaways, and some are on drugs and supporting themselves with sex work. I listen to them and encourage them to listen to their hearts, and to try and change what is making them unhappy. If they are desperate for money or drugs, I ask them to explore alternatives before selling their bodies. But I don't judge them. I give them a business card I made for people who are interested in my artwork, because it works just as well for homeless youth who might want to contact me later. I carry contact information for social services in Thunder Bay, Toronto, and Winnipeg, so I can pass that on in case it might help.

Of course, I also talk with other homeless youth, those who aren't necessarily gay, bisexual, or transgender. For instance, recently I was waiting for a bus when I saw a teenager who looked like he was having a hard time, and I said as much. He replied with hostility, saying, "What's it to you? Why should you care?" So I asked him, "Why shouldn't I? I do care, and I'm willing to listen." He still was angry when he answered me, saying, "You got all day?" I replied, "Yeah, as a matter of fact, I do. I could sit right here and listen to you if you feel like talking to me. I'm an elder and I have good listening skills." So that's how we started talking. He told me about the problems he was having with his girlfriend, and that his dad accused him of things he didn't do, and then hit him. He said that he was sick and tired of it all. I missed the next two buses while listening to him, and then I took him to McDonald's for a soda and we sat together there for a while longer. I asked him if he could stay with any relatives, and he said no. Before I left, I gave him my card and other contact information of people who might be able to help him. I did not hear from him again, but at the bus stop only a few days later, I saw his face on a poster for missing children.

Usually, I never learn what happens to the young friends I meet on the streets, but I have been sad to hear that one of them went to jail, and another who was a heavy drug user died. I always hope that the others have made it off the streets and are doing well now.

VOLUNTEERING AND PARTICIPATING IN LARGE EVENTS

As a lesbian Ojibwa-Cree elder, I am sometimes asked to assist in different political and social activities. There are not many Anishinaabeg of my generation who still speak their languages fluently, and there are very few openly lesbian or gay elders. I have done translation work, like recently I narrated an educational video about elder abuse for the Thunder Bay police to use in their outreach efforts. I have also spoken to different groups about being a two-spirit person. Once in a while I speak to small audiences, like support groups for young people, and at other times to large ones, for instance when I am interviewed for television or newspapers. I also continue to volunteer for AIDS service organizations. In Thunder Bay, I conduct smudging and healing ceremonies before events sponsored by the AIDS committee or the local hospice. Most recently, I became a member of the Board of the Ontario Aboriginal HIV/AIDS Strategy, an organization that provides services to urban and rural Anishinaabeg affected by HIV/AIDS. I also joined the City of Thunder Bay Elders' Advisory Council, which provides the city government with guidance on First Nations traditional practices and ceremonies.

In addition, I have volunteered in several Ontario schools and children's centres to teach children about Ojibwe and Cree languages and cultures. With younger children I usually tell stories, and we make art projects and put on plays together. Most of my stories involve animal characters whose behaviours reflect issues that the children might be dealing with in school, like a wolf who bullies other wolves in his pack. I have done some similar activities with high school students, but they often are more interested in learning about Anishinaabe history, language, and culture, so I spend a lot of time answering those kinds of questions instead. I also have taught university students in Ojibwe courses and language camps in Thunder Bay, Toronto, and Minnesota. Fifteen or twenty young people usually attend those intensive courses. Most of them have some Ojibwa heritage but have never learned Ojibwe, and they are very serious about learning the language. For four days, we only speak Ojibwe from 8:00 a.m. until 8:00 p.m., and after that time they can use English if they want to, but usually they don't. I am not paid for such work, although sometimes organizations give me gift cards or grocery cards, and I usually receive transportation, accommodation, and meals for the courses that involve travel.

In the last decade, I was happy to participate in some annual gatherings of two-spirit people from Canada and the U.S. At each of those events, about fifty of us came together to celebrate the different ways we experience two-spiritedness. We held drug- and alcohol-free discussions, support groups, and dances. Participants represented many different First Nations in North America. Until now, most of the members have been male and in their twenties or thirties. Very few have been older than fifty years of age, and not many can speak their native language. Several gay or transgender men in their sixties attended those gatherings and enjoyed the socializing. A couple of them were politically active and taught younger participants about the history of two-spirit people in our cultures. To date, I believe I am the only female elder to participate in those annual meetings, and the only elder who leads traditional ceremonies. It may be that other two-spirit elders have not heard of the gatherings, or are not interested or able to join them. I also suspect that many two-spirit people of my generation did not survive into their sixties. Like my cousin Angela and my friend Bonnie, many probably experienced poverty, violence, addiction, and disease before dying at a young age. When I attend the two-spirit gatherings, I lead some ceremonies and teach about my traditions. When I am asked, I tell participants about my particular *niizhin ojijaak bimose* (two-spirit journey). I share my understanding of the male and female spirits I have inside of me, and how I embrace them both. I listen and learn from others' stories. Together we work on our healing, have fun, and celebrate the freedom to be ourselves.

In recent years, I also attended large-scale gay pride events in Toronto, and I helped to open the parade one year with a smudging ceremony. Before the ceremony I talked to the crowd about focusing on love, peace, and honouring the Great Spirit who is walking with us, even if bystanders shout unkind things as we pass. When I smudged the people gathered there, I asked the Great Spirit to help us all have healthy lives, to protect us from harm, and to give us strength and courage to face challenges.

Then, in 2011, I was excited when Thunder Bay held its very first "Thunder Pride" week. We had many events, including raising a rainbow flag at city hall, a poetry reading, a film festival, a healing walk and gathering, a youth activity, a drag show, and a family day. I attended everything. I read some of my poetry at the writers' gathering. For the family day event I helped to decorate, and then displayed my artwork there. I led the healing walk and spoke at the gathering afterwards about the difficulties that we have experienced as lesbian, gay, bisexual, and transgender people, and how many of us have been lost to violence and disease. On the Friday night of that first Thunder Pride week, I also dressed up as Elvis and participated in the drag show. Fifty years after I secretly wished to dress like Elvis as a teenager in Ombabika, I finally got to do it. It was fun! At first, the younger people in the audience seemed stunned. Based on the poetry reading and the healing walk, they probably thought that I was just a serious elder. But when I sang and pranced as "Elvis," they laughed and clapped and started chanting my name. I was happy to show them that being a spiritual person and an elder is not all about seriousness and loss (Figure 32). Certainly we have responsibilities and sometimes we face great challenges, but that is all

FIGURE 32. DRESSED UP AS ELVIS FOR THE FIRST THUNDER PRIDE WEEK DRAG SHOW (SIXTY YEARS OLD, 2011). USED WITH PERMISSION OF RACHEL A. MISHENENE.

the more reason to cherish the pleasure, humour, and joy in our lives and the world around us.

We have held two more Thunder Pride weeks since 2011. Four months ago, for the first time, we had a parade as well. I performed a smudging and drumming ceremony to open the week (Figures 33 and 34), praying for positive energy, healing, and safety for us all. Then I helped to lead the parade. When I saw the long stream of people walking behind us on the road, I could not believe how many had gathered together there to participate. There were people on foot, people on bicycles, and even people in golf carts. There were many men and women from Thunder Bay, and many others holding signs from Winnipeg, Kenora, and Toronto who had come to support us. That sight took my breath away. I clearly remember the hostility I faced when I came out publicly in Thunder Bay only twenty-five years ago, so seeing all the people celebrating in the parade was a very moving and a joyful moment for me.

FIGURE 33. LEADING A SMUDGING AND DRUMMING CEREMONY BEFORE THE SLEEPING GIANT AT THE START OF THE THIRD THUNDER PRIDE WEEK (SIXTY-TWO YEARS OLD, 2013). USED WITH PERMISSION OF JEN SMITH.

FIGURE 34. SMUDGING A WOMAN WITH SWEETGRASS AS PART OF THE THIRD THUNDER PRIDE WEEK HEALING CEREMONY (SIXTY-TWO YEARS OLD, 2013). USED WITH PERMISSION OF JEN SMITH.

MY GRANDMOTHER'S GRANDDAUGHTER

Given the discrimination and violence I have experienced in my sixty-three years, it would have been easy for me to become a hateful person. Even today, when I am grateful to lead a peaceful and happy life, there are moments when I feel anger, bitterness, and regret. But those feelings only make me miserable, and I don't want to live like that. I have learned to manage difficult emotions, like the sorrow I experience when I am helping people who are dying, grieving loved ones, or struggling with addiction or a history of sexual abuse. I believe I am whole today because I confront and feel such pain fully. Sometimes, during a crisis, I have to function in the moment, but sooner or later I try to take the time to focus on my loss. I do not let those feelings take over my life. I try to work through them. I take long walks and express myself by writing, painting, or talking with a friend, a counsellor, or my Higher Power (Figure 35). That is the only way I know how to let negative emotions go and move on.

FIGURE 35. *BEAVER TAKING PAIN FROM THE WOMAN*, 2010
WATERCOLOUR.

I also never forget the many reasons I have to embrace and enjoy life. Looking back on more than sixty years, I appreciate all of the good things that have happened to me, and how many wonderful people I have known, and still know, today. I don't only mean my friends, lovers, and family, but also strangers, professionals, and good Samaritans, like my neighbour Renard, who looked out for me when I was a small child, and Mrs. Jones, the teacher who tried to convince my mother not to beat me, and the doctors who healed my broken body when I escaped a violent marriage. Those are just a few, but there are many others. They include my childhood friend Jane, who helped me become sober when I hit rock bottom, my AA contact Herbert, who gave me a chance to be trained in my field, Charlotte and the other social workers who aided me when I was first learning to live with blindness, and the unknown taxi drivers who stopped people from attacking me after I came out as a lesbian on television. Over the years, there have been a lot of people who treated me with kindness and went out of their way to help me, even when it involved serious sacrifice or risk to themselves. These people give me faith in the human spirit, and in all of our potential to be loving and compassionate.

My grandmother, of course, was the greatest example for me. She gave me many tools to help me to survive and thrive, even when I experienced terrible hardships. My *kokum* taught me to find comfort in the natural world and the Great Spirit, to forgive those who harmed me, to cherish the love of a partner and family, and to enjoy humour and laughter with friends, even at the worst of times. At this stage of my life, I often feel my grandmother's presence, especially when I am with my grandchildren and great-grandchildren. I hear her voice when I speak to them. I see her expressions on their faces. I love them the way she loved me. And I hope my love will stay with them and give them warmth and strength throughout their lives, as my *kokum*'s love still does for me.

AFTERWORD

BY MARY LOUISA PLUMMER

HOW WE CAME TO WRITE THIS BOOK

For many years, Ma-Nee Chacaby has wanted to write her life story so that her children, grandchildren, and great-grandchildren can better understand her history, as well as their own. Ma-Nee also wished to record her experiences and understanding for a broader audience. She has lived through important historical transitions and few records of those times are written from the perspective of someone like her, that is, a poor, recovering alcoholic, visually impaired, and lesbian Indigenous woman. However, Ma-Nee faced considerable challenges in writing her life story. As a child, she spoke Ojibwe and Cree almost exclusively. She only really learned English—and reading and writing—in her twenties, after she moved to a city. By Ma-Nee's thirties and forties, though, her vision had deteriorated to the point that she had difficulty seeing words on paper, and, later, on computer screens, which created new barriers. So while Ma-Nee has a love of learning, expression, and new technologies, independently writing an extended piece about her life would have been extremely difficult.

Ma-Nee approached this dilemma with the creativity, resourcefulness, and persistence that are typical of her. Over the last twenty-five years, she identified several friends, family members, and acquaintances who she thought might be able to assist her in writing her biography. At different times, she asked each one to help her in this task, including me. All of us

215

were enthusiastic about the possibility. In fact, several times Ma-Nee began to narrate her life experiences to someone who took notes or audio-recorded her account, with goals varying from writing a short story to drafting a book-length manuscript. However, those efforts rarely extended past a few hours of narration, representing only a small glimpse into Ma-Nee's life, because few people had enough time to record and write Ma-Nee's full history. One short story was published after such a collaborative effort (Baril 2012). That story was loosely based on Ma-Nee's description of boys and girls in her childhood community being taken away to residential schools.

I came to this book project first and foremost as a close friend of Ma-Nee's, but I am also a social scientist and a professional writer. Ma-Nee and I have known each other well for over two decades. Each of us considers the other to be within her small circle of best friends. In the course of our relationship, I have heard almost all of the stories detailed in this book, some of them on multiple occasions. I was motivated to work on this project because I knew how important it was to Ma-Nee. In addition, I believed that many readers would be interested in such a compelling and honest account of an individual overcoming hardship against great odds. I also appreciated that Ma-Nee's autobiography would provide a rare, first-person, published account of the challenges faced by many Indigenous Canadians in the latter half of the twentieth and early twenty-first centuries, particularly lesbians, poor people, and individuals with little formal education. Recognizing that this book may be a valuable contribution to the academic literature, I have tried to follow social science research principles and practices throughout the project. For example, I took a systematic approach to our interviewing, recording, analysis, and writing processes.

Ma-Nee's and my mutual interest in writing her life story, and our pre-existing rapport and trust, made it straightforward for us to work on this book once the right circumstances came together. That opportunity arose in the summer of 2013. I had a gap in my work commitments and realized I could devote six months to the project full time, so I suggested to Ma-Nee that we give it a try. Ma-Nee also had enough time available and was eager to attempt it. Fortunately, we had technology that made it feasible for us to communicate over a great distance, because at that time Ma-Nee lived in Thunder Bay, Ontario, while I lived on the other side of the world, in Dar es Salaam, Tanzania.

OUR INTERVIEW AND WRITING PROCESS

Starting in July 2013 and continuing every weekday for several months, I used low-cost Skype software to call Ma-Nee, either reaching her on her telephone land line or on her computer's Skype account. Our daily talks lasted one to two hours. In the first calls, we focused on what Ma-Nee had been told about her family's history before she was born. She then described her earliest memories, and ultimately addressed each major period of her life in detail. In this way, we carried out a long series of semi-structured and roughly chronological interviews. At the start of each interview, Ma-Nee addressed gaps or answered questions which she or I had identified after the previous day's work. Then she continued narrating her life story, starting from whatever point she had finished with the day before, and responding to my questions as they came up. This process sometimes required Ma-Nee to spontaneously translate from Ojibwe or Cree into English, particularly when describing the first two decades of her life.

Our daily interviews generally followed a chronological sequence, but we revisited each period of Ma-Nee's life on multiple occasions, sometimes to resolve outstanding questions, and sometimes to flesh out events in more detail. Ma-Nee's memories and reports about particular incidents and time periods were very consistent overall. When there were discrepancies, I probed further, engaged in whatever fact-checking I could related to the period or event, discussed how to resolve the issue with Ma-Nee, and/or acknowledged the uncertainty in the text itself. During each interview I typed Ma-Nee's words as she spoke. I usually wrote her words verbatim, but occasionally I truncated them as bullet points. My priority was to record key content and terminology rather than every word Ma-Nee said.

For each hour of interview, I needed an additional five to six hours to incorporate the rough transcript into a working book manuscript. I took a pragmatic approach to this process. I tried to use Ma-Nee's original terminology and exact words as often as possible. My main goal, however, was to write a first-person narrative in simple, clear, and correct English that would be familiar to Ma-Nee herself. I then integrated the different pieces of the account into chronological chapters with thematic sub-sections. A more rigorous academic approach would have involved audio-recording, exact transcription of the interviews, and exclusive use of verbatim quotations in the order that Ma-Nee said them. Such an exercise would have taken years to complete and the resulting manuscript might have been difficult for readers to follow. The advantages and disadvantages of these different methodologies will be discussed later in this afterword.

Some people consider the Ojibwe term Anishinaabeg to mean "the Ojibwe people," while others alternatively, or additionally, believe it refers to all Indigenous peoples (e.g., Agger 2008; Simpson 2011). Ma-Nee subscribes to this latter understanding. All of the Anishinaabe (Indigenous) words in this book are Ojibwe. Ma-Nee spoke Cree throughout her childhood with her mother and grandmother, but she used Ojibwe within her broader community. As an adult in Thunder Bay and Winnipeg, she mainly spoke Ojibwe with other Anishinaabeg because she did not know many Cree speakers. As a result, her Cree is somewhat rusty today. Importantly, there are numerous dialects and spoken forms within both Ojibwe and Cree languages. In addition, many Anishinaabeg speak Oji-Cree, which some consider to be a dialect of Ojibwe with a strong Cree influence, but others consider to be an independent language with its own dialects. This linguistic diversity is further complicated by the varied ways people have attempted to write Ojibwe, Cree, and Oji-Cree using Roman script. Different groups have developed standardized ways of spelling words in specific dialects of those languages, but Ma-Nee was never taught those methods formally. I came to this project with English as a first language and extensive linguistic training and experience in three other languages (German, Mandarin Chinese, and Swahili), but I only knew a few dozen words in Ojibwe. Like Ma-Nee, I was not familiar with standardized ways to spell words in either Ojibwe or Cree.

In the course of writing the book, Ma-Nee and I discussed how to spell the Anishinaabe words she mentioned while narrating her life story. Again, we decided to take a pragmatic approach. First, we carefully spelled those words together as they sounded to us. Then, when possible, we compared our versions to those of electronic and paper Ojibwe and Cree dictionaries. Often we synchronized our spellings with more standardized ones, but sometimes we did not, if Ma-Nee felt the standardized spellings did not accurately reflect her dialect, pronunciation, or knowledge of the terms. Ultimately, this book is a personal account reflective of Ma-Nee's particular languages and experiences.

Once I had completed a full draft of the manuscript, I read it out loud to Ma-Nee via Skype, and she requested edits and deletions. This review reminded her of several relevant experiences which she had not addressed earlier, so I expanded the text to include them. Ma-Nee was very committed to being accurate and comprehensive in her narrative, even when recounting incidents that caused her pain, or for which she felt shame or regret. Like any autobiography, though, this account is likely to be limited by subjective factors, such as recall and individual perspective, as well as other constraints, such as the extent to which a book-length manuscript can reflect sixty-three years of a life. We found it especially difficult to determine the accuracy of dates of events which happened before Ma-Nee was born, some of which she only knows about because of the stories her maternal grandmother told her half a century ago. Usually, we estimated early dates by triangulating whatever information we had available, such as personal records, recalled birth and death dates, and historical events which coincided with them.

After I had read the entire manuscript to Ma-Nee and revised it based on her specifications, we discussed whether to replace all real names that were mentioned in the text with pseudonyms. We were concerned about protecting the privacy of any individuals named in the biography. Many of them or their families are still alive today, and might not want their identities to be known. To protect their confidentiality, we systematically replaced all actual names with pseudonyms, with Ma-Nee's name being the only exception. Generally we selected pseudonyms which reflected the ethnic and linguistic basis of the original name; for example, Ojibwe names replaced Ojibwe names, and French names replaced French names. In addition, we sometimes omitted information from our working draft if we thought it might suggest the identity of a person mentioned in the book, especially children who Ma-Nee knew had been sexually abused.

This new manuscript draft was then circulated to reviewers for their consideration. We are very grateful to Betsy Martin, Catherine Green, Eric Bertram, Gwen O'Reilly, Marni Sommer, and Mustafa Kudrati, all of whom read the draft and provided useful feedback at that stage. We also thank Alana Forslund for her assistance in maintaining Ma-Nee's computer during that time, and for scanning many images used in the book. Ma-Nee and I discussed the reviewers' feedback and agreed on ways to try to improve the manuscript. For example, one reviewer found it confusing to distinguish between the seventy-eight people who are named in the narrative. In response, I drafted a descriptive list of people mentioned in the book to use as a reading aid, and Ma-Nee and I systematically reviewed that list together to expand visual descriptions of each person in the main text. On each occasion that we discussed the book from a new angle, such as when I read this afterword to Ma-Nee, or when we identified figures, selected pseudonyms, or drafted visual descriptions of people mentioned in the text, the revision process prompted new discussion of the material and sometimes resulted in further edits and expansions. All photographs included in this book are from Ma-Nee's private collection, unless otherwise noted.

In summary, from July 2013 to March 2014, Ma-Nee and I conducted more than one hundred hours of semi-structured interviews, and I spent approximately six hundred more hours drafting, revising, and expanding the manuscript prior to submission to the publisher. After submission, and before the manuscript's acceptance for publication, I also substantially revised and expanded this afterword based on helpful recommendations from the University of Manitoba Press, including Jill McConkey, the acquisitions editor; Jarvis Brownlie, the editor of the Critical Studies in Native History series; the editorial board; and two anonymous external reviewers.

After the manuscript had been accepted by the press, Glenn Bergen, the managing editor, and Barbara Romanik, the copyeditor, thoroughly reviewed it. They proposed many thoughtful changes to it, mainly focusing on improving grammar and wording. Then, in October 2015, I read the copyedited narrative aloud to Ma-Nee via Skype and we made revisions to it. Our priority at that time was to identify and replace words and phrasing that Ma-Nee did not know or only vaguely understood with synonyms she would typically use. Betsy Martin and Gwen O'Reilly, two close, long-time friends of Ma-Nee, greatly assisted us at this stage by carefully reviewing the narrative, flagging many terms which they felt Ma-Nee was unlikely to use, and proposing more likely alternatives. Finally, we appreciate that Jess Koroscil, the graphic designer, typeset the manuscript and patiently incorporated our final edits once we reviewed that proof.

WESTERN SOCIAL SCIENCE AND INDIGENOUS KNOWLEDGE-SHARING

The previous section outlined how Ma-Nee's and my work on this book generally was in line with Western social science and oral history traditions (Denzin and Lincoln 1994; Perks and Thomson 1998; Bernard 2002). It should be noted, though, that Ma-Nee's contributions also represent her Anishinaabe conversational and storytelling heritage. Ma-Nee was raised within the Anishinaabe intellectual tradition of teaching, sharing, and entertaining through storytelling (e.g., Culleton 1983; Johnston 1990 c1976; Flannery 1995; Anderson and Lawrence 2003; Bird 2005; Benton-Banai 2010 c1988; Simpson 2011; Doerfler, Sinclair, and Stark 2013). She has become a gifted storyteller and employed those narrative skills throughout our work on this book.

Our writing process incorporated many aspects of what some have referred to as Indigenous research or knowledge-sharing methods, including storytelling, conversation, and a fundamentally relational Indigenous paradigm (Wilson 2008; Kovach 2010). Margaret Kovach, a researcher of Plains Cree and Saulteaux ancestry, explains how this type of sharing and learning works: "When used in an Indigenous framework, a conversational method invokes several distinctive characteristics: a) it is linked to a particular tribal epistemology (or knowledge) and situated within an Indigenous paradigm; b) it is relational; c) it is purposeful (most often involving a decolonizing aim); d) it involves particular protocol as determined by the epistemology and/or place; e) it involves an informality and flexibility; f) it is collaborative and dialogic; and g) it is reflexive" (Kovach 2010, 43). As Kovach and others suggest, the quality of the relationship between the researcher and research participant is central to this Indigenous methodology. A close, multidimensional relationship is perceived positively because of the trust it engenders, rather than negatively as a potential source of bias, as is often the case within Western research paradigms. In describing her research with Indigenous mental health workers, for example, Suzanne Stewart, a researcher from the Yellowknife Dene First Nation, commented:

> An important assumption is that the participants would be
> willing to engage in honest and meaningful conversation with
> me about their experiences of mental health and healing in

counselling contexts. Trust is the foundation of an ethical and authentic research relationship.... For the community agency to trust me enough to partner with me to carry out the research, I had to establish other professional and personal relationships with both the agency itself as an institution and the individuals who worked within it. Thus, what is considered a dual relationship in Western ethical codes of research and counselling could be viewed as both necessary and ethical in Indigenous protocols of research. (Stewart 2009, 60)

This book, like Stewart's work, is broadly grounded in both Western and Indigenous knowledge-sharing traditions. On an individual level, *A Two-Spirit Journey* also is a collaboration between an Indigenous woman and a woman of European heritage. Given the colonial and postcolonial history of North America, a biography such as this one, which was narrated by a First Nations elder and transcribed, written, and edited by someone of European heritage, should be considered within the context of similar works.

MULTIPLE AUTHORSHIP AND VOICE

There is a long history of told-to narratives in which non-Indigenous people recorded stories by Indigenous narrators, and then modified and organized that material prior to publishing it. Non-Indigenous writers often published those texts solely under their names, even while they claimed that the account accurately portrayed the Indigenous narrator's voice. In the 1990s, such practices became the subject of vigorous debate. At the time there was increasing focus on disenfranchised people's rights to speak in their own voices and on their own terms. The "appropriation of voice" in historical told-to narratives was criticized and challenged, and some argued that told-to narratives should be dispensed with altogether.

In her book *First Person Plural*, however, Sophie McCall argues that told-to narratives are not inherently exploitative, and instead can be conducted collaboratively and with integrity (McCall 2011). When that is the case, she notes, they may offer valuable contributions to the broader canon of Indigenous writing. McCall explains:

Aboriginal literature in Canada has increasingly come to mean singly authored texts, as if told-to narratives were synonymous with literary colonization.... [However] In recent decades, as Aboriginal writers, editors, translators, scholars, and community members have become more involved in developing innovative approaches to the task of recording and preserving oral traditions, it has become clear that told-to narratives remain a vibrant form of cultural expression.... Just as the collector-editor selects, interprets, shapes, and determines the form of the narrative, so too does the narrator choose, arrange, and order her memories.... Narrators use a range of strategies, from direct confrontation, to parody, to silence, to avoidance, in order to claim narrative authority in these composite texts. (McCall 2011, 5–8)

In the Introduction to her collaborative work with Elsie Paul and Harmony Johnson, *Written As I Remember It*, Paige Raibmon voices similar sentiments and discusses how told-to narratives may play a positive role in settler societies struggling with reconciliation (Paul, Raibmon, and Johnson 2014). Raibmon notes: "In order for told-to narratives to realize this potential...there are a number of prerequisites. One is...that the collaborative process is conducted with integrity. No told-to narrative, regardless of how positive its intention, innovative its structure, or original in content, can meaningfully model or contribute to reconciliation if this condition is absent. Accordingly, historians, anthropologists, and literary critics alike have argued that the *process* of collaboration is as important in the final multi-authored result" (Paul, Raibmon, and Johnson 2014, 11). Genuine collaboration and communication, mutual listening and respect, and acknowledgement of joint authorship are all critical in creating a told-to narrative with integrity.

Since 1990, a number of told-to narratives have been published in which the collaborators' process and decision-making are clearly explained and scrutinized, and the narrator is acknowledged as a co-author and even the first author, in recognition of her central or leading role in the work. For example, in *They Write Their Dreams on the Rock Forever*, the elder Annie York of the Nlaka'pamux Nation is identified as the first author of the book and the sole author of the chapter based on her word-for-word explanations of red ochre inscriptions written on the rocks and cliffs of the lower Stein Valley in British Columbia (York, Daly, and Arnett 1993).

Discussions about the collaborative process involved in told-to narratives often have focused on how the narrator's "voice"—that is, her syntax, speech rhythms, and distinctive way of speaking—can be accurately conveyed in writing, without undue modification. Adequately representing such oral narratives in written text is challenging, especially in the case of First Nations elders who may have learned English as a second or third language, with little or no formal education. Transcribing such individuals' English speech verbatim can provide a literal, accurate representation of their wording, but if their phrasing is ambiguous or their grammar is incorrect, readers may become confused.

Many told-to collaborators have grappled with these issues. For instance, to create *Lived Like a Story*, three Yukon elders of Athapaskan, Tlingit, or combined ancestry—Angela Sidney, Kitty Smith, and Annie Ned—narrated their life histories to Julie Cruikshank over a ten-year research period (Cruikshank et al. 1990). Cruikshank audio-recorded and transcribed a total of 160 hours of discussions with the three women. In transforming those transcriptions into a manuscript, she aspired to stay as close as possible to the women's original wording, in order to keep the "texture" of their oral narratives. However, Cruikshank found this problematic, as the resultant text was sometimes difficult for readers to understand. Describing one of the women's exact transcripts, Cruikshank explains, "The narrative conventions she uses...may plunge an unfamiliar listener into a dense, incomprehensible world without the leavening of context" (Cruikshank et al. 1990, 267). Cruikshank found it necessary to systematically edit the material in several ways: to remove information that the narrators wanted omitted; to create a continuous, flowing narrative (thematically and in terms of paragraph structure); to reduce repetition; and to correct grammatical errors (e.g., personal pronouns, subject-verb agreement, and subject order in sentences).

Other recent told-to collaborations have faced similar challenges and arrived at similar compromises. To produce *Written As I Remember It*, Sliammon elder Elsie Paul worked with a number of researchers who recorded, summarized, transcribed, interpreted, wrote, and edited her teachings over many years (Paul, Raibmon, and Johnson 2014). At first she collaborated with two professionals, Janet May and Arlette Raaen, with whom she engaged in one and a half years of interviews which were either audio-recorded or written down in detailed notes when Paul spoke. That material was then used to develop a typescript of each session— representing a close approximation of Paul's words, but not verbatim transcriptions—and it was further organized into a manuscript. In reviewing that draft, though, Paul's children and grandchildren said it did not sound like their grandmother. They felt her character, tone, and sense of humour did not come across. Paul and her family then enlisted the assistance of a different researcher, Paige Raibmon, who arranged for all of the existing audio-recordings to be transcribed verbatim, and for Paul to be re-interviewed and audio-recorded on all of the topics which had not been audio-recorded in the first round of interviews. That second stage of recording, transcription, writing, and editing required several more years and presumably substantial additional funding.

This process resulted in thirty-six hours of audio-recording transcripts, which Elsie Paul's final two collaborators—Paul's granddaughter, Harmony Johnson, and Raibmon—tried to transform into a word-for-word narrative with minimal edits. However, people who were invited to read portions of the new manuscript complained that Paul's direct speech was difficult to decipher. Like Julie Cruikshank, the two writers ultimately edited the manuscript to a greater extent than they had originally intended. Raibmon explains: "We started to look for an appropriate path—one that preserved the orality and style of the original narration while achieving readability.... Our work was more compositional than editorial, much closer than I had first anticipated to the process of crafting a historical argument.... Working in this way first required us to understand [Paul's] teachings and then to convey them through the composition of the manuscript" (Paul, Raibmon, and Johnson 2014, 27). In the end, the collaborators carefully modified the transcripts in both wording and structure. For example, they deleted information that Paul wanted omitted; replaced pronouns with specific descriptors; reduced repetition; removed Paul's false starts and their own questions; and organized the chapters thematically. Paul's family members reported that this final manuscript better represented her unique voice than the first one had.

In summarizing their attempts to accurately reflect Paul's oral narrative in written form, Raibmon comments: "The translation from oral to written might be more usefully seen as a trade-off rather than an absolute loss. Gains can also be achieved in the process of turning oral speech into text. These might include sharing knowledge with a wider audience, and the oft-cited and debated benefit of 'preservation.' Of course these gains exist as such only if the narrator judges them so. Elders themselves are aware of the potential trade-offs, and they weigh the pros and cons of written formats just as they do when deciding whether to narrate in English" (Paul, Raibmon, and Johnson 2014, 26–7).

Cruikshank, Raibmon, and their collaborators strove to reflect each narrator's authentic voice by audio-recording all interviews and formal discussions, by transcribing them verbatim, and by editing them to a minimal extent. Critically, such an approach is extremely time-consuming, labour-intensive, and costly, either in terms of salaries paid to people working on the project, or lost income for those who conduct research without compensation. Even with such rigorous standards, the desired outcome is not guaranteed and compromises may be unavoidable. In both of the above books, the authors eventually found it necessary to substantially modify the verbatim text to produce readable and publishable manuscripts.

A different approach to collaborative biography than those previously described was carried out by Helen Agger and her mother, Dedibaayaanimanook Sarah Keesick Olsen, over ten years of conversations (Agger 2008). The two women employed an informal methodology in which Olsen recounted stories from her life to her daughter in Ojibwe, and Agger replied in English while jotting notes in English on the side. Eventually Agger organized her notes into a coherent sequence to publish as her mother's biography.

Ma-Nee and I took a similar approach to writing this book. We tried to make the project practical and feasible, and we prioritized producing a text that is "user-friendly," that is, not difficult for readers to follow. Like the other Indigenous elders described above, Ma-Nee has a unique voice and way of speaking that reflects her rich and varied experiences. Although she mainly learned English informally as an adult, she has a remarkably broad and subtle English vocabulary, and she is very good at communicating and expressing herself in it. Nonetheless, it is not unusual for her to speak in grammatically incorrect sentences. These might confuse unfamiliar readers if they were unedited, and also, very few publishers would consider publishing a manuscript in such a form, so I wrote the manuscript in grammatically correct English. However, even if we had wanted to create a narrative made up entirely of Ma-Nee's exact words, I would not have been able to do so. Coming into this project with only six months to devote to it full time—and at the most another six months to give to it part time, if needed—I knew I could not follow such a strategy or I would never complete the book. This led to the methodology described earlier in this afterword, that is: rough transcription of Ma-Nee's words as she spoke; prioritization of her original terminology and verbatim quotations when I composed the narrative shortly afterward; organization of the material chronologically and thematically; and production of a first-person narrative in simple, clear, and correct English. In addition, Ma-Nee and I closely reviewed multiple drafts of the manuscript together and modified it to better reflect her "voice," while also making any other changes which she felt were necessary.

MA-NEE'S STORY WITHIN THE BROADER LITERATURE

In addition to considering how the process of creating this book was similar to or different from those of other biographies of Indigenous women, it is worthwhile to consider how the content of Ma-Nee's story complements other Indigenous biographies. Writing in 1990, Cruikshank commented that most told-to Indigenous life histories published to date had documented men's lives (Cruikshank et al. 1990). She noted that such texts typically focused on historical events and particular crises, either in the life of the man or in the life of his community. Recently published or re-published first-person accounts by Indigenous men address more of men's day-to-day lives. For instance, *Call Me Hank,* the autobiography of Henry Pennier (1904–1991), describes in detail his life as a Stó:lō man working in the white-dominated British Columbia logging industry for four decades (Pennier 2006). Similarly, the told-to narrative of William Berens (1866–1947), *Memories, Myths, and Dreams of an Ojibwe Leader,* largely focuses on stories and myths, but also provides some detail about his life hunting, trapping, fur trading, engaging in commercial fishing, and working as a guide and an interpreter (Berens and Hallowell 2009).

Cruikshank notes that Indigenous women's life histories typically have differed in their focus from both Indigenous men's and non-Indigenous women's narratives (Cruikshank et al. 1990). She explains that, in

Indigenous women's accounts, "The recurring theme is one of connection—to other people and to nature. Connections with people are explored through kinship; connections with land emphasize sense of place. But kinship and landscape provide more than just a setting for an account, for they actually frame and shape the story" (Cruikshank et al. 1990, 3). Indeed, both family and nature—the bush—have been central to Ma-Nee's life and are recurrent themes within this book, as they are in the other women's biographies mentioned above.

Of the Indigenous female elders whose life histories have already been discussed, four (Annie York, Angela Sidney, Kitty Smith, and Annie Ned) were born between 1890 and 1904, the fifth (Dedibaayaanimanook Sarah Keesick Olsen) was born in 1922, and the sixth (Elsie Paul) was born in 1931, so they represent earlier generations than Ma-Nee, who was born in 1950. Five of those women also came from different geographic, linguistic, and ethnic backgrounds than Ma-Nee, in present-day British Columbia and the Yukon. Dedibaayaanimanook Sarah Keesick Olsen, however, was born and raised in the Ojibwa community of Namegosibiing Trout Lake, Ontario, approximately 500 kilometres west-northwest of Ombabika, Ontario, where Ma-Nee grew up.

Despite many differences, all of these women share striking similarities with Ma-Nee which contribute to each woman's extraordinary knowledge of her particular languages and cultural traditions. They all grew up in rural or remote areas, and spoke one or more Indigenous languages fluently. Like Ma-Nee, three of the women were raised by their grandmothers, while two were close to a grandfather or a great-aunt, and the sixth was responsible for caring for her invalid mother throughout her childhood, which kept her near home and the elders in her community. Each of the women could recall and narrate their elders' stories and legends well, and they also possessed many traditional skills. Several had hunted or trapped animals, and two, like Ma-Nee, were so skilled that they had supported themselves through such activities, whether single or married. Four of the women never went to school or attended it very briefly before withdrawing. The other two attended school for only two years, similar to Ma-Nee, who intermittently attended the one-room school house in her community for three years. Annie York did not attend school because her father was half-white. Under the Canadian laws at the time, she was not considered to be

Native and thus was not eligible for Native residential school education. Commenting on this while describing York's life, her collaborator Richard Daly notes: "While her contemporaries were having their languages and cultures scrubbed out of them at mission schools, Annie was learning hers, obtaining an informal Native education from Interior Salish elders who were happy to impart their knowledge to someone whose head was not cluttered by the partial learning and emotional problems gained in the notorious schools. Spences Bridge elder, Mary Andersen, [who] also avoided formal government-regulated schooling...told us, 'I didn't go to school. That's why I know so much!'" (York, Daly, and Arnett 1993, 35).

All of the biographic texts described above devoted great attention to linguistic and cultural teachings. As Raibmon comments: "Whether through the interventions of scholarly collaborators and editors, the choices of narrators themselves, or, most likely, some combination thereof, autobiographies of Indigenous women tend to emphasize women's roles as wives, mothers, and preservers of cultural practice (as basket weavers, language teachers, and button-blanket makers, for example)...and minimize the narrator's work in the paid labour force, and implicitly position her on the precarious fulcrum between tradition and modernity as 'the last of her kind'" (Paul, Raibmon, and Johnson 2014, 42). While these biographies typically provided an overview of the narrators' lives from their earliest memories to the current day—including acknowledgement of major events, such as marriages and deaths—few have examined the women's emotional lives in much depth. Elsie Paul's new book represents a positive step in that direction, particularly in her discussion of suffering, grief, and healing. Nonetheless, in her book those topics are mainly presented as teachings from her perspective as an elder, healer, and community worker, rather than from her in-depth examination of her personal experiences. In several of the texts, the elders acknowledged that alcoholism had ravaged their personal lives and those of their broader communities, but they refused to discuss this in detail.

In A Two-Spirit Journey, Ma-Nee has chosen to address this topic and other personal issues with great honesty and depth. A wide range of emotions run through Ma-Nee's life history as told in the book, including fear of physical and sexual abuse, courage in the face of danger, sorrow at her vision's deterioration, elation at falling in love, anger over injustice, trust in the Great Spirit, grief when loved ones died, happiness when playing with grandchildren, and empathy for others who are struggling. Ma-Nee offers an extraordinarily frank view into her emotional life, and her descriptions of the many traumas she experienced are remarkable for their unwavering honesty.

In this way, Ma-Nee's narrative is similar to first-person accounts documented in a few autobiographies and anthologies based on the lives of younger and at-risk Indigenous women. For example, Maria Campbell, a Métis elder of Cree, French, and Scottish descent, published a memoir in 1973 at the age of 33 in which she recounted many experiences which are similar to Ma-Nee's early life (Campbell 1982 c1973). These include both cherished memories, such as a beloved grandmother and trapping with her father, and harsh, brutal, experiences, such as growing up amidst alcoholism and poverty, an abusive early marriage, and addiction and hardship on the streets as a young woman. Like Ma-Nee, Campbell describes the many obstacles she had to overcome on her path to recovery and healing.

Similarly, in the book *In Plain Sight*, Leslie Robertson and Dara Culhane present told-to narratives based on interviews they conducted with seven poor and/or homeless women in Vancouver's Downtown Eastside from 2001 to 2003. Explaining their goal in producing that book, Robertson and Culhane note: "Our intention is to open a space for the voices of women who are seldom heard on their own terms, women who are highly visible on the street and in media representations but whose daily realities remain largely concealed" (Robertson and Culhane 2005, 7). When discussing those women's backgrounds, they add, "Perpetual, repetitive, relentless experiences of tragic loss permeate the lives of individuals and families in this community" (Robertson and Culhane 2005, 127). Like Ma-Nee, most of the women who shared their stories had been sexually molested during childhood and some were physically abused by alcoholic mothers. Each of these women had known great losses, such as the death of a child. The majority also had experienced violent relationships with husbands or boyfriends, either before or after they came to Vancouver's Downtown Eastside, and all had repeatedly been beaten or raped by other men after they got there. The majority of the women had had serious injuries or illnesses while living in the downtown area. All but one had struggled with addiction; the remaining woman managed serious mental illness for many years. Several of these individuals described great difficulty finding and keeping jobs, and striving to pay for housing and food on very limited social assistance.

A Cree woman in that anthology, with the pseudonym Laurie, matter-of-factly mentions having had lesbian partners while living on the streets. Her description of those relationships is not unlike the lesbian relationship Ma-Nee witnessed between a cousin and a childhood friend when the three of them were frequenting bars in Thunder Bay in the early 1970s. This last point touches on one aspect of Ma-Nee's life history that is perhaps the most unique in the existing literature, as there are very few published accounts by Indigenous lesbians (Cooper 2003).

Ma-Nee's experience of living with two spirits, including coming out and embracing social activism in the 1980s, reflects one of many broader cultural and societal changes she has both witnessed and participated in over the course of her life. Ma-Nee also experienced other great socioeconomic transitions, including those from traditional to modern labor, from rural to urban living, from epidemic alcoholism to large-scale sobriety initiatives, and from historical trauma to the First Nations healing movement. Her rare, first-person perspective provides insight into how racism, homophobia, violence, substance abuse, and poverty have shaped Indigenous women's experiences in Canada. Because of its difficult content, her account may be challenging to read at times. Nonetheless, Ma-Nee's story is an inspirational example of courage, resilience, and healing against great odds. We are fortunate that she has shared it with us.

PEOPLE MENTIONED IN THE BOOK

*The following list briefly describes people mentioned in this book.
All names are pseudonyms.*

Abigail – Daughter of Diana and Randy, and granddaughter and foster daughter of Grace and Ma-Nee. She was raised by them from the age of four until adulthood (1996–2009).

Adrienne – Daughter of Victoria, and younger half-sister of Bonnie.

Andy – Adopted son of Deborah and Gabe, and younger brother of Ma-Nee. He was raised by Ma-Nee from the age of nine until his mid-teens (1968–1974).

Angela – Daughter of Renee and Aziinii, and younger cousin of Ma-Nee.

Aziinii – Husband of Renee, and uncle of Ma-Nee.

Barbara – Daughter of Ma-Nee's cousin, Gilbert, and granddaughter of Renee and Aziinii.

Barry – Son of Gabe, and older stepbrother of Ma-Nee.

Bonnie – Daughter of Victoria, and cousin of Jane.

Dr. Boyle – Eye doctor who Ma-Nee knew in the 1970s.

Charlotte – Social worker who Ma-Nee knew in the 1980s.

Christopher – Husband of Leliilah, and maternal grandfather of Ma-Nee.

Claude – Son of Christopher and Leliilah, and maternal uncle of Ma-Nee.

Claudia – Older teenage girl who Ma-Nee knew in the 1960s.

Darrius – Adopted son of Ma-Nee's daughter, Talia.

Deborah – Ma-Nee's biological mother.

Diana – Adopted daughter of Ma-Nee's partner, Grace.

Edith – Wife of Phillip, who may have been Ma-Nee's biological father.

Edmond – Friend of Ma-Nee in the late 1950s and early 1960s.

Edna – Woman who Ma-Nee knew in the 1950s and 1960s.

Ethan – Husband of Ma-Nee's cousin, Flora.

Flora – Daughter of Renee and Aziinii, and much older cousin of Ma-Nee.

Frank – Man who Ma-Nee was involved with in the early 1970s.

Fritz – Man who Ma-Nee knew around 1960.

Gabe – Husband of Deborah, father of Matilda and Barry, and stepfather of Ma-Nee.

Gilbert – Son of Renee and Aziinii, and much older cousin of Ma-Nee.

Grace – Ma-Nee's second female lover (1991–2004).

Gus – Ma-Nee's first husband (1966–1970).

Hank – Friend of Ma-Nee in the late 1950s and early 1960s.

Harry – Friend of Ma-Nee in the 1970s.

Helene – Girlfriend of Ma-Nee's cousin Justin.

Herbert – Man who hired Ma-Nee in the late 1970s.

Irene – Godmother of Ma-Nee.

Ivan – Friend of Ma-Nee in the late 1950s and early 1960s.

Jacques – Son of Christopher and Leliilah, and maternal uncle of Ma-Nee.

Jane – Daughter of Karen, and Ma-Nee's closest friend in the 1960s and 1970s.

Jonathan – Ma-Nee's second son.

Mr. Jones – Hudson's Bay Company store manager who Ma-Nee knew in the 1960s.

Mrs. Jones – Schoolteacher who Ma-Nee knew in the 1960s.

Joshua – Older boy who Ma-Nee knew in the early 1960s.

Justin – Son of Renee and Aziinii, and older cousin of Ma-Nee.

Karen – One of Ma-Nee's mother's friends, and mother of Jane, Ma-Nee's best friend in the 1960s and 1970s.

Ken – Boyfriend of Ma-Nee's daughter, Sarah, and father of Valerie and Susannah.

Dr. Lambert – Medical doctor who Ma-Nee knew in the 1960s.

Leah – Ma-Nee's first female lover (1988–1991).

Leliilah – Ma-Nee's maternal grandmother, who raised Ma-Nee in the 1950s and early 1960s.

Lori – Girlfriend and later wife of Ma-Nee's brother, Andy.

Martin – Son of Ma-Nee and Gus, and brother of Sarah.

Matilda – Daughter of Gabe, and older stepsister of Ma-Nee.

Matthew – Fiancé of Ma-Nee's granddaughter, Valerie.

Max – Friend of Ma-Nee in the 1950s.

Mitchell – Son of Ma-Nee's cousin Justin and his girlfriend Helene.

Namiid – Daughter of Valerie and Matthew, and great-granddaughter of Ma-Nee.

Nancy – Friend and housemate of Ma-Nee in the early 1990s.

Nate – Ma-Nee's second husband (1980–1987).

Nick – Son of Karen, and older half-brother of Jane.

Noah – Adopted son of Ma-Nee's daughter, Talia.

Paige – Friend who Ma-Nee first met in the late 1980s.

Pascal – Childhood friend of Ma-Nee, and cousin by marriage.

Paula – Daughter of Renee and Aziinii, and cousin of Ma-Nee.

Mr. Percy – Employment officer who Ma-Nee knew in the 1970s.

Phillip – Man who many believed was Ma-Nee's biological father.

Quinn – Son of Diana and Randy, and grandson of Grace and Ma-Nee.

Randy – Boyfriend of Diana, Grace's daughter.

Renard – Neighbour of Ma-Nee in the 1950s.

Renee – Daughter of Christopher and Leliilah, and maternal aunt of Ma-Nee.

Richie – Father of Phillip, and possibly Ma-Nee's paternal grandfather.

Rose – Woman who Ma-Nee knew in the 1950s and 1960s.

Sabrina – Daughter of Ma-Nee's cousin Angela. She was raised by Ma-Nee from the age of one to five years (1976–1980).

Sarah – Daughter of Ma-Nee and Gus, and sister of Martin.

Shiigohbii – One of Ma-Nee's closest friends in the late 1950s and early 1960s.

Stacey – Sister of Gus, and sister-in-law of Ma-Nee.

Susannah – Second daughter of Sarah and Ken, and Ma-Nee's granddaughter.

Tabitha – Friend who Ma-Nee first met in the late 1980s.

Talia – Adopted daughter of Ma-Nee.

Tracey – Woman who Ma-Nee knew in the late 1980s.

Valerie – First daughter of Sarah and Ken, and Ma-Nee's granddaughter.

Victoria – One of Ma-Nee's mother's friends, and mother of Bonnie, who was a close friend of Ma-Nee in the 1960s and 1970s.

William – Son of Abigail, Grace and Ma-Nee's foster daughter.

GLOSSARY

See the afterword for an explanation of Ojibwe word choice and spelling below.

amik – beaver

aniinah – expression of surprise, equivalent to "What are you doing?" or "What's up?"

Anishinaabe – Indigenous person, also used in the text as an adjective ("Indigenous") to describe other nouns, e.g., Anishinaabe medicine, Anishinaabe family, or Anishinaabe history

Anishinaabeg – Indigenous people

bimose – journey or walk

eya – yes

giizaagiyin – I love you

giizhik – cedar

gitchi – great or big

Gitchi Manitou – Great Spirit

jiimaan – canoe

kokum – grandmother

maamaa – mother

madayigan – drum

madodoigan – sweat lodge

makizin – pair of moccasins

makwa – bear

manitou – spirit outside of a person, like a god (not a ghost)

mashkikiiwazh – medicine bag or bundle

mashkodewashk – sage

miigwetch – thank you

miinikaa – place with many blueberries, or a blueberry patch

miiweh – expression of closure, as when ending a story, like "that's it"

nagwaniian – snare

nasemaa – tobacco

nichi – friend, also the name of one of Ma-Nee's dogs

niizhin – two

niizhin ojijaak – two spirits or souls

odaabaan – vehicle

ojijaak – person's spirit or soul

onaagan – trap

shkiizhig – my eyes, also the name of one of Ma-Nee's dogs

tikinagan – traditional swaddling cradleboard

Wanamikiikwe – Thunder Flight Woman, the name of Ma-Nee's kayak

wiidigewaagan – spouse

wiigiwaam – dome-shaped building made from a frame of arched poles or saplings covered with birchbark

wiigwaasi – birch

wiigwaasi jiimaan – birch canoe

wiiskwemushgan – sweetgrass

windigo – beast or monster

windigo odaabaan – train, literally a beastly or monstrous vehicle

zhooniyaa – money

BIBLIOGRAPHY

Agger, Helen. 2008. *Following Nimishoomis: The Trout Lake History of Dedibaayaanimanook Sarah Keesick Olsen.* Penticton, BC: Theytus Books.

Anderson, Kim, and Bonita Lawrence, eds. 2003. *Strong Women Stories: Native Vision and Community Survival.* Toronto: Sumach Press.

Baril, Joan. 2012. "The Scoop, 1955." *Room* 35, 3: 77–80.

Benton-Banai, Edward. 2010 [1988]. *The Mishomis Book: The Voice of the Ojibway.* Minneapolis, MN: University of Minnesota Press.

Berens, William, as told to A. Irving Hallowell. 2009. *Memories, Myths, and Dreams of an Ojibwe Leader.* Edited by Jennifer S.H. Brown and Susan Elaine Gray. Montreal: McGill-Queen's University Press.

Bernard, H. Russell. 2002. *Research Methods in Anthropology: Qualitative and Quantitative Approaches.* Walnut Creek, CA: AltaMira Press.

Bird, Louis. 2005. *Telling Our Stories: Omushkego Legends and Histories from Hudson Bay.* Edited by Jennifer S.H. Brown, Paul W. DePasquale, and Mark F. Ruml. Peterborough, ON: Broadview Press.

Campbell, Maria. 1982 [1973]. *Halfbreed.* Lincoln, NE: University of Nebraska Press.

Cooper, Nancy. 2003. "Arts and Letters Club: Two-Spirited Women Artists and Social Change." In *Strong Women Stories: Native Vision and Community Survival,* edited by Kim Anderson and Bonita Lawrence, 135–43. Toronto: Sumach Press.

Cruikshank, Julie, in collaboration with Angela Sidney, Kitty Smith, and Annie Ned. 1990. *Life Lived Like a Story: Life Stories of Three Yukon Native Elders.* Vancouver: University of British Columbia Press.

Culleton (Mosionier), Beatrice. 1983. *In Search of April Raintree.* Winnipeg: Pemmican Publications.

Denzin, Norman K., and Yvonna S. Lincoln. 1994. *The Handbook of Qualitative Research*. Thousand Oaks, CA: Sage.

Doerfler, Jill, Niigaanwewidam James Sinclair, and Heidi Kiiwetinepinesiik Stark. 2013. *Centering Anishinaabeg Studies: Understanding the World through Stories*. Winnipeg: University of Manitoba Press.

Flannery, Regina. 1995. *Ellen Smallboy: Glimpses of a Cree Woman's Life*. Montreal: McGill-Queen's University Press.

Johnston, Basil. 1990. c1976. *Ojibway Heritage*. Lincoln, NE: Bison Books.

Kovach, Margaret. 2010. "Conversational Method in Indigenous Research." *First Peoples Child and Family Review* 5, 1: 40–48.

McCall, Sophie. 2011. *First Person Plural: Aboriginal Storytelling and the Ethics of Collaborative Authorship*. Vancouver: University of British Columbia Press.

Paul, Elsie, in collaboration with Paige Raibmon, and Harmony Johnson. 2014. *Written as I Remember It: Teachings (ʔəms taʔaw) from the Life of a Sliammon Elder*. Vancouver: University of British Columbia Press.

Pennier, Henry. 2006. *Call Me Hank: A Stó:lō Man's Reflections on Logging, Living, and Growing Old*. Edited by Keith Thor Carlson and Kristina Fagan. Toronto: University of Toronto Press.

Perks, Robert, and Alistair Thomson. 1998. *The Oral History Reader*. New York: Routledge.

Robertson, Leslie, and Dara Culhane, eds. 2005. *In Plain Sight: Reflections on Life in Downtown Eastside Vancouver*. Vancouver: Talonbooks.

Simpson, Leanne. 2011. *Dancing on Our Turtle's Back: Stories of Nishnaabeg Re-creation, Resurgence and a New Emergence*. Winnipeg: ARP Books.

Stewart, Suzanne L. 2009. "One Indigenous Academic's Evolution: A Personal Narrative of Native Health Research and Competing Ways of Knowing." *First Peoples Child and Family Review* 4, 1: 57–65.

Wilson, Shawn. 2008. *Research is Ceremony: Indigenous Research Methods*. Black Point, NS: Fernwood Publishing.

York, Annie, Richard Daly, and Chris Arnett. 1993. *They Write Their Dreams on the Rock Forever: Rock Writings in the Stein River Valley of British Columbia*. Vancouver: Talonbooks.

Critical Studies in Native History

(continues Manitoba Studies in Native History)

A NOTE ON THE TYPE

The text of this book is set in Minion Pro (11/14), designed by designed by Robert Slim-
bach in 1990 for Adobe Systems. The title text is set in DIN Next, designed by Akira
Kobayashi and Sandra Winter in 2009 for Linotype GmbH (now Monotype GmbH).